A gift from my
Sister, CAROL, in
Spring of 2020(?)
THANK YOU, CAROL.

Love,
Jack
July 19, 2023

D1570833

Anfractuous

Stories and lessons from
a winding, bending, curving life.
One man's path, filled with angry
pancakes, perilous blowholes,
and Chupacabra roadkill.
But, then again...whose isn't?

Tim e Holder

LifeRich PUBLISHING

LifeRich Publishing is a registered trademark of
The Reader's Digest Association, Inc.

LifeRich Publishing books may be ordered
through booksellers or by contacting:

LifeRich Publishing
1663 Liberty Drive
Bloomington, IN 47403
www.liferichpublishing.com
844-686-9607

ISBN: 978-1-4897-3742-7 (sc)
ISBN: 978-1-4897-3744-1 (hc)
ISBN: 978-1-4897-3743-4 (e)

Library of Congress Control Number: 2021915695

Print information available on the last page.

LifeRich Publishing rev. date: 09/27/2021

Jesus, I love you. Thank you for your mercy and your grace. You rescued me from isolation, loneliness, fear, guilt, and shame. Your nonstop, unrelenting pyrotechnic display of love, acceptance, kindness, and understanding continually presses me further into you. You're never dull. I never know what you're going to do next. But I do know you're with me. You're the adventure. You provide the courage and confidence I need to navigate this serpentine, anfractuous journey while solidly gripping your hand. This book is yours. Did I say I love you? I do. I can't wait to see you face-to-face. What a day of rejoicing that will be. You'd best be ready. Brace yourself for the most fiercely intense body slam in the history of mankind. Until then, lead on, my Brother, my Rescuer, my Savior, my truest, most faithful Buddy!

Creative Living, you listened. You believed. You laughed and cried. You told me I should, I could, and I'm capable. I can't begin to show my gratitude for your encouragement. I've watched and experienced the mighty hand of God move through your prayers. You gave me the chance to pursue my dream. Sometimes I look around the CL gathering on Sunday mornings and think, *This is a perfect, genuine image of our future. All together forever.* Quite often, I take a heart picture.

Bramble Market, in a legitimately substantial way, this book would not be in print if not for your love and mission. Observing and being part of allowing God space to breathe life into your dream is far more than a job. It's peace. It's joy. It's anfractuous. It's hearing people come through the door and tell us, "There's something different about this place." The Holy Spirit is thriving, dancing, and ripping all around those tin walls. Thank you for the baked potato farm-to-table dinner.

Dear Jack,
Enjoy!
SHINE! Daniel 12:3

Conquerors will march in the victory parade,
their names indelible in the Book of Life. I'll lead
them up and present them by name to my Father
and his Angels.

—Revelation 3:5 MSG

Every God-begotten person conquers the world's
ways. The conquering power that brings the
world to its knees is our faith. The person who
wins out over the world's ways is simply the one
who believes Jesus is the Son of God.

—1 John 5:4–5 MSG

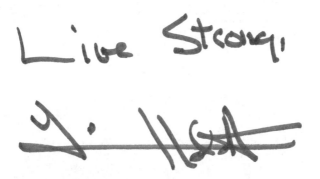

Live Strong!

Daniel 1:13

Live Strong!

contents

Acknowledgments

To all of you who ate a baked potato, whether literally or vicariously: this book wouldn't have been possible without you. Your generosity speaks to your belief in my gifts and the realization of my dream. Thank you.

By extension, there have been times in my life when I found myself in desperate need. Many of you reading this will know you chose to provide, love me, and give, many times sacrificially. I can't even begin to list everyone; I know I'd inadvertently leave someone out, which would generate great heartache for me. As I write this, the Lord floods my mind and heart with faces and memories. Thank you. You lived out the promise: "You'll be—and experience—a blessing. They won't be able to return the favor, but the favor will be returned—oh, how it will be returned!—at the resurrection of God's people" (Luke 14:14 MSG).

David Rice and everyone at the Bramble Market: David said, "I have an idea, and you can't say no."

Ruth Danner: In 1972, you were a drum major, and I was a second-chair trombone player. Who'da thunk it? Almost a half century later, you are still leading well, and I am still following direction. Thank you for your patience, insight, honesty, encouragement, and outright grit while editing this project. I couldn't have finished this without you. Through the onslaught of run-on sentences and sentence fragments, you heard my voice. You gave these walls of words a fresh coat of paint.

The entire Holder and Lefler tribe (and G): Our parents imprinted on us the beautiful legacy that there's almost always a reason to laugh. Jesus had a great sense of humor. Even when it got us in trouble—which was more often than not—we chose joy. We discovered the priceless truth that finding joy, not because of the struggle, but during the struggle, is eternal. We have the stories to justify it. The ability to unearth humor in almost any experience runs deep. What a gift.

The questioners: I love that you're all part of this project. You've made these words feel like a party. Like home.

Scot and Michelle Waldo: Cinnamon rolls and cookies. Excellent idea.

Introduction

You will be woefully disappointed if you read this publication expecting a theological exegesis on ecclesiastical truths or a tutorial in parochial imperfections. And yes, I used a thesaurus to confirm the correct usage of those words.

I'm in no way an educated biblical scholar. I've read through the Bible a few times, even the book of Numbers, which is, in my opinion, the colonoscopy prep of the Bible.

I do possess, however, a considerable amount of years under my ever-expanding belt loops. I have learned lessons, some from observation and many hard-earned through the fires of life events. I have never given up on the reality of where my strength comes from and on whom my hope and trust rest. My heart craves a more constant desire to profoundly expand the never-ending relationship I've established with Jesus. He inhabits my deepest desires. The author of my faith and my wildest, craziest dreams, Jesus is my truest companion and ally.

Several years ago, I left my job as worship leader for Celebrate Recovery at a huge church. I loved that job, and when it was over, I questioned whether there was still work for me to accomplish while on this side of the veil. I spent several months seeking God's direction for my future, wondering if there was to even be one.

Of course, his plan for me remained intact; I was just too self-involved to immediately see it. I began attending a church that encapsulated what I'd been missing: First Assembly of

God in North Little Rock. The pastors, staff, volunteers, and members are outwardly focused yet equally fixated on caring for each other. I sit in unabashed amazement when we take special contributions. First Assembly is a generous, giving, Jesus-loving and -honoring church. The teaching is always biblically on point and progressive. I use the word *progressive* carefully but deliberately. It's progressive in that we are willing to change the methods but never sacrifice the message. What is the message? It's the flawless, unbeatable truth found in the faithful Word of God. Jesus is now and will forever be the one true answer. He is our gateway to heaven. He loves us. He loves you. He shed his blood and died a cruel yet eternally necessary death. He took the punishment we deserve. He died instead of us. He carried our sin to the tomb. Three days later, he obliterated death and walked out of that tomb very much alive. He's back in heaven now with his Father. As for those of us who have put our hope in him, well, Jesus is preparing our home there, and he knows, by design, explicitly what we like.

On Sunday mornings, someone grabs my hand as I enter the lobby, authentically happy to see me. I meander through the hallways, linger in the coffee center, and breathe in and absorb the atmosphere surrounding me. Hugs, smiles, and handshakes. Palpable joy and expectancy. It feels good. I'm in a safe, God-honoring, praise-filled environment. I never wait for God to show up. He's already there.

I began attending a Sunday morning Connections class called Creative Living. I remember being invited to a leaders' meeting one Sunday night. I attended because I was told there would be food. And there was. We always have lots of food. That makes me very happy.

One of the teachers for the class was stepping back, and the leaders needed someone to help teach the opening ten-minute segment—kind of a warm-up to the morning to get people awake and energized. They asked me if I would take over that small chunk of class time every other Sunday, sharing the responsibility with Patricia Knott. That added an extra level of angst, as Dr. Knott is, well, brilliant. I glanced out on the room and noticed a lot of heads nodding. I specifically remember Greg and Julie Hillegas. Julie, as always, nodded with her comforting, encouraging smile. Greg, as always, nodded with his goofy "No duh" grin.

I hadn't written anything of magnitude or planet-cracking substance since the third grade. I emphatically informed the twenty people in the meeting that I wasn't gifted in that arena. After much cajoling and the guarantee of a perennial supply of sausage balls, I finally, reluctantly acquiesced to a six-month trial period. If, at the end of the experiment, they felt I was best suited to explore other life goals, I'd be dismally depressed and disturbingly bitter. But I'd understand and sluggishly attempt to move forward.

That was eight years ago.

When I read one of my essays, class members would often encourage me to compile my stories into a volume. So that's exactly what I've done.

Every chapter is its own stand-alone essay or story. Some are funny. Some are more serious—thought-provoking, hopefully. Some are a combination of both. My time limit in Creative Living class caps at ten minutes. When reading out loud, ten minutes equals five double-spaced pages of 12-point Times New Roman font. Anyone should be able to read any given essay in less than ten minutes. Yeehaw! Years in the making, I told an editor I thought I wrote the book and the publishers did everything else. She said, "Oh no. Writing a book is like giving birth to a child." I said, "Okay. Well, I'm at about eight centimeters. I'm ready for the epidural. Get this thing out of me!"

Oh, another thing: you will occasionally find, if your memory is better than mine, a snippet of one essay in another story later in the book. Don't worry. You're not experiencing déjà vu. Sometimes I felt more lessons could be learned from one adventure.

After compiling a number of essays or stories that I hoped would entice readers to continue the journey, I discovered fifty-four stories were assembled—one for each week of the year, plus two. I don't much care for the idea of happenstance, so I concluded there must have been a transcendent reason.

I enlisted an army of friends from all over the country who have been pivotal players in my life journey and implored them to come up with questions for each chapter—conversation starters, if you will. I found the responses fascinating. I knew my theme and my endgame for each story. Others were able to read them subjectively, producing intriguing alternative ideas for consideration. You will find a brief description of each questioner next to his or her name. I want you to know them. I have tons of friends. Just look at my social media pages. If you weren't asked to offer suggestions, it's in no way a reflection of my love for you. Don't take it personally. You can call me to task when we get to heaven.

If you would like to use this book as a group tool for discussion, do it. It'll be a year-long endeavor, saving money from buying other less intriguing, less soul-stirring, and otherwise bland, boring quarterly study guides. I'd love to hear how the essays ministered to you. Or don't.

If instead you want to read the stories privately and spend personal reflection time with the questions, do it. I'd still love to hear how they touched you or gave you reason to laugh a little. Or don't.

If you want to read the stories and completely ignore the conversation starters, go for it. It's all about you!

I hope you learn a little from the words here. I hope you get a chuckle or two along the way. God knows we need more laughter these days.

At any rate, for whatever reason you chose to own a copy of this twisting, curving, bending, anfractuous adventure I call life, I thank you. From the guts of my soul.

Anfractuosity

IF YOU SHOULD ever hear me for some random, arbitrary reason yell out, "Anfractuosity!" don't be alarmed. Anfractuosity is merely the act or state of being anfractuous, which is an adjective meaning "full of bends and curves" and "intricately winding but not breaking."

A lot like life.

There are absolute, turning-on-a-dime moments or experiences in my life when I know change has just happened or when I can sense something is about to change. Many times, it's part of my journey that I have no control over. Sometimes it's totally due to user error. But a shift in focus is inevitable.

I've spent a lot of time thinking about the anfractuous paths our lives tend to follow. I wonder how many of these paths are due to mere circumstance and how many are the direct hand of God. I've lately been savoring a statement my pastor, Rod Loy, made in one of his recent teachings: "The message will always be consistent, unchanging. But the methods should always change."

Twists, turns, curves, bends—anfractuosity.

Even with a never-changing message that is clear and sharper than any double-edged lightsaber, I never stop being surprised by the unexpected, serpentine bends and curves in the road. I wish God would give me a heads-up when something is about to change. If he would just yell, "Plot twist!" maybe I would have adequate time to prepare and then maybe I could handle it all on my own and not have to depend on him. Yeah, that always works.

Psalm 139:16 (MSG) says, "Like an open book, you watched me grow from conception to birth; all the stages of my life were spread out before you, the days of my life all prepared before I'd even lived one day."

God always knows. When I spend my time trying to do it all on my own, it's easy to forget that he is actually on my side and knows what's best for me. I'm fully aware that he has a plan for my life that was laid out by him before I was even conceived. He knows when I want something that is not his best for me, even when it's ministry-oriented. He knows when it's time for me to let go of my dream, even if it's beautiful, because his plan is better and, in the long run, will satisfy me and leave me more fulfilled. He will sustain my gifts and grow me into that plan.

A couple of years ago, I prayed hard about a volunteer position that might open for me in Celebrate Recovery, a ministry I dearly love that, frankly, saved my life. But I couldn't get past the feeling that God wanted me to grow in a different place. I wrestled for weeks. Finally, I heard him say, "Give up what you think is good for what I know is better."

When I finally let go, when I finally surrendered, I felt a wave of overwhelming peace and freedom. Real freedom. I was giving the Lord room to do something new. Then, a couple of years later, the door of that ministry reopened, and I found myself in a position of cleared space and heard the Lord say, "Now it's time."

Anfractuosity.

I sent one of my essays to my sister, Jacqui. Although she uses social media, she never reads lengthy stuff, including mine, so I told her she was required to read my latest essay. Reluctantly, I'm sure, she acquiesced. She's a Jack Russell terrier: once she gets her teeth in something, she refuses to let go. She texted about two hours later and told me to go to timeholderblog.com. She'd started a blog site for me. She'd caught the vision that my writing should be in print and available for others to read. A new adventure began because I cleared out space and gave the Lord room.

Just when we think we could never love anything more than using our gifts precisely as we always have, we need to be ready and prepare for anfractuosity. God will grow and challenge us, and he will use our gifts for his glory. There will be a bend in the road, a burnished new key turning in a locked door, or a shifting season. The brave decision is allowing our hearts to surrender and our methods to change to display his unchanging message of hope.

David wanted to build the temple. God told him it would be not his to build but his son's. David must've felt disappointment. But God's plan for David was better. I believe part of the reason the temple wasn't David's to build was because through his line, the Savior of the world would come. So Jesus descended not from a man who built a temple but from a man after God's own heart. David gave up his dream to receive what God knew was best.

Anfractuosity.

Another way I'm trying to escape the traps of human conditioning is to change my view of change. If I expect change, my knee-jerk reaction is to think, *I have to lose something for change to happen. What am I going to have to give up?* Maybe that's why so many people hate change. The word itself has terrible connotations. Maybe that's why so many are afraid to give their hearts to Jesus. *If I accept Jesus, what will I lose?*

What if we looked at it from a different vantage point? What if we made Isaiah 43 our touchstone instead? Isaiah 43:19 (NIV) says, "See, I am doing a new thing! Now it springs up; do you not perceive it? I am making a way in the wilderness and streams in the wasteland."

God is doing a new thing.

What if we allow him room to do a new thing in us instead of changing something? Maybe we do have to give up something we love so he can give us our new best dreams. I find the adventures of life far less scary when I think of them as new things rather than changes.

He's doing a new thing. To me, that says it all. He's doing it, and it's new. It's going to be fresh water in a wasteland. Sounds like an oasis to me.

Anfractuosity isn't about how steep the mountain is or how sharp the curve is. It's about the adventure of what's just around the next bend. What's the next part of my story that God is about to reveal for his glory?

As exciting as the new thing can be, excitement doesn't necessarily mean happiness. Life events can ofttimes leave us drowning in a brackish swamp-water puddle of pain and heartache before we get to fresh water.

I have two precious friends I've known for more than two decades. We all attended church together. Billy worked as the youth minister, and Christi was married to the senior pastor. Coincidentally, a few years later, both of these families felt called to move into different seasons of their lives at about the same time. Christi and her family relocated to another state to do a church start-up. Billy and his family moved back to their hometown.

Only a few years into leading their new church, Christi found herself at an insurmountable impasse. After a painful divorce, Christi packed up her daughters and moved back to their hometown.

Meanwhile, Billy struggled with many health issues that culminated in several strokes. He lives in a retirement village now, is divorced, and is only fifty-three years old.

Because they now reside in the same city, Christi regularly visits Billy. She wrote to me,

> Billy continues to digress. He appears to be displaying symptoms of dementia or Parkinson's maybe. He reminisces about his friends and speaks longingly of you. The stroke has left him in a frustrating state. He recognizes his cognitive functions are lessening all the time, and it scares him. So I ask for your prayers on his behalf! It would be a gift for you to visit with all of us. Especially Billy. Beyond that, I ask for prayers on his behalf. Love ya, Tim.

Soon after, she sent another message:

> So I'm struggling and feel great terror about finances and being alone. Will you pray for me? I'm grieving and feel something between fear and terror. I need Jesus! I want things to be different, and they're not. It's difficult to know what is an emotional stirring versus a real change. Either way, it's too late. It's done. It's over. My miracles are used up. And to be honest, I recognize that it's not about miracles. It's about accepting the things I cannot change. This is a tough one to accept.

I processed for a few days before I was able to respond. My heart ached for everyone involved. I love them all dearly. I remembered the great times we'd shared and how promising life had looked back then, and I grieved for all the losses. I looked for new things. Could my feeble words help? I spoke from my heart what I knew to be true.

I don't know that the terror you feel is anything abnormal. It may be that any kind of terrible, traumatic change brings up the *f*-cubed instinct (fight, flight, or freeze). You're brave. You've always been fearless.

I'm remembering back to when I felt God calling me to a life of singleness. It wasn't easy. And I think I initially kind of railed against that reality. It was hard to grab hold of the idea that Jesus was going to have to prove he's really enough. He is enough; that's true. But as beautiful and surprising as he is around every life turn, I don't feel him physically hug me. I don't get to throw my day at him while we grill out together. He's not physically there to drop by and fix a can of chicken noodle soup when I'm sick. We don't laugh till we cry over the goofy stuff the dogs or mutual friends get into.

I do talk to him all the time, though, and hope I will feel a response. I do hear him. Very clearly.

So I think even if it's occasionally been a bit unconscious on my part, I've been forced to look deeper, know him on a soul level more intimately, and plan out more time to spend with him. Sometimes that rationale doesn't make living alone any more comfortable. But sometimes it does.

Everything is a season. That's pretty much my mantra nowadays. I can look back and safely say that every circumstance, experience, crisis, crisis of faith, broken promise, need, failure, and decision, right or wrong, has somehow always managed to come to an acceptable resolution. Not always—very rarely, in fact—the perceived purpose I would have chosen. But in hindsight, always right.

And I'm still standing. Leaning into the almost constant winds of change has made my roots stronger and made me more durable and bendable, resilient. It's all, everything, just another season. And somehow it works out.

Sometimes, at night, when I turn out the lamp and crawl under the covers, if I look extraordinarily hard, I catch a glimpse of his eyes.

Christi wrote back,

Some of it has been brave, and some of it has not been brave. Some of it has been a lack of trusting God! Yet even when I didn't trust God the way he asked me to, he was still watching and waiting and guiding and covering and all-consumingly loving me, all in the midst of my disbelief and my belief! That is an amazing God!

I hung out with Billy today, and though he won't recall the words I read to him from your message, in that moment, that pivotal, powerful moment, as I read, "I catch a glimpse of his eyes," he said, "Oh wow, I can just be still finally and focus and reflect on that." He got it! And it was powerful to him! Thank you for creating a powerful moment for me. Thank you for creating a powerful moment for Billy. Thank you for creating a powerful moment for all of us together!

How do we get through and survive the anfractuosity of this life?

Jesus is ahead of us, peering with perfect precision around the curve, the next bend, preparing the way, and we get through it together. The powerful moments for all of us together.

May his grace be evident with every step you take. May the anfractuosity of your life overflow with all things new.

CONVERSATION STARTERS
BY LORI LEE LOVING

Lori Lee and I are kindred spirits. We have mastered the art of finding comedy in a plethora of unintended life calamities. I knew this story would inspire her. Lori Lee skips around every bend, every anfractuous curve. She's acutely aware of who's leading the way. She's really pretty.

1. Sometimes we misinterpret what to do, and sometimes we just flat out make the wrong choice. Either way, it can push us to move in a new direction. Tim invited me to comment in his book because I once ate the whole sacred loaf of bread by mistake at a communion service. *Um, what?* It was a predicament that only Tim might stumble into. We make plans. We do what we think we are asked to do and can still entirely misread a situation. I'd never seen a whole loaf of bread used in a service. When it was handed to me, I took a bite directly out of it like a hoagie sandwich. I thought, *Well, they couldn't want it back now*, so I carried it back to my seat and ate the rest. I thought everyone had a loaf. I thought *they* were the weird ones. I have no idea how they finished out the service for others. Were they forced to crumble up old crackers or mints? That's a crazy, lighthearted situation of doing the wrong thing. Other days, we've all certainly made seriously poor choices or experienced the consequences of other people's choices. That's when the road diverges. Thankfully, we serve a God who "will make our paths straight," as mentioned in Proverbs 3:6.

2. Have you ever completely misread a situation or taken the wrong path? Discuss.

3. Were you blessed by a new road you could not have predicted? It doesn't always change in an instant. Take a moment to remember how it felt to have God walk beside you around the bend.

4. Are you willing to put one foot in front of the other and trust where God's Spirit has prompted you to go?

BONUS CONVERSATION STARTERS FROM TIM e HOLDER

Originally, I wrote conversation starters for this story. But then I realized this was perfect for Lori Lee, so I asked her to help out. She got first chapter, top billing. Here's a little about me: I have five dogs. I live in the country outside Little Rock, Arkansas. I live on two and a half acres of woods, weeds, and more than a little poison ivy, in a small house made of wood. I live in *The Blair Witch Project*.

1. Does change frighten you? Or do you dive into the adventure and ride the wave just to see where the current takes you? Does change mean more work or planning? How do you handle big changes? Stress? Anxiety? Excitement? Passion? Zeal? Hysteria? How differently would you feel if you made it a habit to recognize life events as a way for Jesus to turn change into a new thing for his glory?

2. *Anfractuous* means "winding, twisting, bending, and curving but not breaking"—like life. Life can be hard.

Talk about an experience in your life when you were afraid you might shatter. When you felt you were given more than you can handle. What tools and resources did you use to regain your footing, your strength, and your hope? Did you reach out to others for support to hold you up with physical needs? Did they hold you up with prayer and comfort? What hope can you wrap around someone struggling right now?

3. Are you in the middle of a life event that is burying you? Do you feel alone and desperate for care and answers? Let me tell you one of the top-five strengths I've gained over the years I've worked the Celebrate Recovery program: we were never made to walk this journey alone. The most courageous thing you can do is seek help and wise counsel from others. Be brave. Tell someone where you are mentally and emotionally. Be honest and specific. The truth is, we all need it sometimes. We're all an ex-something. If you're in a group setting right now, talk about it. Be strong. God will find a way, as impossible as it seems in the moment. Ask him for more faith. He will use your horrible situation and make it a new thing for his glory. Wait for it. God is doing a new thing. It will be a spring in the wasteland, and oh, you will have such a story to tell.

The Squirrel from Hell

ONE BRIGHT, CRISP autumn morning, I was leisurely driving to work. Surveying the route ahead, I noticed a squirrel sitting in the middle of the road.

After living in the country for twenty-some years, I've become reasonably adept at maneuvering around live critters. Mostly.

I swerved to miss the adorable little fellow and didn't feel a bump. I was happy.

I looked in the rearview mirror to make sure he'd made it across the road and was running off to scamper and frolic with his squirrely little friends—and I was horrified to see him break-dancing like a trout on hot asphalt in the road.

My heart, as usual when an injured animal is concerned, jumped straight into my throat, effectively cutting off oxygen to my brain and, by extension, any rational decision-making processes.

I slammed on the brakes and turned my car around. The only solution—totally abhorrent to me—was to go back and run over him again to put him out of his misery.

I'd already gotten misty-eyed, not to mention a bit nauseated. Apparently exhausted from thrashing, the bushy-tailed rodent now lay on his side, motionless, as I approached.

I feared he had already passed into a glorious eternal place with a street paved with acorns and stolen birdseed, when another car traveling in the opposite direction passed him. He flopped onto his belly, sat upright, and stared straight ahead.

I let out a pained howl that sounded not unlike a screech owl being neutered without anesthetic.

I parked on the closest dirt crossroad, jumped out of the car, and raced back. He was still sitting there, looking off into the distance, perhaps trying to decide whether or not he should go toward the light. Whatever he was thinking, I know he felt like he'd done been eat' by a bear and crapped off a cliff.

I was already blubbering as I apologized profusely. Then, for some insane reason, I crouched down to see how close I could get.

He was obviously in shock. I chose to pat him on the head a little. I then carefully picked him up, carried him back to my car, and set him gingerly on the floorboard between my feet. I turned the car around and drove back two blocks to Doubletree Veterinary Clinic, where I work, so Dr. Peck could check him out to see if he would live or not.

Slowly, cautiously, I parked the car outside the clinic. My next move involved, once again, care, compassion, and love. As I reached down between my legs to painstakingly pick him up, he miraculously shifted from shock to a radical state of distress. This surprising turn of attitude moved me into the same state of bug-eyed panic.

He, obviously not as injured as I'd first suspected, began bolting from ceiling to floor to door to dashboard, banging against the windows, to the back dashboard thing, (whatever that back dashboard thing is called) shaking more from agitation than distress at that point. All the while, I was trying to calm both of us down. I reached for him, and he began leaping again with great abandon. He landed on the back dashboard thing again, and

I froze. Actually, both of us froze. We were very still for a while. A short while. He disdainfully glared at me as if saying, "I will shank you."

Okay, sidebar. I think this minimutant was actually working with a domestic terrorist cell, and I had, in fact, thwarted his evil world-dominance plan from a suicide-bombing attempt aimed at destroying our nation's power lines.

Trying to be inconspicuous, I slowly turned and leaned over the back of the driver's seat with arms stretched out, trying to nab him. Apparently, fearful of an upcoming cast-iron-skillet event, he lurched at me with paws, complete with razor-sharp talons, outstretched and scratched my face as he passed, landing squarely on my back.

There I was, leaning at my waist over the seat with arms out in front of me, with a squirrel sitting on my back. And he didn't jump. He didn't move. He just sat there. On my back.

I began to jiggle a bit. He didn't budge. I jiggled more. He didn't shift. I vainly attempted to reach behind me, and that was when he dove to the passenger floorboard.

I swiftly, with great agility, reached down and grabbed his tail. He hopped forward a few inches. There was a moment of stunned disbelief on his face—and, I'm sure, mine—as I raised my clinched fist. We both gaped slack-jawed at the tuft of hair left in my grip. Then we both moved our gaze to take in the plucked carnage that used to be a thick, fuzzy, fluffy tail.

I chose to seize the moment. In perhaps not the wisest choice of my life, I grabbed again and got hold of his back.

Until that moment, I'd never really appreciated the agility or dexterity of those frisky little nut-snatchers.

He, in turn, reached around and sank his teeth into my index finger—deep—and didn't let go. I jerked my hand up and found him resolutely hanging from my finger. I shook my pointer three times. With each jiggle, he turned his defiant, furious eyes at me as if to say, "Is that all ya got?"

After deciding he had toyed with me long enough, he released his fangs of death. He nimbly dropped to the floorboard, dove, and hid beneath the passenger seat.

At that juncture, I was bleeding like a stuck pig. I thought if I moved the seat back and forth, it might encourage Rocky the Flying Incubus to come out. But the seats are, alas, electric and travel about a tenth of an inch every fifteen to twenty seconds. I finally realized he was secure in his fortress of solitude and wasn't going to budge.

I staggered into the clinic, looking as though I'd been in a wrestling match with a barbed-wire fence. The staff just looked at me with jaws dropped.

"What happened to you?" someone asked.

"I just got bit by a squirrel—in my car."

Hysterical laughter erupted. "No, seriously. What happened?"

"I just got bit by a squirrel in my car!"

No one could believe such butchery had actually been executed by a squirrel, until I took my coworkers out to the car, and they saw the foul personification of evil now sitting in the passenger seat.

After finding a Band-Aid for my finger, my coworker Jenny and I tried in vain to capture him by corralling him toward a portable kennel placed outside the door.

After twenty or so minutes, a passive observer said, "Why don't you just back away and let him jump out?"

Oh. Yeah. Good point.

I backed away from the door and watched as he jumped out, plowed into the side of the open door, and bolted headfirst into the trunk of a nearby tree. Once again stunned senseless, shaking his battered head, he gathered what little dignity he had left and slowly crawled up the trunk of the tree.

After a call to my doctor about antibiotics, pain meds, and the distinct possibility of rabies shots, I eventually healed—physically.

Word to the wise: if you're driving down Kanis Road close to Ferndale, Arkansas, and a precious, adorable, darling little squirrel crosses the road in front of you with a bunged-up, disfigured tail, speed up! Or at the very least, call Homeland Security immediately!

CONVERSATION STARTERS FROM DAVID AND MICAH RICE

David is my boss. He's a devoted friend, father, husband, and businessman. He's the guy everyone wants to have as a friend. He amazes me with his heart for Jesus and the way he seeks how he can best serve the Lord. He never shies away from telling others about his relationship with God. He looks for moments to connect with the Holy Spirit. I'm thankful he's in my life. I love my job. Micah, David's wife, is an amazing mom. She watches her kids for ways to cultivate their unique, God-given gifts. When you talk to Micah, it's easy to unconsciously segue any conversation into what God is doing in our lives and revealing to us the ways in which he is loving us. We text songs and sermons to each other. She's really, really pretty.

1. If you were a squirrel, would you willingly exit the vehicle and the embrace of soft, cuddly-hearted, tall, bald-headed Tim?

2. If you could interject any dialogue between Tim and squirrel, what would it be in the story, and when would it occur?

3. Suppose Tim was wrong, and the squirrel was actually not a terrorist but instead a resolute, crime-fighting squirrel hero with a dark but overcome past. What was his life story and mission?

Laodicea Revisited

MY FRIEND LISA Fischer's mom, Sherry Gibson, died on July 13. Soon after the memorial service, Lisa and I were talking. Lisa said, "Let me tell you how the Lord walked me through the experience of my mom's death. Our family felt sure her memory problems stemmed from dementia. At the same time, Dad dealt with the effects of a stroke. They both worried about the other. Mom worried about what would happen to Dad if she died first. Dad worried who would take care of her if he died first."

Lisa struggled with how the situation should be handled. When she began to feel fearful, unsure of her next move, or anxious, she pleaded with God. Her eyes glistened as she told me, "And then I heard the Lord say, 'Lisa, I have this. Stop being afraid.'"

The family finally received a diagnosis of dementia and began plans to identify the right medications that would benefit Sherry. Sadly, two days after everyone learned the news of her dementia, Sherry passed away. Lisa told me she remembered how many times the Lord comforted her spirit with the knowledge that everything was okay. He was taking care of her mother. In true Lisa Fischer style, she smiled as she remembered, "He told me to hush up and sit down."

Lisa listened as God whispered to her heart. She went to him and asked for his mercy. The Lord's desire was that Lisa allow him and give him the privilege to be an active part of her story.

During our conversation, I shared with Lisa the story of my buddies David and Micah Rice and the birth of their daughter Aila Sage. David and Micah are my granola friends. They do pretty much everything naturally. When it came time for Aila Sage to enter the world, Micah made herself as comfortable as possible in their bathtub, surrounded by a midwife; her mom, Connie; and David sitting close by. The delivery went smoothly, and Aila Sage was born.

She wasn't breathing.

The midwife immediately exercised every procedure necessary to support Aila Sage. Nothing worked. David sat helplessly next to them and prayed, asking the Lord to help his child survive. He heard the Lord say, "Let me in."

David kept praying, "I am. Please, Lord, help my baby breathe."

Horrified, everyone struggled with the heart-wrenching possibility that Aila Sage might not live.

The midwife and Connie performed CPR, with Connie doing compressions and the midwife breathing for Aila Sage.

Still nothing.

David quietly cried out and begged the Lord for help. He distinctly remembers hearing the Lord say, "David, let me into this."

David kept quietly praying, "Lord, I am letting you in. Please help."

They were now at the five-minute mark, and still no breath. The midwife urgently implored someone to call 911.

Again, David heard the Lord say his name. "David, let me into this."

David, desperate for the life of his newborn daughter, jumped to his feet and cried out, "In the name of the Lord Jesus Christ, let my baby breathe!"

Aila Sage breathed.

Later that night, their older daughter, Prairie, came to David and told him she had prayed when her sister wasn't breathing. As soon as she asked Jesus to let Aila Sage breathe, Aila Sage breathed.

When Micah told me this story, she informed me that Aila Sage's name, in Scottish Gaelic, means "From the strong place." I asked her if she learned any big lessons from the birth. She said her takeaway was that Jesus wants us to invite him into our experience. That thought stuck with me. When I shared it with Lisa, she said it reminded her of Jesus saying, "I stand at the door and knock."

I know the verse and the accompanying image. I've always thought it was a great picture of evangelizing the world. I'm sure I've used that verse at some point when encouraging an unbeliever to accept the Lord. I decided to find out exactly what Jesus meant when he said it.

The letter, in Revelation 3, is a message to the church in Laodicea. It is the last of the letters to the seven churches and arguably the most scathing.

Among other hindrances to the Laodiceans' faith, their lives reflected neither hot nor cold. That made them disgusting to God.

I learned, when I read the letter to Laodicea, that it convicted the church. It didn't entice nonbelievers. When Jesus declared, "I stand at the door and knock," he was telling those of us who already know him to let him in. In essence, he said, "Hey, I'm standing right here. You know who I am. You've accepted me into your heart. Invite me in."

Too many Christians cry out to Jesus when they are in desperate need of help. Most certainly, he hears their hearts and answers accordingly. But they fail at asking him to be an active part of their ordeal. It's as though they want to sit back and let Jesus perform a miracle while they watch. They pray for help and guidance but keep him at arm's length.

Jesus keeps knocking and saying, "Open the door, and let me in. I'm right here. I'll come in and eat supper with you. I'll stay with you."

In biblical times, sharing supper together signified friendship or affection. It meant intimacy. When Jesus said, "You're neither hot nor cold, but lukewarm," he was saying, "You can't be noncommittal with me. You've accepted me into your heart, but have you invited me into your experience?"

What if we're missing out on one of the most beautiful parts of our journey with Jesus by knowing who he is but never really allowing him to be an active player in our story? How much are we missing out by feeling comfortable with him sitting in the stadium but never asking him to join the game? What would it feel like if he were sitting at the supper table with us on a regular basis, even when we didn't need help?

Jesus gave them the answer. He needed them to wake up to what they elected to miss. He was saying, "Here's what you will receive if you open the door and let me in. I conquered death and took the place of honor right by my Father on his throne. Open the door. Invite me in. And when the time comes, you will be a conqueror just like me, and you will sit right next to me on my throne. You will have experienced complete victory."

There is a difference between committing to the Lord and asking him to be an active participant in our ongoing adventure. His love and affection for us are so powerful, sure, and complete that he won't settle for less than a determined, deliberate relationship through every undertaking, every trial, every pursuit, every failure, and every dream. He'll just keep on knocking.

Of course, it's not easy, but I'm going to do my best to always leave the door wide open.

CONVERSATION STARTERS
FROM NANCY J. KLINE

Nancy's testimony is worthy of a book. I watch her work with women whose hearts are shattered and without hope, and I see them flourish with renewed faith and relationships with Jesus. Why? Partly because of Nancy's words. Partly because of her story. But mostly because of her overflowing heart of love. Anyone who knows her knows Jesus a little better. Anyone who's around Nancy knows love. And she's really pretty.

1. Can you describe a time when you cried out to the Lord in desperation, as David was doing?

2. Tim describes the importance of inviting Jesus into our ordeals, our experiences, our suppers, and our adventures. How can you do this in your own life?

3. What makes you think Jesus wants to be involved in your everyday life experiences?

4. Lisa heard the Lord say he had her fearful situation. Have you heard the Lord's voice say something that surprised you?

5. Do you feel like you know the Lord well enough that trust comes easy in all situations?

Best Turkey Ever

For even the Son of Man did not come
to be served, but to serve, and to give
His life as a ransom for many.

—Mark 10:45 NIV

I WILL SIT in front of the TV on Thanksgiving morning to watch the parade. I've certainly seen my fair share of Thanksgiving Day parades. I still love them—all the gliding cartoon balloons, decorated floats, and marching bands.

As I prepare to head over to enjoy an outrageously excessive meal, raucous laughter, and love with friends, I will, as is my custom, ask the Lord to bring my mind and heart all the blessings he has lavished on my life, all the points of praise, and all the moments of clarity in my journey with him. I will thank him for the grace he has poured over me through his only Son's blood.

I will thank him for people he has strategically placed at specific places in my life who have been influential in encouraging me to be the man I'm becoming. Faces and places will race through my mind, and I, of course, all misty-eyed, will thank him for his mercy and love. I will praise him for these precious people and ask him to bless them on this day.

Almost always, he brings to mind events and people from previous years. One Thanksgiving morning, he pulled me up short at a long-forgotten person and time. I called Mom and asked if she remembered the lady's name. Mom thought it might have been Tilly Matthews.

I was somewhere between six and eight years old. Dad was the preacher at Cedar Bayou Church of Christ in Baytown, Texas.

I can't remember how we became acquainted with Tilly. But I do remember driving across the Cedar Bayou Bridge to her house near the railroad tracks. We drove every Sunday night to pick Tilley up and take her to church with us. I use the term *house* loosely. It was more of a shanty, a shed, down by the bayou. I expected to find it collapsed on itself in a pile of rubble every time we approached. It leaned to the right in a dangerously precarious position. The slant was so defined Tilly would struggle to open the front door, which seemed to be constantly jammed. She obviously could see us coming down the hill, under the bridge a few hundred feet away, and would begin the battle of the door before we ever got to her house.

Dad never had to honk. She must have been standing by her window, watching and waiting for us. We would watch in horrified fascination the weekly ritual of woman versus gravity. There was always a small light from a lamp behind her in the house. When the door finally surrendered and Tilly threw it open, we heard it slam back against the inside wall. We watched as the light behind her formed a silhouette of this little old lady fighting to get out and fighting to close the door behind her. We silently watched, spellbound by her determination to meet us.

She had a frail, tiny frame. A whisper of a body. A leathered, life-worn face so wholly covered with wrinkles and creases that more than once, I got in trouble for counting. Lips that were so pursed with furrows they seemed perpetually chapped. Eyes that, although milky with cataracts, were a paradox of sorrow and life, wisdom and childlike curiosity, and immense love.

Tilly draped herself in the same old thread-bare brown tweed overcoat that engulfed her body. I never saw her out of it, even in the middle of a humid, sweltering Texas summer. She was equally proud of the ancient hat she always wore, which was adorned and battened with tired, nondescript flowers and petals I was never able to identify.

A selfish child, I always anticipated what she held in her hands. Walking with a determined gait to the car, she never failed to have candy for my brothers, sister, and me. I got perturbed at Mom for imploring Tilly not to give us candy. It was years before I comprehended that. Mom didn't care about our having sweets; she realized what a huge sacrifice it must have been for Tilly to give out of her desperate poverty. I did recognize, at least from a child's perspective, Tilly's childlike joy at seeing our ecstatic reaction to her gifts.

For quite a while, we believed Tilly made all the candy herself. She often brought out the treasure placed perfectly on a beautiful plastic plate that she insisted Mom keep. Years later, Mom told me Tilly didn't make candy. She bought candy, unwrapped each individual piece, and daintily and purposefully arranged the pieces on the platter. Now I understand why Mom would sigh and turn to look out her front-seat window.

One particular Sunday night, Tilly struggled more than usual with her front door, fighting like a gladiator to get it open with one hand. The whole shanty shuddered. From her silhouette, I saw that her occupied hand held something more significant than a plate of candy. The unidentified object was more significant in circumference than Tilly and must have weighed at least fifty pounds.

As she approached the car, an enormous, almost mischievous grin turned her face into a grill of corrugated pleats and furrows. I had to laugh, until Mom gave me *the look*.

Tilly's burden proved to be an enormous frozen turkey. Mom gasped and said, "Tilly, what—"

Tilly stopped Mom's disapproval by raising an old, gnarled, arthritic hand and, with her finger to her lips, whispered in her smoky, crushed-opals-on-burlap voice, "Happy Thanksgiving."

On the way to church, we kids marveled at the gift. Tilly smiled, sheepishly fulfilled, while quietly tapping the frozen bird in her lap. Mom found a way to stay occupied, focusing on some point far off in the distance.

At the time of that long-ago Thanksgiving season, I didn't understand why that turkey brought up such an emotional response in my young heart. I've devoured many turkey legs since that day. They are all unique. I remember how early Mom used to wake up to put the turkey in the oven, but it seemed Mom worked extra hard to make Tilly's turkey better than any we'd ever prayed over before. That day, I somehow knew that turkey was beyond exceptional. It was costly—priceless.

Even though my parents routinely implored Tilly to come home to have a meal with us, she never did.

On that day, I wondered how Tilly would celebrate her Thanksgiving. Did she have family or friends to enjoy the day with? Or would she be alone, joyfully plotting her next plate of candy?

Did she have any idea how precious every bite of that turkey would be that day? Did any of us, in that moment, have a full understanding of how special that meal would be or how that act of kindness, one sacrificial gift, would be remembered and impact our lives a half century later?

Will any of us know before heaven how one small act of service we perform today will echo through the halls of eternity?

We moved away from Baytown a few years later, and I never saw Tilly again. I wonder who was privileged to be the next recipient of her goodness. Her love. Her joyful sacrifice. Were there other kids who would one day, many years later, think of Tilly on a cold Thanksgiving morning and remember her extraordinary kindness? Would they thank God for that moment in time when they were given a glimpse of his goodness? Remember his own sacrificial giving? Would they wonder, as I do, if they had ever given as much as that little least of his? Did she know how thankful this grown-up would one day be for her life? For the lessons she taught me just by living a life of service to others?

Today, Lord, I'm thankful to you for placing Tilly in my life and my heart. I thank you for giving me this precious, priceless eternal memory. Thank you for teaching me that the greatest leaders are the ones who live to serve. Tilly led me well. And one day may I have the honor of serving Tilly in heaven as she served me here on earth! Today, with all my heart, I'm thankful for Tilly Matthews.

Be ready with a meal or a bed when it's
needed. Why, some have extended hospitality
to angels without ever knowing it!

—Hebrews 13:2 MSG

CONVERSATION STARTERS
FROM BARRY NAPIER

I've known Barry for somewhere around forty-five years. We lost track of each other for a few decades but then reconnected through Celebrate Recovery. He is a smart, funny, focused, redeemed friend. We played together in a CR band for many years. He's a great guitar and mandolin player. Yeah, I looked for songs so he could play the mandolin. He took my leadership and made new things out of some really hard songs. He's a great friend and father and husband to Cindy. I love this dude. I'm thankful God opened the door so we could work together. He wrote five questions. He's always been an overachiever.

1. A friend once told me, "Some people are so poor all they have is money." In what ways was Ms. Tilly wealthier than people who are financially rich? What riches did she have that money could not buy?

2. Matthew 6:2 instructs us to give of our means in a way that doesn't draw attention to ourselves. Think of an experience in which you gave or did something for someone else anonymously or confidentially. Share an experience in which you were the recipient of a confidential or anonymous gift or deed.

3. There is a difference between people-pleasing and serving as God and the Son instruct. People-pleasing involves doing something for someone else so he or she will like you or be impressed. Godly service involves doing something for someone else strictly for the joy it will bring to him or her. Do a quick inventory of your

past behavior, and ask yourself: What has been your motivation when serving others?

4. I remember an old song that goes, "Brother, let me be your keeper. Let me be as Christ to you. Pray that I might have the grace to let you be my servant too." Do you find it difficult to receive a gift or kind deed from someone less fortunate than yourself? In this regard, discuss the difference between pride and humility.

5. Years after you have passed on, will thoughts of you come to someone's mind? If so, how will you be remembered?

Horror Movies at Midnight

I'VE ALWAYS LOVED to read. It's a passion. The past few years, though, have been so life-busy I rarely find time to read like I used to. When I was a kid, one of my favorite things to do was grab the thick Sunday morning edition of the newspaper; unfold it; and sit down to read the comics, *Parade Magazine*, and the *TV Guide*.

I sat in front of the TV with my box of Cap'n Crunch cereal and a gallon of milk. At the same time, Mom tried valiantly and semisuccessfully to get everyone, including herself, dressed for church. Dad would be shaving while he mentally went through his sermon outline for the morning service, many times wishing he could come up with a great object lesson for his main point.

As I said, I loved reading. I was totally engrossed in the *TV Guide*. I read the synopsis for every episode of my favorite shows and looked specifically for which horror movie would be showing on the late Friday night scare-fest.

One thing consistently puzzled me as I read all those little snippets of my favorite shows. The confusing anomaly was almost exclusively confined to the summertime. I went to inquire of my father. He was, of course, shaving.

"Dad, I don't understand something here."

He absentmindedly asked, "What's that?"

"I'm reading what the show is going to be about. It says, 'Lucy has a bit too much Vitameatavegamin and embarrasses Ricky at a commercial shoot.' And then it says, 'Repeat.' So I go back and read it again, and it says the exact same thing: 'Lucy has a bit too much Vitameatavegamin and embarrasses Ricky at a commercial shoot. Repeat.' Dad, I've read it five times, and it says the exact same thing every single time!"

I think Dad cut himself with the razor and sported toilet paper to church. When Dad used the incident as his illustration that morning, the congregation erupted into hysterical laughter. Object lesson. Main point.

Most Friday nights, we kids were allowed to stay up a little later since it was a weekend. Being the rogue child, I always begged for more TV. Dad usually relented, rattling off rules I'd heard thousands of times before already and could recite from memory. I could watch TV for a while with the volume turned down to the third-lowest notch on the knob. I was forbidden to watch the horror movie. I was required to turn the TV off before the Mummy, Dracula, or Godzilla crossed our black-and-white screen.

Dad turned off the family room light, the last remaining light in the house, and headed down the dark hallway to bed. I knew if I played my cards right, I would hear his heavy breathing, meaning he was totally asleep, in approximately 4.7 minutes.

I slid off the couch, and with all the stealth I could muster, I tiptoed to the TV, turned down the volume so only I could hear it from the couch, and changed the knob to channel 2, one of only three channels in existence. I crawled back onto the sofa, hid up to my chin with a blanket, and waited, heart pounding, for the opening credits.

Obviously, I had no other option. I already knew which black-and-white monster to prepare for, since the previous Sunday, I'd read the synopsis in the *TV Guide* twelve times.

It didn't take long before I was quivering in fear. Which end of the couch was the werewolf crouching behind, waiting for me to uncover one inch of flesh from the *the blanket*?

Everyone knows that any skin or body part covered by *a blanket* is impervious to attack or dismemberment. A single hair uncovered, though, means certain death.

I'm not sure at what point the fear became too overwhelming, and I fell asleep. It was always before the end of the movie. I never knew who conquered the Creature from the Black Lagoon. I never found out if the good guys shoved Dracula into the sun and burned him to a crisp. And what about all those secondary characters—which, of course, included me—who got eaten by the werewolf?

All I know is that I slept during the movie's climactic end. I sawed logs while the Native American, in full headdress, performed sign language to the Lord's Prayer. Finally, I was jerked awake by the annoying test-pattern screen with the one piercing tone that droned on till the next morning, when the station awoke once again.

I quivered, mentally making sure all body parts were covered by *the blanket*. I listened intently, making sure there was no other movement in the room as I tried to fall back into my terrified sleep.

Then there were steps. Distinct footsteps coming from the hallway.

If I screamed, the Creature from the Black Lagoon would know where I was, and my short, uneventful life would be over. Of course, the slimy creature couldn't see me, thanks to the magic of *the blanket*. If I didn't scream, there was always the possibility it would move right past me to the next room and eat one of my brothers.

So I waited, vainly attempting not to give myself away by breathing or shaking too much. Suddenly, the TV went silent, and the steps moved to the edge of the couch. *The blanket* was thrown to the side, and there in the darkness, I made out my dad's form towering above me.

He was ominously quiet.

He couldn't yell at me without waking the entire household. As custom dictated, Dad walked to the TV and pressed the power button, rendering the room completely black, except for the blistering square residue from the TV test pattern now burned into my retinas. Dad reached down and took my hand, lifted me off the couch, and began the 347-mile trek down the dark hallway.

Pitch black, that hallway. As Dad and I walked, I expected Frankenstein's monster to lumber out of my already dead sister's bedroom to attack. We passed the bathroom, where the sightless four-foot-tall spider would crawl out of the toilet to pull me into its commode web.

But oddly enough, now I wasn't afraid. Actually, I felt like the hero of the tale. I knew nothing was strong enough to overtake me. I could walk through the blackest night, the darkest ink of life, as long as I held tightly to and never let go of my father's hand.

Minnie Louise Haskins, a twentieth-century British poet, penned one of my favorite quotes in her poem "God Knows":

> I said to the man at the gate of the year: "Give me a light that I may tread safely into the unknown." And he replied: "Go out into the darkness and put your hand into the hand of God. That shall be to you better than light and safer than a known way." So I went forth, and finding the Hand of God, trod gladly into the night. And He led me towards the hills and the breaking of day in the lone East.

So do not fear, for I am with you: do not
be dismayed, for I am your God. I will
strengthen you and help you; I will uphold
you with my righteous right hand.

—Isaiah 41:10 NIV

Everyone needs a hand to hold in the dark.

CONVERSATION STARTERS FROM RITA STONE

Rita always looks for ways to make everything around her better. She finds the good in everything and takes joy in bringing it out in people and experiences. If you ever see pictures of her cooking expertise, it's equivalent to a work of art. She's funny. She listens well and gives amazing, God-filled encouragement. She's a good person to have on your side. She's very pretty. She loves her husband, Kent. He's a good guy too.

1. Do you have an activity that gives you the same adrenaline rush as a horror movie? What draws you to that activity?

2. Tim's dad represented both deserved discipline and protective love. How did the adults in your life communicate these principles to you?

3. Were you the rogue kid in your family? If so, how did your free spirit play out? Did you grow out of it? Or do you still have moments? Give a couple of examples.

4. When Tim was young, his passion was reading. What was your earliest passion? What hobbies did you love doing? Have you lost a passion that you long to rekindle? An early passion may be a gift from God, part of his plan for you. What can you do to resurrect those dreams?

Patty Duke and "Eve of Destruction"

I KNOW IT will be hard to believe, but when I was eleven years old, I was the skinniest kid at Shady Oaks Elementary School in Hurst, Texas, and possibly the least athletic kid in town.

I never understood how I could excel at games like hide-and-seek, red rover, and dodgeball with neighborhood kids. When put in any organized athletic endeavor, I became a beached jellyfish.

I always dreaded when physical education tests happened every spring, when we were forced to do a specific number of sit-ups, jumping jacks, deep knee squats, and sprints of more than ten yards. I would panic, shiver like a horse shedding flies, and break out into flop sweats. It was the most miserably heartbreaking time of my life. Until fifth grade.

Patty Duke was nineteen years old when she starred in a movie called *Billie*. It's the story of a tomboy who loves sports. When the high school track coach sees her run, he asks her to join the school team. Her inclusion on the formerly all-male team causes a stir, especially with her father. He is typically supportive of Billie, but now he worries her shocking behavior will cost him his bid for mayor. Nervously, he starts setting Billie up with dates, unaware that she has a crush on her classmate Mike.

The reason Billie is so good at running is because she hears the beat. Patty Duke nods her head to the beat of the song she hears in her mind, and when the race starts, she runs to the rhythm of the song. As the competition progresses, she mentally speeds the beat of the song up and, therefore, runs faster, winning every single race, becoming the sweetheart hero of her school.

Well, I thought that was the best idea ever.

I couldn't wait for the running of the fifth graders a few days later. I was going to conquer the race with sheer dogged determination.

I specifically and deliberately chose "Eve of Destruction" by Barry McGuire as my driving beat.

I practiced for days. When the event day finally arrived, I felt confidence and dedicated focus as every male in the fifth grade lined up on the touchdown line at the end zone of our elementary football field.

I was channeling the beat. I'd never been more prepared for anything in my life. The whistle blew, and I felt sure turbo-thruster fire was shooting out the bottoms of my dress shoes, and possibly my ears, as I launched off the starting line. I ran like the wind as I heard the beat pounding in my head.

At just the right moment, I jerked the needle from 33 1/3 rpms up to 78. I completely skipped 45. I forced my skinny legs to move beyond what I thought was possible for me. With the chilly spring wind whipping past my face, I knew that if I had been wearing a nun's hat, I would have taken off like Sally Field.

The end zone was in sight, and I revved up the beat just a bit more to make the percussive explosion of speed as impressive as I possibly could.

Then it was over. I finished the race approximately fifty yards behind everyone else.

Truth be told, it was at this point I began to wonder why the beat thing wasn't working. Somehow, no matter how hard I tried, I couldn't get my legs to speed up as fast as "Eve of Destruction" was playing in my head.

Every other kid waited by Mrs. Smith, my teacher. She was obviously, even though I didn't want to believe it at the time, doing her best not to laugh outright as I caught up to the rest of the class already walking in the doors back to class. I never wanted to step foot on those yard lines ever again. Ironically, I passed through that accursed field every day. The back of our property butted up against the school playground.

For the rest of my life, I have resented Patty Duke. If I'd possessed a clearer understanding of the law at the time, I might have tried to sue her for intentional infliction of emotional distress.

It wasn't until I was in my twenties that I began to understand the mystery of running the race. I wanted to be in better shape. I joined a gym and got a trainer. I chose not to use my car as much, so I rode my bicycle to wait tables. I taught aerobics at the most exclusive studio in Nashville. I ran five miles six days a week, rain, sun, snow, or ice. I was at 3 percent body fat. As I ran, girls would drive by with their windows rolled down and whistle. It was awesome.

At the time, there weren't a lot of competitive outlets for athletic endeavors, other than the occasional 5K or 10K for charity. I calibrated my mind so I was exercising for the benefits of building strength and energy and having some discipline in my life. I realized that mastering one area would bleed into every other area of my life.

Many Bible verses mention running. I love Hebrews 12:1 (MSG): "We'd better get on with it. Strip down, start running—and never quit!" In other words, I'm running a race that has been specifically designed for me. All of us are. And guess what? There is a prize at the end of this race.

Even though you run your race with purpose and dedication, you need to remember that you have a responsibility to stand as part of a great cloud of witnesses. You must be conscious of the ones running the course with you, and when you sense they are strengthening their stride, let them hear your applause.

If you have extra baggage slowing you down, be careful you don't trip over it. Be vigilant, and watch to make sure it doesn't impede your rhythm. Even if it's equipment you think you need, give it a close inspection. More than likely, you'll find you can dump it if it causes you to lose focus on the goal.

By the way, don't worry so much about the prize. That's already yours. But focus on it. Keep it in sight. Keep Jesus in sight. Be brave, and keep running. Endure through the sizzling heat of an asphalt life. Keep running when every step seems to climb a bit steeper than the last. Go for broke when the path is straight and flat.

Breathe. Take time from running to stroll in the cool evening breezes, and listen for the sounds of the Lord walking through the spring flowers. Psalm 119:32 (MSG) says, "I'll run the course you lay out for me if you'll just show me how." As we run the race out of obedience, the Lord will expand our compassion. He will make room in our hearts for the wounded, bruised, and lonely outcasts who have forgotten and lost their direction.

Keep training. Read the playbook. Even in the middle of the race, we are still training.

We love to watch sporting events, hoping we will see records broken that edge against the limit of human potential. Mike Powell is a great example. He holds the world record in the long jump. At the Olympics, the long jump was once a marquee event.

But not any longer. Why is the long jump no longer the spectator draw it used to be? What happened? Mike Powell happened.

At the 1991 World Championships in Tokyo, Powell was ready to show the previous world champion, Bob Beamon, how to jump.

Powell was such a no-name at the time that when he got up to jump, he looked up and saw Beamon leaving. Powell took it as a slap in the face. According to Powell, his "whole life story, even today, is being the underdog." Even now, after seeing the video hundreds of times, he says, "Every single time I see it, I go right back to the moment. I smell the air in the stadium."

His biggest competitor during the event was Carl Lewis, who held the Olympic record. In long-jump qualifying, Lewis leaped more than a foot farther than anybody else.

Powell jumped before Lewis in the thirteen-man order. His first jump out of six was horrible, just twenty-six feet. He was so amped up he was hyperventilating. Lewis went four jumps later and jumped farther than Powell's personal best.

Powell moved into second place on his second jump, but Lewis responded with the longest jump of his career on his third. Powell, so error-prone he used to be called Mike Foul by his coach, was over the board on his fourth, meaning he stepped across the board where the jump was to begin.

Lewis watched from behind. His next two jumps posted the greatest back-to-back long jumps in history. He sat on the grass to watch Powell's fifth jump.

Powell puffed his cheeks, waved his arms like a pro wrestler, and propelled off the board with room to spare. He panted as his body arched in the air. He gave in to gravity and dug into the dirt with a thud that caused screams from a crowd of some sixty thousand.

Powell immediately rose from the pit, raising his arms, pointing his fingers, and roaring with focused intensity. He clapped as he awaited the distance reading. Lewis, who'd sat during Powell's jump, stood up.

Then Powell saw the results: 8.95 meters—a new world record.

"Everything I did during my whole life until that point was encapsulated in that jump," he said in an *NBC SportsWorld* article. "Everything in my life that I had not achieved. Every girl that turned me down for a date. Every time I didn't learn something. That was my moment to show the world. You're going to need a crowbar to get this smile off my face."

Mike Powell jumped 29 feet, 4 1/4 inches.

That's just shy of three stories, people. He has held the world record for twenty-six years, and it's almost universally accepted that this record will never be broken.

Run the race. Focus on the process. Be deliberate and scheduled with training. Don't give up. Run with purpose. Don't run alone. Applaud others who hear the beat. Focus on the goal, but don't worry about the prize.

It's already yours.

CONVERSATION STARTERS FROM GREG AND JULIE HILLEGAS

Greg and Julie are a big part of the reason these stories all came into existence in the first place. They nodded when I was asked to help teach the Creative Living Connections class. Greg is a guy you can sit with and talk to about pretty much anything for hours. He makes you feel accepted and comfortable. Julie is completely devoted to everything important to her: her husband and two sons; her extended family and friends; and, most importantly and passionately, Jesus. She's really pretty.

1. What are current distractions you have that hinder you from focusing on the goal?

2. What's a goal or accomplishment you have achieved or overcome?

3. If you could ever participate in the Olympics, what event would you choose, and why?

Epic Failures

I THINK EVERYONE has moments, points of reference, in their lives they wish never happened. But alas, too many people know about the distressingly awkward incident to show grace enough to ever allow you to live it down.

One typical, uneventful Sunday morning, I stood in the choir room at 8:20, getting ready to go onstage to worship. All the choir members usually gather upstairs by eight fifteen to run through the choir song and then just hang until we single-file it downstairs and onto the platform.

Coffee decided to set in.

I knew I had about ten minutes to spare, so I dashed to the men's room. It would have to be a quick trip—no reading the newspaper. I raced into the stall. Dropping my pants, with my bechunkis hovering over the throne (yes, when all is said and done, you may feel the need to slaughter a pig to get this visual out of your head), I noticed clean toilet paper in the bowl, so I reached behind me, grabbed the handle, and flushed.

For some unexplainable, unforeseeable reason, the commode exploded. Water went everywhere in a nanosecond. I was apparently in shock; I just stood there waiting for the tide to ebb back out to sea. Or maybe I was waiting for Moaning Myrtle to come screaming from the depths of the Chamber of Secrets. Nonetheless, a few seconds passed before I realized water was all over the floor, swirling around my dropped khakis and out the stall door.

When I finally became conscious, I grabbed my pants up. I grabbed them up so fast, in fact, my wallet and iPhone, nestled snugly in my back pockets, popped out and into the small creek forming around me in the stall. I wasn't sure what to grab first: my pants or my wallet-and-phone combo. I was in *The Matrix*. The blue pill or the red pill? I grabbed the combo. They were both soaked. I laid them on top of the double toilet paper dispenser and then grabbed my pants up. They too were drowned. But just the back of them was soaked. The front rested comfortably on my wet shoes.

I knew it was only a couple of minutes before my presence needed to be onstage. I couldn't see how bad the wetness was since most of it was on the back of my pants. I ran into the now empty choir room, threw the wallet-and-phone combo into my music locker, raced down the stairs and onto the risers, and deliberately stood in the back row so no one could see me from behind. I sang with all the gusto I could muster as toilet water ran down the back of my legs and pooled onto the riser at my feet for approximately twenty to twenty-five minutes.

Of course, worship time would soon come to an end, and the choir would climb back up the stairs to the choir room. Being in the back row, I would climb the stairs in front of everyone else. You have no idea how difficult it was to climb up fourteen steps backward with forty people watching me make a complete dipstick of myself. Or remove all doubt from their previously undecided minds.

Anissa Hodges, climbing the stairs right behind me—or in front of me, depending on your point of view—furrowed her confused brow as I ascended backward up the stairs. Before she could comment, I tried to answer her baffled expression. "The commode exploded—not my debris—and my pants were on the floor. They're soaked in the back."

By that time, we were in the choir room, so I turned and continued my journey. Then Anissa said, "Oh, that's why there's toilet paper on the back of your pants."

I just knew she was joking. "Stop it! That's not even close to funny."

I could feel the red rising from my forehead to the back of my neck as she said, "Well, not exactly toilet paper. More like toilet-paper beadlets."

"You have got to be kidding me."

A concerned bass was right behind her and said, "Um, there really is. Come on." He ushered me immediately into the bathroom, grabbed paper towels, and courageously and dauntlessly proved what a true friend looks like. He began swatting the back of my pants with paper towels.

Suddenly, a tenor walked into the bathroom and froze midstride, just staring. The bass, not missing a beat, said, "Somebody had to do it."

When he'd removed all the offensive beadlets, we went back into the choir room. I grabbed the wallet-and-phone combo out of my music locker and began wiping them down. I tried unsuccessfully to get the cover off the phone, when Anissa said, "Did your phone get wet?" I nodded.

She grabbed it out of my hand since I was obviously a total dolt at getting the OtterBox off it. Before I could even get "You know how to get that thing apart?" out of my mouth, Anissa had wholly disassembled the phone. Totally. In less than five seconds. Impressive.

I took it back, wondering what to do next, when Anissa punched my arm and said, "Don't put it back together!" I was attempting to do that very thing. She made sure I understood I was to take the disassembled phone home and not try to use it till I'd buried it in rice overnight. I nodded in obedience to her command.

At that point, I went back to the throne room to see if I needed to mop up any water that might have missed the drain in the floor. The grate, not draining, apparently needed as much repair as the offending depository.

With my normal good fortune in place, I walked in to find Pastor David Richards, our beloved choir director, grabbing paper towels out of the dispenser by the handful and throwing them into pools of water. He briefly glanced at me and continued his exercise as he said, "I'm afraid someone will slip and break something."

I lowered my head in shame and not a little mental discomfort and whispered, "I think—well, actually, I'm pretty positive—I caused this."

He paused and shot his eyes in my direction for the slightest moment, just long enough to mutter, "Why am I not surprised?"

I'm sure, if we're honest, we've all experienced a few of our own epic failures, whether they are from mistakes of our own choosing or from bad choices by others and whether they are remembered with heartache or grief or even laughter through embarrassment. We all have and will experience them.

A few months after the toilet-paper debacle, I began my thirty-first Celebrate Recovery step-study at a men's correctional unit. Twenty men sat around me as I explained the program and the guidelines and how the meetings would take place every week. Close to the end of the session, just before we stood shoulder to shoulder and said the Lord's Prayer together, one of the guys said, "What a refreshing change to get to come to a place and not be afraid to just be me."

I feel the same way. At the beginning of every study, I say pretty much the same thing to the guys. Before I begin, I silently ask the Holy Spirit to stand guard around that room, and every time, I feel a sense of protection, a vacuum. It's a wall that's impenetrable. The Enemy can't get through.

"Guys, this space every Monday night will be a safe place. We'll make it safe. I know where you are as much as you do. And I know that you've been put in a position that screams 'Failure!' But I'm here to tell you it doesn't matter why. You're here. It doesn't matter what you've done in the past. The Creator of the universe, the one true God, has a plan for you. He's prepared you for extraordinary things. You've made mistakes, sure. But we all have.

"Look at Peter. He walked with Jesus. He watched Jesus turn water to wine, heal blind people, raise cripples to walk, and forgive the unforgivable. He heard words and saw actions proclaiming forgiveness. And then, with just four words, Peter committed possibly the most epic failure of all time: 'I don't know him.'

"But here's the miracle of the story. Jesus—while fully aware Peter would soon deny him, turn his back on him, and walk away—reminded him his name was Peter, and on that rock Jesus would build his church. And the gates of hell would never conquer it. God's plan for Peter never failed or changed. It stayed constant and sure and true. Just like God. And you are no different. Proverbs 23:18 (ESV) says, 'Surely, there is a future, and your hope will not be cut off.'

"Here's the truth of you. And here's what I know the Lord wants you to know. You are God's masterpiece. He created you anew in Jesus Christ, so you can do good things he planned for you to do long ago, even before the world was put into orbit around the sun. His plan for you was in his heart before you were born, and he even wrote about those plans in his book before you were conceived. If you're worried about what he thinks of you sitting here all in white, feeling like a failure, remember Peter. Your failure is nothing compared to his.

"God's plan for you has never changed. He will see it revealed and completed if you choose to do the hard work and, like Peter, find the trust and courage to say, 'Yes, Lord, you know I love you.'

"We've all failed in one way or another. We've all messed up the plan in one way or another. You've listened to voices all your lives that have told you you're not good, you'll never amount to anything, you're stupid, or you're destined to fail. And you've believed those lies, and you've lived those lies. They haunt you, and you hear them in your waking and sleeping. It's what you've been taught. It's all you know.

"Now it's time for you to work. God wants to renew the plan for you that he laid out so long ago. If you let him, he will equip you with everything good to fulfill that plan that will be pleasing to him. His heart is to use you to bring glory to him and his Son, Jesus. And you can rest, knowing that the ripples from his plan for you will reverberate against the shores of heaven forever and ever."

The room is always filled with supernatural activity. I make it a conscious choice to lock on the eyes of every guy there at some point while I'm talking. They are transfixed by the words, which, trust me, come not from me but from a Father who loves them dearly. I often read hope in their eyes and a renewed resolve to trust the work and the process—some for the first time in their lives.

My final words to them are always "Encourage each other this week. If you're out on the yard or walking to chow and see one of your classmates, just say, 'You are God's masterpiece.'

"I know some of you think that it isn't true for you. You've failed too much. God couldn't possibly love you. Let me tell you what's true about those beliefs. You cheapen and devalue a unique and rare gem the Lord has created. That, my friends, gets to be your last failure. His plan for you is real and has never changed.

"There's a phrase in the Bible that I love but never really understood until recently: you are the apple of his eye. In ancient times, the pupil in the eye was believed to be a round, solid object, like an apple. And since the pupil is essential for vision, calling someone the apple of your eye meant you cherished them.

"The Bible says you are the apple of his eye. Why would he say that? Because when he looks in your eyes, he sees the reflection of his Son. It means you are treasured. It's okay if you are afraid to believe because of the hurt, pain, guilt, and shame you've experienced in your past. It's okay not to believe that right now. Just because you don't believe it doesn't make it any less true."

Then we stand arm in arm, shoulder to shoulder, a band of brothers and begin: "Our Father, who art in heaven, hallowed be thy name ..."

CONVERSATION STARTERS
BY LORI LEE LOVING

Lori has been a friend for close to forty years. We experienced many of the golden years of Christian music activity in Nashville. We lived life with a crazy group of people, finding new and creative ways to encourage each other in our journeys with Jesus. I have many great memories of Lori Lee. I'm blessed to have her in my life. And she's so pretty.

1. I think we've all been there with Tim in an embarrassing moment. I once walked an entire mall with a tail of toilet paper hanging over my skirt. As we grow, we learn that admitting the failure up front takes much of the steam out of it. We laugh first and with others so they can all be in on the joke. In the same way, we admit our missteps to others so they, in turn, feel free to admit theirs. It gives us all the opportunity to support someone who is sharing a failure and needs to be reminded that God forgives us when we seriously blow it. With honesty over a goofy mistake or honesty in causing heartache, it's best healed when it's all out on the table to be dealt with. Psalm 15:1–2 (NASB) says, "Lord, Who may settle on Your holy hill? One who walks with integrity, practices righteousness, And speaks truth in his heart." Sometimes we're the toilet paper, and sometimes we're the shoe. Sometimes a bad situation sticks to us, and sometimes we walk right into it. Was there a situation in which being completely honest and up front about your mistake helped to heal a wound? Talk about it.

2. Is there a situation today in which you can encourage someone that honesty will set him or her free?

BONUS CONVERSATION STARTERS FROM TIM e HOLDER

I came up with questions for this one and then decided I wanted Lori Lee's input on this as well. She gets the sheer joy of occasionally laughing at, learning from, and sharing our inconvenient adventures. Here are my thoughts.

1. Everyone has experienced at least one, if not incalculable, epic failure that, in the moment, seemed as if it would haunt you and cause excruciating embarrassment for the rest of your miserable, pathetic existence. Share an event that still makes you cringe. Be honest. Let the group laugh with you.

2. Peter and I are much alike. He's one of the biblical characters I most look forward to hugging when I get to heaven—after I body-slam Jesus and hold on to him for like a thousand years, of course. Even after reading how Jesus restored Peter, have you ever felt God can never thoroughly forgive you for hurts and pain you've caused in the past? He does, you know. He really does. It's his desire to see you healed and whole. Process as a group why this lie is ominously pervasive in our culture. How can you lovingly work as a group to encourage healing from the guilt and shame of your past?

3. God intimately and with intention imagined a specific plan for you before he laid the foundation of the earth. Yes, you! Do you feel you are living out his perfect plan

for you? His plan will always lead you to a pure, authentic relationship with him and those around you. That is the litmus test. If you get the sense you're missing out on using your gifts the way God wants you to use them, ask the Lord to lead you to fields of opportunity where you can flourish for his kingdom.

4. Wait! What if you're not sure of your strengths? Everyone grab a pen and paper. List every person in the room. Write down next to his or her name the single most positive characteristic of that person. Then go around the room one recipient at a time, and have all the members of the group expound on the strengths of that one person. It's life-changing when you hear several people encourage you. Reflect on the gift of encouragement given to you by those around you. What did you learn about yourself? How can this new knowledge translate into a renewed focus on God's plan for you? If you're not in a group setting, call friends, and ask what they feel are your greatest strengths. Be courageous.

A Flat Tire, a Leaf, and a Hummingbird

I LOVE THE -*ber* months from September through December. My favorite season is October. In my memories, all things autumn are encapsulated in that one month, October.

One crystal, sunlit morning, I left my house for work. As I walked to my car, I noticed the front left tire was perilously low. *Great. Just great. Come on, God. I need to just get to the bottom of the hill.* The local convenience store, complete with air pump, sat conveniently three miles down the road.

At the bottom of the hill, I heard the all-too-familiar rattle of a tire going flat. I knew it was too far for me to try to make it to Bear Creek Country Store, where I could have shoved down my stress with a bacon, egg, and cheese biscuit. *God, come on!*

The next-closest safe zone, as there is no shoulder on Ferndale Cutoff, is the 4-H center. I pulled into their parking lot and climbed out. The tire was a tragedy. I walked to the back of the car and lifted the hatch. A distinct tightness snaked into my shoulders, and I felt a distressing, foreboding, nameless dread, almost nausea. As I lifted the panel in the back of the car, I remembered: no spare tire. Even worse, I'd taken the jack out while cleaning the car a few months earlier, and it was sitting in my sunroom. Don't judge me!

I walked back to the driver's seat and sat there swigging a bottle of A&W root beer from a brown paper bag. I was close enough to the veterinary clinic where I worked that I decided to walk there. I figured I could make some calls and find a tire place who could send someone to come take the tire off, run the shredded tread to their store, put a new tire on the rim, and bring it back. Easy enough.

Half an hour later, I walked into the clinic, told the staff what was going on, and made the calls. Come to find out, no one offered the service I needed. A person had to physically take the tire in, which made no sense to me. *How can you take the tire in if it's flat?* They acted as though everyone had a spare tire and a jack in the back of their car.

The only thing I could think to do was walk toward home— three miles away—to grab the jack, come back, take the tire off, and figure out what to do from there.

I began my walk.

Almost immediately, old patterns began to seep into the vulnerable corners of my mind. All-but-forgotten tapes began to play. *You are so stupid. Why did you leave the jack out of the car? Why haven't you figured out a way to get a spare tire? You are completely irresponsible. Worthless.*

Before I let it go too far, I determined that I would not allow the Enemy to turn the experience into a martyr or bonehead attitude of despair. I asked the Lord to walk with me and help me see his specific plan in that situation.

I told him I would sing. I told him I would sing and smile the whole way, even if part of the way it was a forced grin, which may or may not, in retrospect, have looked creepy to cars passing by. I thanked him that instead of four wheels that went flat, I was walking on two legs with a motor that had lasted almost ten times longer than the one in the car. I needed the exercise anyway. I thanked him that my paycheck had been direct-deposited the night before, so I could pay for a tire. I began to sing one of my favorite songs by Plumb, "Exhale": "It's okay to not be okay. This is a safe place. This is a safe place. Don't be afraid. Don't be ashamed. There's still hope here. There's still hope here."

Suddenly startled, I felt something brush against my neck. Out of the corner of my eye, I examined a lonely red leaf as it floated past my shoulder and silently landed on the warm pavement at my feet. I glanced up to study the towering oaks and prickly pine trees that spread their canopy of branches over the cutoff. I watched the sparkle of sunlight as it danced and reflected on the asphalt around me and marveled at a Creator who, season after season, placed every leaf individually on every tree on the planet.

I stopped, pulled out my phone, and took a couple of pictures.

I used to think he made all this beauty just so I could enjoy it. But the truth is, if I sat on my deck at home and spent all summer counting the leaves on just one of the trees in my yard, I'd never be able to finish the job. It would be impossible. And that's just one tree. Yet every spring, God faithfully replaces every leaf on every tree—not for me to enjoy, since I too often take the leaves for granted, but to show his glory.

I listened to the rustling of the leaves as the wind passed through them, applauding the One who strategically placed each one of them. I thanked him for decent enough eyesight to see his glory all around me. I even clapped a little myself. *Hey, God!*

> You will go out in joy and be led forth in peace; the
> mountains and hills will burst into song before you,
> and all the trees of the field will clap their hands
>
> —Isaiah 55:12 NIV

I couldn't help but think, as I watched a few more leaves fall in front of me, of a scene from one of my favorite theatrical productions, *Cyrano de Bergerac*.

Cyrano has received a mortal wound on his head from an enemy. He has made his way to an abbey to see the lady he's secretly been in love with for many years. Roxane has never known of Cyrano's love for her. She's also unaware of Cyrano's wound. They are talking, mostly of trivial things, when the autumn leaves begin to fall. Roxane notices them in the failing light and says, "They are Venetian yellow. Watch them fall." Cyrano replies, "How well they fall. In this short journey from the branch to the earth, they succeed in showing a final beauty, and in spite of their fear of rotting on the ground, desire this fall to assume the grace of flight."

I sang, "Oh God, we breathe in your grace. We breathe in your grace and exhale. Oh God, we do not exist for us but to share your grace and love and exhale."

A buzzing from the side of the road interrupted the moment. It didn't quite fit the reflective posture I was creating and the peace I was beginning to experience. I searched the brush to find the source of the unwelcome intrusion.

Across the ditch, I saw a hummingbird—my favorite bird. They're fascinating little critters. Their wings can beat seventy times per second, in the shape of a sideways 8, like an infinity symbol. They are able to fly forward or backward, and they can hover like living helicopters, which was what I thought that little feller was doing. I love to watch them. I stood and marveled at how the delicate creature could stay so still in midair.

But something wasn't right. It took me a few seconds to finally realize he wasn't hovering at all. In fact, he was writhing, frantically struggling to free himself from a spiderweb.

Not sure where the spider was, I moved quickly. As I got closer, I could see he was becoming more and more frightened. I walked closer to figure out the best way to release him.

Finally, I put an index finger on each side of the web and pulled the sticky threads back. Although that action ultimately freed him, it acted more like a slingshot, catapulting him through the air, until he found his equilibrium again a few yards away. He stopped and hovered. He turned, and we considered each other for a few precious moments before he pivoted in midair and disappeared.

I thought, *Well, Lord, I know you regard your creation. You watch and care deeply over every single creature. You said, "But ask the animals what they think—let them teach you; let the birds tell you what's going on. Put your ear to the earth—learn the basics. Listen—the fish in the ocean will tell you their stories. Isn't it clear that they all know and agree that God is sovereign, that he holds all things in his hand—Every living soul, yes, every breathing creature?" (Job 12:7–10 MSG). So if my having a flat tire is part of your plan to save this smallest of your mighty hand, then I gladly find your glory there. Thank you for letting me be here at just the right moment.*

I sang, "Just let go. Let his love wrap around you and hold you close. Get lost in the surrender. Breathe it in until your heart breaks; then exhale."

I continued on my adventure for no more than five steps. I was still pretty much wrecked from the hummingbird moment, and tears were flowing, when my phone rang. It was Cliff Peck, my buddy the veterinarian. He said, "What are you doing?"

I said between sobs, "I just got to save a hummingbird."

"What? Where are you?"

Gathering myself together as best as I could, I said, "I'm just taking a walk."

"Well, where are you walking? The girls said you have a flat tire."

"I'm about halfway up the hill."

"Up your hill? Where's your car?"

"Look. Dude, you have to work. I'm a big boy. I can handle this."

"Is the flat fixed? Where's the car?"

"It's back at the 4-H center. Seriously, go to work."

"Well, where are you going?"

"I'm going home to get my jack."

"Your jack is at your house? And you're going to carry it back down the hill all the way to the 4-H center? And then what?"

"Well, I'm going to figure it out from there. Go to work."

"Okay. Well, head back to the 4-H center. I'll meet you there." He hung up.

He drove up the hill and picked me up.

Cliff, never shying away from finding ways to help others, said, "I'm off today. We're going to Texas, and Deane has some work to do on a podcast before we go. She's busy. So I'm good."

I said, "I'm sure you have more important stuff you need to be doing to get ready to go."

He looked over at me, feigning exasperation, as if I should have known better. "Tim, this is what friends do."

The good doctor turned around and took me back to my car. He had his jack with him. Weird, I know. He got down on his knees, and while he took the tire off, we remembered a specific flat-tire scene from *A Christmas Story*.

Cliff took the tire off, threw it into the back of his truck, drove me to Sam's, ran some errands, picked me and my tire up, drove back to the car, got back down on his hands and knees, and put the tire back on. Then he climbed into his truck and turned it around to leave. As he drove off, he rolled down his window and yelled, "Put your jack back in your car!"

A few minutes later, on my way to work with a brand-new tire, I thought about Cliff and the hallowed ground I stand on in the presence of such a godly servant's heart. I thought about the God whose bountiful, inexhaustible generosity is clearly evident in the forever family he has mercifully lavished on me. I thought about the brilliant creativity of the great Star-Breather on display in the expert uniqueness of a single leaf that brushed against my shoulder. I thought about the aerodynamically impossible design and strength of the fragile, delicate hummingbird flying with purpose from flower to flower, remembering every single dew-holder he has gathered nectar from. I knew he would drink as much sweet dew as his slight frame could hold, preparing for his long, lonesome, arduous twenty-hour flight across the Gulf of Mexico to vacation for the winter in warmer climes. I thought, *Not even Solomon, in all his splendor, is clothed as richly as I am.*

I breathed in, and I exhaled.

CONVERSATION STARTERS
FROM DEBBIE REES

She's so pretty. Debbie and her husband, John, were leaders of our community group for almost as many years as the church we attended has been in existence. They helped form a community of friends who have been a source of fun and spiritual strength for decades. They've weathered the good, calm, and bad seasons with joy, determination, and commitment. It's good to have a tribe.

1. Name a time in your life when you knew God could have answered your prayer immediately, but in his wisdom, he chose to answer in a way seemingly more difficult for you and, in doing that, gave you a blessing you'll never forget.

2. Name a situation in which someone went out of his or her way to show love and a servant heart toward you. How did that act make you feel? Humbled? Grateful? Indebted?

3. The Enemy grabs our attention first in our mind. He wants us to doubt God's love and live discouraged. How did Tim combat this feeling? How would you?

The Great WWGM Caper

IT MIGHT BE difficult for you to believe, but I have not always been the serious, poker-faced, brooding person who stands before you today. In fact, there were a few decades of my life when this deadpan and humorless shell of a man didn't exist.

When I lived in Nashville, Tennessee, from 1980 to 1990, rarely a stretch of days passed when I wasn't actively involved in some sort of practical joke, some form of tomfoolery that kept me almost always on the precipice of trouble—trouble that, to me, was merely a minor, pesky nuisance and certainly not a deterrent to the fun I was having. I figure God has a sense of humor. Genesis says we were created in his image, and if we humans have the ability to see and express humor, then so does God.

I drove everyone crazy. I never made jokes or performed pranks that would hurt or humiliate people. In fact, even as a child and later in college, I let my friends come up with the ideas. They always said, "Go get Holder. He'll do it." And they were correct. I'm assuming it was my weird way of feeling accepted.

Over the years, I've finally come to grips with the reality that I enjoy engaging in crazy capers. Somehow, I knew my practical jokes would eventually become great stories for future generations.

Early on, I landed a job at WWGM radio station as a disc jockey. I would put the vinyl on the turntable, set the needle on the record, and pull the stop-latch until it was time to release it and let the tune travel through the airwaves.

As a gospel station, WWGM only occasionally played music. I worked nights and weekends. I spent most of my time occupied with threading reel-to-reel tapes of fifteen-minute to hour-long sermons by famous pastors of the era. Though wonderful people, the owners and managers of the station were not necessarily cool people hip to the new contemporary Christian music scene coming out of Nashville studios.

While more progressive stations were playing Farrell and Farrell, Amy Grant, and Russ Taff, WWGM hung on to tried-and-true gospel favorites, such as Yolanda Adams, the Kingsmen, the Gaithers, and the Happy Goodman Family.

I attempted to move the station forward by introducing the manager, Lorna Harrison, to Amy Grant, Michael W. Smith, and DeGarmo and Key but with little success. So as revenge, I would regularly find ways to make Lorna laugh while she was on air. Lorna, a beautiful, Jesus-loving, sweet mahogany-skinned lady, always came into the office impeccably fashioned and accessorized. She was gifted with a radio voice that melted butter, and I'd stop whatever I was doing to listen to her deliver the news. I would have been just as intoxicated if she had been reading a stock market report from the newspaper.

WWGM occupied an older building in an older section of a Nashville subdivision. A huge, ancient oak tree protected the two-story white clapboard home better suited to somebody's grandparents. The second story housed the owner's office. Small, cozy bedrooms on the first floor had been converted for administration and recording.

When you walked up the concrete steps on the right side of the house and through the front door, you found yourself in a large reception area, which I assume was formerly a living room. The receptionist's desk ran down the right side of the room, giving her a perfect view of anyone approaching through the front door to her left. The control room was to the receptionist's right. Separating the reception area and the control room was a huge pane of glass beginning about three feet off the ground and climbing to the ceiling, looking directly into the control room. From the reception area, you could clearly make out the back of a counter crowded with control panels. The disc jockey or newscaster, on the opposite side the control panels, faced the picture window and, therefore, anyone coming in the front door or loitering in the reception area.

Curtains in the control room could be pulled shut if the DJ didn't feel like being sociable. It was weird. I suppose the arrangement was so the disc jockey could see any artist coming for an interview enter the station and could wave excitedly, setting the celebrity at ease. The curtains were usually open, allowing everyone some sort of contact.

I usually worked from around four o'clock in the afternoon till midnight, and frequently, I was the only one there.

But on one particular night, Lorna was hanging out to do some catch-up projects and needed to be in the control room. She said she would just do the DJ stuff until she finished with her other work.

So I waited my turn, watching TV in the reception area. I heard Lorna say on air that she would be right back with the news after a commercial break.

Unfortunately, at that moment, my ADHD kicked into overdrive. I glanced at the receptionist's desk. My eyes landed on an extensive array of pencils and pens methodically organized by color and length.

I have no idea what came over me, but the next thing I knew, I was crouched down outside the picture window with a pencil stuck into every possible facial orifice I could find. I waited until Lorna was about a minute into the newscast before I slowly raised my head into view. I looked something like this:

I don't know. Maybe slightly reminiscent of a character in *Hellraiser*. At any rate, the ultimate reaction far outdid my initial hopes.

Lorna, the quintessential professional, never wavered in her ability to keep her composure on air. She kept reading the news as though she were a nightly news anchor—for about a minute. Then there was an arduously, painstakingly long pause that ended with a button click going straight into a commercial for Joyce Landorf's newest book, ironically titled *Your Irregular Person*.

Lorna flew out of the control room, alternating every fifteen seconds between howling laughter and attempts at professional anger. Howling laughter won out in the end. It always does. I think she gave up trying to do any work, and we just sat around and talked for another hour between taped sermons and commercials. Bonding comes in a lot of forms. It was a good night.

I'm usually a bit anxious in the moments before I actually go in for the kill with my practical rascality. I guess I hope it ends up as a good story rather than with me in jail or sporting a black eye.

WWGM was one of the first stations to connect to cable. The format changed so that we went off the air nightly at 7:00 p.m. and switched over to cable. I was a little miffed about that. I was the night person. In order to hear the station at night, you were required to have a cable hookup at your house, and you paid for the cable service. As much as the gospel artists were loved, who in his or her right mind was willing to pay for a cable hookup to listen to a gospel AM radio station? Realistically, at that time, the prelude to the techno era, no one did.

One night—I don't know what came over me—I cued up an hour-long reel-to-reel tape of a popular pastor who sounded remarkably like Linus's school teacher, Miss Othmar. I wasn't listening. I went to the reception area and started watching a documentary called *The Secrets of the Baobab Tree*.

I was frustrated. I saw the evening as a waste of time. When the reel-to-reel had almost finished, I went in and, out of spite, cued up "Stubborn Love" by Kathy Troccoli.

I'd been strictly forbidden to play that particular song, even though it was off Kathy's first album. Apparently, the song didn't actually say the word *God* anywhere in it, so it didn't meet station's standards.

Anyway, I cued it up. As soon as the pastor said, "Good night," I came on with a couple of commercials. Then I said—and it was like an out-of-body experience—"When we come back from the commercial break, we are going to have a huge contest, so stay tuned."

My mind raced as I thought of the possible ramifications of what I was about to do. But somehow, I felt the punishments would be worth it and would be wholly justified.

After the break, I went on air and set up the colossal event. "Okay. Let's do an instant contest. When you hear the brand-new hit single by Kathy Troccoli called 'Stubborn Love,' be the first person to call into the station, and you're going to win a huge prize! You're going to completely own WWGM radio! Yes, it's true. If you're the first person to call in, this station is yours! Just come into the station Monday morning. We will have all the contracts ready, and you just put your John Hancock next to the space marked with an *x*, and you'll own your very own gospel radio station."

Then I went to some commercials and a couple of songs. My palms were sweating as I waited to release the play button. I took a deep breath, and I don't think I inhaled for the next four minutes and thirty-seven seconds.

I released the stop-latch button.

"Stubborn Love" started.

I sat there with my eyes glued to the push-button phone, with all five yellow buttons for outside lines blankly staring back at me.

It seemed like forever. Obviously, no one was going to call after the first two minutes of the song. I let my breath out with a long *whoosh*. I got up and threaded the next fifteen-minute pastor reel-to-reel on the spindles.

As the song slowly began its last chorus, I looked at my watch and knew there were only about thirty seconds left. No one, of course, was listening. Point made.

Then, at four minutes and twenty-seven seconds, the first line lit up. There was no sound from the phone in the control booth, in case someone called while we were on the air. But it was there. The unmistakable steady blink of the silent yellow light was deafeningly loud to my psyche.

I felt every pump of blood as it drained out of my head, into my face, and down into my chest cavity, rendering me incapable of any rational thought. My brain no longer functioned as it swirled somewhere around the center of Dante's third level of hell. You know what they say happens just before someone dies. I saw my third-grade class.

My mouth went completely dry as I picked up the receiver and choked out, "Hello. This is WWGM radio. How may I help you?"

After a slight pause, the guy on the other end of the line said, "Uh, isn't this Pizza Hut?"

My body, which moments before had been a two-by-four plank of fear, slowly became a massive pile of poured-out, gelatinous flesh. I sank into and became one with the cushioned seat of my swivel chair. I choked out, "No, this is a radio station. And by the way, it's eleven o'clock. Pizza Hut closes at ten." The phone went dead.

I must have sat there for a good fifteen minutes in the silence before I realized it was, in fact, silent. I'd never pushed the button to start the next reel-to-reel pastor.

But then again, who cared? Nobody was listening. No one!

CONVERSATION STARTERS
BY JACQUI LEFLER

I loved getting my sister, Jacqui, up for school by finding new and horrifying ways to wake her. I made orange-iced rolls for breakfast and put the delicious orange icing on only four of the eight rolls. Guess which ones she got? I hid under her bed in the dark when she came in from dates, just so I could grab her ankle. This is a mere smidge of the torture I routinely inflicted on her. It's amazing she turned out as stunning as she did. She's so pretty.

1. Does God really have a sense of humor? Does the Bible specifically indicate this? In Psalms, David reveals a very intimate relationship with God. We see a God who cares, who listens to David's cries of anguish, who cries with him in times of distress, and who also rejoices with David. "Take delight in the Lord and he will give you the desires of your heart" (Psalm 37:4 NIV). The word *delight* means "to take great pleasure" or "to give keen enjoyment." This delight, this enjoyment, is given to us from the Lord, and we are invited to participate in it with him. God even gives us guidance on when to express our emotion. In part, Ecclesiastes 3:2–8 (NIV) says, "There is a time for everything, and a season for every activity under the heavens ... a time to weep and a time to laugh, a time to mourn and a time to dance ... He has made everything beautiful in its time. He has also set eternity in the human heart; yet no one can fathom what God has done from beginning to end." Ecclesiastes 2:24 (NIV) finishes that thought: "A person can do nothing better

than to eat and drink and find satisfaction in their toil. This too, I see, is from the hand of God."

2. My business brain wants to know what would have happened if someone had actually called in wanting to come get the keys to the radio station. I suspect the following: you would have been terminated immediately—duh! There would have been an attempt to appease the winner with a cash gift. Likely, they would not have wanted a radio station no one listened to, so they would have accepted said gift. Or there would have been lawyers involved. One will never know, because God once again saved you from yourself.

3. I need to know: Did Lorna ever know you almost gave away the radio station? (The answer is no.)

The White Stone

BACK IN THE summer of 1975, I joined a group of college students on a mission trip to East Brunswick, New Jersey, where we held Vacation Bible School for local children. Eight of us spent the entire summer living in the preacher's home, where the garage doubled as the church auditorium.

Close to the end of our stay, the team leader gave us a surprise exercise during one of our group devotionals. He wanted us to make lists of all the good qualities we perceived in each team member's character or what we saw as God-given strengths and gifts in each other.

Over the years, I have processed that experience, and I have never forgotten the impact it made on me. I don't remember the comments I made about the other members of the team or even the comments made about me. However, I do remember fearing that when the group leader called my name, there would be dead silence from the others. I was horrified that everyone would surreptitiously glance around, praying someone would conjure a positive character trait to pin on me, or that, in trying to be benevolent, they would utilize trite, obviously impossible attributes, such as "I fully believe you will be president of the United States one day" or "I will be shocked if you don't win hundreds of Academy Awards in your lifetime." Then everyone else would nod a little too briskly and affirm a little too loudly the fake sentiment behind the statement. Or, unable to find any good qualities, they would take the opportunity to point out all my idiosyncrasies and character defects and give me pointers on how I might fare better the next time I was a participant in a similar exercise.

But none of that happened. As I look back, I remember every person's expression as we went around the room and validated and verbally appreciated one another. I remember expressions on people's faces. Most of them, I'm sure, reflected the same fears and apprehension I'd experienced just before my name was called.

As the exercise continued, a completely different spirit filled the space. Tears fell from every eye as humble holiness enveloped that small living room. Every person there received a cherished gift, as though we were pinning a value tag on each heart that read, "Priceless."

James 3:17–18 (MSG) says,

> Real wisdom, God's wisdom, begins with a holy life and is characterized by getting along with others. It is gentle and reasonable, overflowing with mercy and blessings, not hot one day and cold the next, not two-faced. You can develop a healthy, robust community that lives right with God and enjoy its results only if you do the hard work of getting along with each other, treating each other with dignity and honor.

It wasn't uncommon for God to be a name-caller. He changed Saul's name to Paul, which means "Humble." Peter, of course, became the "Stone" on which the Lord built his church. Moses means "Drew out."

One of my favorite characters experienced a name change from Mirab-Baal to Mephibosheth, which means "Exterminator of shame." The name Eunice, which belonged to Timothy's mother in the Bible and to my own mother, means "Good victory." Obviously, what these people were called, even their given names, represented something. The name often described to outsiders what the person's character was like or was at least meant to be when he or she was first named by his or her parents. Names helped define people for those just meeting them. Often, their names changed later on to fit their new identities.

One day we will all be given new names. Revelation 2:17 (MSG) says, "Are your ears awake? Listen. Listen to the Wind Words, the Spirit blowing through the churches. I'll give the sacred manna to every conqueror; I'll also give a clear, smooth stone inscribed with your new name, your secret new name."

I remember names I was called when I was growing up that weren't particularly good. In fact, I remember more of those names than the ones I should have been called. But even back then, there was a stone already hewn, hidden in the heart of God, inscribed with my real name, the name he has specially designed for me. And it describes me perfectly. One day, when I see it, when he hands it to me, I will finally realize all he planned for me to do and be, and I will exclaim, "Of course that was my name!"

It wasn't a typo in James 3 when he instructed early Christians to do the hard work of getting along. It isn't easy all the time to find the best in another fallen, sinful human being. But amazingly, it's there, and we are called to honor each other with the dignity only we can give.

I remember the honor I felt that night in 1975, not only in receiving words of affirmation from my friends, people I respected, but also in the tears that fell as my heart swelled with the knowledge that I was speaking streams of life into other tender hearts.

There was a distinct reverence in the confidence that some, like me, were hearing, maybe for the first time. Those friends were valued for their gifts. What they offered was crucial and far-reaching for the kingdom of God. They were essential. It was just as much a gift for the giver of the consequential words as it was for the recipient.

I have been involved in many step-studies with Celebrate Recovery over the past couple of decades. Two exercises in the participant guide always amaze me. They amaze me because, to a study, the results are almost exactly the same. One exercise says, "Name some of the negative things you've done in your life." The other says, "Name some of the positive things you've done in your life." It's no longer surprising to me that the answers to the first could fill a book—every participant's response. On the other hand, for the second exercise about positive things, the responses are surprisingly short. Some participants even leave the space blank.

What are we listening to about ourselves? Do we hear the names we heard as children so often that we believe them to be true? Do we still call ourselves those names today? Do we hear the name Failure, Worthless, Ugly, or Stupid in our hearts when we turn out the lights to sleep? Do we run through all the wrong, embarrassing, irresponsible things we did that day? Is our life inventory filled with only the negative things we did in the last twenty-four hours? Do we dwell on the names we were called, even the ones we gave ourselves?

If we are honest, do we truly believe those names are the ones the Creator of the universe, the One who uniquely made us, wants us to hear and believe?

Or do we hear the names God has given us? I think we all intellectually know that real truth is found only in God's Word. I defy anyone to show me a verse in which God says we are a mistake. So why is it so easy to believe the negative things about ourselves, the things our culture believes are so important, over the truth revealed to us from the very heart of God?

I'm guessing it's because we are so inundated with what's expected of us. We have allowed media and what we're taught is valuable by the world to extinguish the truth—so much so that we begin to believe the lie of the Enemy that we have no value.

I choose to begin my day with his truth about me. The truth that says I am fearfully and wonderfully made. That I am his treasured possession. That I am the apple of his eye.

He has called us names all right! Chosen. Blessed sons and daughters. Saint. His. Heirs. Not condemned but accepted. Victorious. A new creature. Set free. Redeemed and forgiven and given access to the very throne room of God. We are light in the Lord. We are citizens of heaven. We are complete in Christ, hidden with Christ in God. We will be revealed with him in glory. He has supplied all our needs. We have been chosen by God, and he has made us holy and beloved.

We're usually called something after we've lived out a dream or accomplished something big. But God calls us before we do it, just as he did with men and women of the Bible. The world might see us as creative or smart or annoying. But God sees us as world changers, radical leaders, and peacemakers.

Listen carefully. Tonight, as you go through the events of your day, take responsibility for what you need to take responsibility for, and let go of things you were not responsible for. As you begin to drift to sleep, if you hear any voice other than *You are mine, and you are breathtaking*, you aren't listening to Jesus and what he says about you. You're not listening to the One who holds together all of creation and is intimately interested in the next breath you take. The Lord may give you a name himself. In fact, I know he has. But he may also ask you to be the life-giver of a name for someone else. It's hard work. But it just might change the course of someone else's life, including your own.

CONVERSATION STARTERS
FROM MELANIE HASSELL

Melanie is a college buddy. I don't recall ever being around Melanie when we weren't laughing about something. I love friends like that. Mel is a wonderful wife, mom, friend, and teacher. She grows flowers in her garden in Tennessee. She has a big old dog and a quiet home with Mike. She loves to cook. What a good life. And she's so pretty.

1. What is the best compliment you could receive today?

2. What qualities do you want acquaintances to quickly notice about you?

3. What do you believe is your strongest God-given gift? How do you believe God can use that gift to further his kingdom? What new name do you want God to give you?

The Albatross I Own

A FRIEND OF mine recently posted a picture on social media that conveyed my life in an extraordinarily powerful way. It was a black-and-white sketch of a scruffily bearded young man's profile. He wore a wide, toothy, squinty, wrinkle-eyed, joyous grin. Whatever the reason, he was wearing on his face what he wanted others to see and believe.

There was also a gut-wrenching cutaway of the side of his head, showing what was going on internally, the real him: a little boy crouched down against a wall barefoot with his knees protectively pulled up to his chest, his arms wrapped tightly around them, and his head lowered into his arms, hiding, buried in his aloneness. On the floor beside him, leaning against him as if clinging for dear life, was his teddy bear.

I've posted a lot of stuff I've written on social media, and occasionally, people find those posts funny enough or worthy enough to share. This picture, promoting mental health awareness, got an exceptional response. It received a bunch of likes. What surprised me even more was that 180 people felt the message was important enough to share. That's pretty dramatic. I don't know how many of those 180 have family or friends who struggle with depression or if they themselves combat that insidious disorder.

Whatever the reason, I believe there is a different story for every person who struggles. Every single one of those people is essential and significant. For that reason, I feel compelled to open up about my own personal albatross.

In 1798, Samuel Taylor Coleridge published his longest poem, *The Rime of the Ancient Mariner*. In the story, an albatross leads an icebound ship out of a dangerous, deadly area. The storyteller, for some idiotic reason, kills the bird with a bow. The crew become angry, and they force him to wear the dead bird around his neck.

Thus began the legend that albatrosses are, metaphorically, a psychological burden that feels like a curse.

However, these creatures are, in fact, majestic birds with wingspans up to ten feet and lifespans as long as fifty years. They are incredibly social and have strong communities, thus making the albatross my second-favorite bird. As I've said, my favorite are hummingbirds, which are substantially smaller and don't live nearly as long. But I digress. The point is that in the story, the punishment for killing the bird becomes synonymous with a burden to be carried.

I don't remember a time when depression hasn't been a massive part of my life. My battle. My thorn. My mountain. In this one area of my life, God has been merciful but quiet.

My days are pretty much a regular routine for me. I work, I go to church, and the rest of the time, I sleep. I sleep a lot.

Every night, when I get home from work, I plan for tomorrow. I will wake up. I will clean the house and do laundry. I will spend time writing. I will take my vitamins. And every morning, I wake up with a heaviness in my chest and a dark black cloud just below ceiling level. I am filled with anxiety, depression, and fear that the cloud will burst at any second. So I go back to sleep.

My dreams are always stress- and anxiety-driven. I force myself to get out of bed every morning, take the dogs for their morning constitutional, feed them, maybe eat a little breakfast, and then crawl back into bed and sleep until I'll be late for work if I don't take a shower and go.

It's not laziness. It's not a lack of desire to be motivated. It's not a lack of positive thinking. It's not wishing my house were clean enough to have friends over for supper. It's not even a lack of spiritual health. I spend time with the Lord every single day. I love being with him, my Rock, who I know understands. I often pray Psalm 61:1–2 (MSG): "God, listen to me shout, bend an ear to my prayer. When I'm far from anywhere, down to my last gasp, I call out, 'Guide me up High Rock Mountain!'"

I don't talk about it much. I don't want people to think I'm attempting to elicit pity or sympathy. In fact, I can't stand that thought. I'd rather carry it alone than burden anyone else with it.

And why is that? I want people to know me as a lighthearted, laughing, joyful, loving guy devoted to friends and Jesus. After all, that's who I am at heart. That's the true me. And I have to remind myself that the knowledge of my disorder is what keeps me grounded. If I depend on my emotions, this disorder will overtake me.

But depression isn't the real me. I have to remember and accept that my absolute best day will probably never quite reach most people's normal day. I don't experience fewer reasons for joy or sadness, anger or fear, disgust or happiness, or wonder or surprise. I have no more substantial or smaller life choices or problems than anyone else.

But there is always the cloud. A heavy chest. Chronic fatigue. The wish that it would be more comfortable. The prayer.

I have a few close friends who I know pray for me. Those are the ones I run to when I have the slightest energy. I look for them at church, the grocery, or anywhere else. They're the important ones, because they bring me moments of escape into joy. If I can make them smile or laugh, mission accomplished. They know who they are.

Many other friends of mine have themselves been touched by depression in a personal way. Many have spouses, friends, or family who struggle with depression. Many fight it themselves. Many have spouses, friends, or family members who have lost their battle with depression or mental illness.

And by the way, depression is an illness.

For several years, I tried antidepressant after antidepressant with no measurable positive result. One doctor, after testing, gave me a prescription for a generic medicine for ADHD. Although I did feel somewhat better for a time, I suddenly found myself strongly considering taking my life. If I'd owned a gun back then, I would not be typing this right now. It was that serious.

I began to research the meds and found that one of the possible side effects was suicidal thoughts. I remembered the psychologist asking me several times before he prescribed the medicine if I'd ever thought about suicide.

I never had considered taking my own life before. When I read the side effects, I stopped taking the drug. Almost immediately, thoughts of taking my life went away, never to return.

Depression is so pervasive and overwhelming that I have taken the word *suicide* out of my lexicon. Instead, I choose other words: "My friend died of depression," "She struggled with anxiety and fear," or "He just wanted the pain to stop."

For the record, I'm confident that believers who have desperately struggled with addiction, depression, or mental health problems will be in heaven. On this side of the veil, they couldn't handle the pain of life any longer and chose to go to the One who truly understands.

A friend told me once that taking one's own life is like showing up to a party where we weren't yet invited.

It's called grace.

When I was a senior in high school, we read a poem by Edwin Arlington Robinson called "Richard Cory." Until recently, I never understood why it resonated, even then, so profoundly with me and why I remembered it so well for nearly forty-five years. Now I know.

Richard Cory
Edwin Arlington Robinson

Whenever Richard Cory went down town,
We people on the pavement looked at him:
He was a gentleman from sole to crown,
Clean favored, and imperially slim.
And he was always quietly arrayed,
And he was always human when he talked;
But still he fluttered pulses when he said,
"Good-morning," and he glittered when he walked.
And he was rich—yes, richer than a king—
And admirably schooled in every grace:
In fine, we thought that he was everything
To make us wish that we were in his place.
So on we worked, and waited for the light,
And went without the meat, and cursed the bread;
And Richard Cory, one calm summer night,
Went home and put a bullet through his head.

I was diagnosed twelve years ago with a disorder called transverse myelitis (TM). It's sort of a first cousin to multiple sclerosis (MS). The symptoms of both are the same; TM just doesn't progress as MS does.

In my research, I discovered that TM and MS are the two strongest disorders causing depression and one of the major contributors to people considering or succeeding in taking their own lives. Although, rest assured, ending my life is not in my thoughts, I understand how others can feel so alone and isolated that dying is more comforting. It's called an invisible disability for a reason.

I choose to live as an emotional, empathetic, compassionate humanoid. That's how my precious Jesus, my best Bud, created me. On the other side of that same coin (sobriety chip), I recognize that constant knowledge of this disorder and the possible contributing factors are critical to my survival. Knowing it's there keeps me away from the shadows. I finally realized that if there's a shadow, there has to be light somewhere.

There are specific things I will do and things I will not do.

I will continue the fight, even when I'm so tired I can't see past the next hour.

I will seek the Lord in all things. I will fight this fight with him. He carries the sword in front of me.

I will not listen to or respond in anger (hopefully, prayerfully) when someone says, "If you just prayed more," "If you found the right meds," "You can be delivered from this," "The Lord told me …," or "It's a sign of weakness or sin."

I've sincerely, with everything in me, tried countless times all of those things, and here I am, still struggling. Those types of responses, usually said out of ignorance or self-protection, are a strong sign of lack of research.

Many Christians throw doubt and lack of faith together as an excuse for depression, but it's neither. It's real. It's pervasive in our culture and our churches. We need to display mercy and compassion. We must be aware of those around us. We must love them and move to keep them from isolating. We must be vigilant to be accountable to them and hold them accountable.

It's not a choice to isolate. It's a condition. It's not a choice to feel afraid, tired, and anxious. It's a disorder. It's horrible, it's awful, and it's debilitating.

I don't know if it's a lifelong part of my journey. But I can tell you this: I know it's not eternal. On the really hard days, I think of my future home, as portrayed in Isaiah 25:6–8 (MSG):

> But here on this mountain, God-of-the-Angel-Armies will throw a feast for all the people of the world, a feast of the finest foods, a feast with vintage wines, a feast of seven courses, a feast lavish with gourmet desserts. And here on this mountain, God will banish the pall of doom hanging over all peoples, The shadow of doom darkening all nations. Yes, he'll banish death forever. And God will wipe the tears from every face. He'll remove every sign of disgrace from his people, wherever they are. Yes! God says so!

My heart is set on things above. When the Lord calls me home, it will be a great day. The best day. The heaviness I have always felt will finally fall away, and the dark cloud will disperse as the veil is lifted. I will see the Love I've waited to see all my life, the One I've leaned on for protection, hope, truth, answers, and salvation. I will finally see my precious Jesus face-to-face.

I used to hear and believe that we die alone. That is absolutely not true. I've never been alone, and I will never be alone. The moment I close my earthly eyes, I'll see the One I've longed for all my life: Jesus.

I will see all my friends and family who have gone home before me waiting at the gate. The joy I've longed for will be mine because I am in the presence of pure Love. The trivial, normal things that seemed monumental here because of this disorder will no longer matter. All the dreams that seemed impossible to accomplish here because of constant sadness and fatigue will finally be fulfilled.

I'll lift my head and breathe in the crisp, clean air of knowing what it means to be free of pain and sorrow. I know these feelings are no different, in kind, from the feelings of all others who have given their hearts to Jesus. We will be there together, laughing, praising, worshipping, working, and living out the truest of dreams—truly, finally living. It will have been worth it all.

And I will fly!

CONVERSATION STARTERS
FROM CAROL SKIBA

Carol is my word-for-the-year buddy. If I need someone to pray, I text Carol. I know she'll do it. Carol's story communicates the redemptive power of God and how he loves his kids into relationship with him. She exudes the love and grace of God. When you see her, you see the reflection of Jesus. I am honored to tell people she's my friend. She's a blessing. And she's really pretty.

1. What is your personal albatross? How can you allow Jesus to help remove it from your neck?

2. How has depression touched your life? In what ways does it affect you?

3. How can you, as a Christ follower, help those who are suffering from depression or mental illness?

Sasquatchville

Key fob is a word used to describe a key chain and several other similar items and devices. The word *fob* is believed to have originated from watch fobs, which existed as early as 1888. The *fob* refers to an ornament attached to a pocket-watch chain. Key chains, remote car starters, garage door openers, and keyless entry devices on hotel room doors are also called *fobs*, or *key fobs*.

—Webpedia

DRIVING HOME FROM a TobyMac concert (row 6, seat 14) late one night, I was about a mile from home on Congo Ferndale Road, which is way out—I mean *way* out, the *Deliverance* part of Ferndale, with nothing but woods for miles—when I saw a huge something on the road ahead. As I got closer, I realized it was a deer someone had hit and killed.

Naturally, my first thought was to ask God to let it run free and happy on my property in heaven, where I would gladly take care of it when I got home. My next thoughts were not as kind. I wondered what horrible human being would just leave it in the middle of the road. Didn't they consider that another driver might run into the carcass? It could wreck a vehicle or maybe even send it careening into a ditch while the driver tried to swerve.

I turned around and went back. I stopped, angling my car to the left so the headlights would shine on the deer lying in the opposite lane. My plan was to drag the poor creature off the road.

I climbed out and carefully set the door against my still-running car—just enough to let it click but not close. I walked toward the deer and noticed a truck coming from the other direction. Applying more than a little effort, I grabbed a hoof and lugged the poor creature into the ditch, waved and smiled at the truck, and walked back to my car.

Feeling good about my selfless deed, I reached down and pulled on the door handle. It was locked. My headlights were still shining brightly. The inside lights were still on. My cell phone was snugly secure in the passenger seat. The car was idling smoothly. But somehow, my driver's door had locked itself behind me. All the doors were locked.

I went into mild shock.

I tried both driver's-side doors. Locked.

The truck pulled up, and the lady inside rolled down her window. I said, "The doors locked." She just looked at me. I repeated, trying in vain to hide the terror in my voice, "The doors locked all by themselves. I live just on the other side of Colonel Glenn. If you could just drive me to my house, I have an extra fob there, and I can get it unlocked."

She just said, "Oh, uh ..."

I don't know why she seemed hesitant—we were just out there by ourselves shortly after midnight in *The Blair Witch Project*.

I said, "Look, I just left a TobyMac concert—row 6, seat 14, by the way. I'm a Christian. I love the Lord. I would never hurt you."

I guess she felt bad and had, in fact, watched the whole dragging-the-dead-deer thing transpire. Although it was after midnight and no one was on the road, I don't think I looked all that menacing. I had all my teeth. So she let me get in her truck.

She said, "Well, do you live with someone?"

I realized at that point she did not intend to drive me back to my car. I told her I would wake up my neighbor and have him drive me to my car.

As she turned her truck onto my drive, I glanced to the right and saw Jeremiah, my neighbor, working in his garage. While rummaging in his tool chest, he glanced up to see the unknown truck pulling into my driveway. Probably he wondered who would have been arriving at that hour. He might've even felt a moment of alarm for the safety of his family and his parents. Both his parents' house and mine were at the end of the long drive, a length of two acres away from the road, way back in the woods.

As we got to my house, I thanked the lady and jumped out of her truck. She turned the truck around and sped away. I ran to the house, which, like my car, was also locked. But I remembered the sliding glass door by the front door was never locked. It was nearly impossible to slide open. I managed to maneuver it enough to wedge myself through; push away all the dogs, who were scrambling to get outside since they had been locked in the house for the past seven hours; grab the extra fob; and run back across the two acres of dirt driveway to Jeremiah's house. He was still standing by the garage window.

I feel certain Jeremiah was a little startled when he saw a human standing at his window at midnight, waving at him. He opened the garage door, and I told him what had happened.

"My car is sitting in the middle of the road, locked, with the inside lights on, headlights on bright. My phone is on the front seat. And the car is running."

He said, "What were you doing out of your car at midnight and locking the door?"

I was beginning to sweat. "We need to hurry! Just drive me up there. I'll tell you on the way."

He was unimpressed with my emotional collapse and said, "Okay. But come look at what I'm doing."

With more than a little angst, I toured the man cave he was building with a new deck. I said, "That's so cool. But if anyone drives up Congo Ferndale right now at midnight and sees a car sitting there locked, running, with the inside lights on, the headlights on bright, and a cell phone on the front seat, idling out in the middle of Sasquatchville, they're going to break a window and steal it or at the very least assume foul play has recently transpired and call the cops. We gotta go."

So we jumped into his truck with his dog, Pearl, and headed to the car. When we got there, Jeremiah turned his lights on bright to survey the situation better and said, "The lights are on. It's still running."

"Yes," I said. "I'm fully aware of that. Wait here so I can make sure the battery in this fob isn't dead."

The battery in the fob was dead.

I went to the car and pressed the unlock button several times, but to no avail. I frantically shook the fob up and down like an old-time mercury-filled thermometer, hoping I could squeeze one last drop of energy back into the ancient battery, which was as dead as the animal I'd pulled into the ditch earlier.

At least internally, and quite possibly externally, I panicked. "This is not happening. This cannot be happening. No, no, no, no!"

I looked back toward Jeremiah in his truck with his dog, Pearl. I couldn't see him, because I was looking directly into his headlights. I'm reasonably sure I mouthed something toward those headlights that I'm not particularly proud of right now.

He jumped out of the truck and came up to my car. I said, "The fob is dead. It's really dead. I'm not sure what to do now. I may have to use your phone to call my insurance agent, who will call a locksmith. You don't have to wait around. It'll probably take them a while to get here, so I'll just wait here by the car. Although I fully expect to hear a banjo start playing somewhere in the woods as soon as you drive off."

Years earlier, when I'd worked as a server at a Nashville restaurant, people would ask for something weird, and there was no way I could respond without making them look like a total moron in front of their friends. For example, occasionally, someone would ask for a Caesar salad with Thousand Island dressing. This was one of those moments. There was no way Jeremiah could respond to the situation without me looking like a complete bonehead. He pointed to a small hole just under the car door handle and said, "Um, well, you do know that fob has an actual key attached to the end of it, right?"

"Oh."

CONVERSATION STARTERS FROM TRICIA WALKER (WWW.BIGFRONTPORCH.COM)

In the early 1980s, Tricia bid on an old house at an auction in Ashland, Tennessee, outside Nashville a ways, and she made the highest bid. Many friends spent at least a year driving from Nashville to Ashland City, tearing out old walls, putting in new walls, getting blisters, doing plumbing, painting, sanding, getting splinters, and decorating. Finally, an amazing refuge hideaway emerged. There were music festivals, birthday parties, cookouts, dress-up-like-the-1950s parties at a nearby diner, and music. There was always music. She's so pretty.

1. What are three situations in which you were able to fully and completely laugh at yourself (e.g., looking for your cell phone when it's in your hand)?

2. What is your go-to strategy for confronting fear?

3. What are some ideas you have for practicing mindfulness or being in the moment ("You know there's a key on the end of that fob, right?")?

Fear versus Knowledge

MY MOM LAY in a hospital bed in Searcy for almost a month. We four siblings made sure she was comfortable and knew at least one of us would always be there with her.

With congestive heart failure, she needed medications. At that time, she had a tough time breathing. The problem was so dramatic she could barely put three words together without having to pause to catch her breath. Walking ten feet to the bathroom in her hospital room left her dizzy and exhausted. She would close her eyes and take shallow breaths until she felt a little better.

Nutrition was a challenge. Food or drink would sometimes travel down her windpipe into her lungs. The flap in her esophagus wasn't functioning properly. So she swallowed anything liquid mixed with a thickener. It was like drinking a soft gel. We secretly discovered that she preferred Dr. Pepper with thickener or a thickened Route 44 sweet tea.

She also suffered from atypical pneumonia, which is similar to severe bronchitis. Specialists discovered her aortic valve didn't work correctly, so the doctors tried to make her strong enough to have heart surgery.

After much trial and error, Mom's doctor explained that his plan hadn't worked, and she was sent to Little Rock for surgery. Alarmed and scared, we kids prepared for an uncertain future. Would this be Mom's final journey before heaven?

Mom, of course, loved having us there. She bragged about us to all the nurses and doctors. Even though she struggled to breathe and get words out, the staff would, in their hurried kindness, listen and encourage her.

One night, sitting beside her on her hospital bed, I rubbed her arm and held her hand. She smiled and then looked away for a minute. She turned back to me and, with a serious, searching look in her eyes, said, "You know, the older you get, the more you look back at your life and realize you didn't always make the best choices for your kids. Sometimes you wish you handled things differently."

I smiled, brushed back her hair, and leaned down and kissed her on her forehead. I squeezed her hand. "Well, Mom, there are no perfect parents. And there are no perfect kids. All of your kids love Jesus. All of us are involved in the church. The ones who have kids have raised them the same way. None of us are drug users or alcoholics. None of us have ever gone to jail. Well, except that one time after a late-night play rehearsal in downtown Nashville, when I ran a red light and the officer sitting at the opposing green light pulled me over and discovered my tags were expired, and I already owed ticket for that, so he hauled me in for a couple of hours. Other than that, in spite of our flaws, eccentricities, drama, and self-imposed dysfunctions, you did a pretty good job. I think you did an outstanding job."

Her sweet eyes glistened as she reached up, brushed my cheek with the back of her hand, and whispered, "I never regretted any of my babies."

The doctors worked hard to get Mom strong enough to have a procedure called transcatheter aortic valve replacement (TAVR).

I felt intense anxiety, not knowing if that was right for her. Then Christina, the TAVR coordinator, came in and meticulously explained the strength building and tests needed to get her as prepared as possible for the procedure. She gave me several brochures to read, with pictures so I could understand better.

I devoured every page. TAVR is much less invasive than open-heart surgery. Instead of having to crack the sternum, the doctors go in with a tube through the groin, knock the old valve out of the way, and replace it with a new one. It expands outward and takes over the work of the original valve.

During that period of waiting, I heard from several friends who had experienced the same procedure or had family members who were walking around with the little miracle device, which looks like a crown. They willingly shared how the procedure reduced recovery time and said they'd observed almost immediate and noticeable improvement in the patient's health.

I felt calm and reassured after reading the information and talking to other people. Peace replaced fear. I had knowledge and understanding of the procedure instead of insecurity and the mystery of not knowing, which dispelled apprehension and worry.

We stood around her bed, all her babies and a couple of nurses, and prayed. The attending nurse wheeled Mom into the surgery room, and we waited. After two hours, Dr. Glover came and told us the procedure had been successful. We went to her room later and hugged her. Each of us told her we loved her and encouraged her to sleep. She did.

The next morning, when I walked into her room, she would not shut up. She talked nonstop, and her cheeks were pink and pinchable. Her coherent words came in complete sentences without her stopping every few seconds to breathe. It's incredible how good she felt when blood actually flowed through her body again.

I said, "Mom, do you hear yourself?"

She stopped talking just long enough to smile and then said, "Yeah." She continued her verbal torrent about the hospital's overuse of carrots in some form or other on every food tray.

It was a miracle. Mom returned to rehab in Searcy for a couple of weeks and then moved back to her assisted living home. All her friends waited for her to come in sipping on her unthickened sweet tea and jump into an aggressively vicious game of bingo.

When I was a child, we didn't talk much about heaven. One Bible verse seemed to restrict discussion about our future home. In 2 Corinthians 12, Paul says he knew a man who was caught up to Paradise and heard inexpressible things that no one was permitted to tell us. Since no one was allowed to tell us, apparently, we all assumed we weren't supposed to talk about it.

I was much older before I began to wonder why nothing ever brought me complete joy, happiness, or a sense of any project being perfectly finished. When my thoughts turned toward heaven, I couldn't feel excited about being a disembodied spirit in a place that could become fairly boring after a while, even with Jesus there.

So I began a journey to discover if there was something more I had missed.

And guess what? There was.

I found a book that has become like my second Bible: *Heaven* by Randy Alcorn. I read it and have just started rereading it. I have never looked at this life and planet the same since devouring this book.

Again, it's about knowledge. Not knowing or believing I had a right to search out information about heaven left me unnerved. What could I reasonably expect about my forever home?

Knowledge has made all the difference. We will not be strumming harps all day. The extraordinary, magnificent reason no earthly experience has ever felt ultimately fulfilling to me is because God has put eternity in my heart.

The knowledge of heaven has changed how I live. Our future home is vibrant and bright with color—colors we can't even imagine. We'll have real bodies and real jobs that were originally created for us to do.

Heaven is rich and full with the presence of God, the star-breathing Creator of the universe. We enjoy perfect relationships with each other and close face-to-face, lying-in-the-grass, looking-at-stars conversations with Jesus.

We'll eat, drink, work, play, travel, worship, and discover a New Earth as God always meant it to be.

We will see God and fully realize he is the one we have longed for all along. In his presence, all the dreams that seemed to continually diminish here on Earth will forever expand.

I love how Randy Alcorn paints a portrait of heaven:

> We, on this dying Earth can relax and rejoice for our loved ones who are in the presence of Christ. As the apostle Paul tells us, though we naturally grieve at losing loved ones, we are not "to grieve like the rest of men, who have no hope" (1 Thessalonians 4:13). Our parting is not the end of our relationships, only an interruption. We have not "lost" them, because we know where they are. They are experiencing the joy of Christ's presence in a place so wonderful that Christ called it Paradise. And one day, we're told, in a magnificent reunion, they and we "will be with the Lord forever." "Therefore, encourage each other with these words." Picture it. Think of friends or family members who loved Jesus and are with him now. Picture them with you, walking together in this place. All of you have powerful bodies, stronger than those of an

Olympic decathlete. You are laughing, playing, talking, and reminiscing. You reach up to a tree to pick an apple or orange. You take a bite. It's so sweet that it's startling. You've never tasted anything so good. Now you see someone coming toward you. It's Jesus, with a big smile on his face. You fall to your knees in worship. Then He pulls you up and gives you the biggest bear hug in all of history. Every kingdom work, whether publicly performed or privately endeavored, partakes of the kingdom's imperishable character. Every honest intention, every stumbling word of witness, every resistance of temptation, every motion of repentance, every gesture of concern, every routine engagement, every act of worship, every struggle towards obedience, every mumbled prayer, everything, literally, that flows out of our faith-relationship with the Ever-Living One, will find its place in the ever living heavenly order which will dawn at His coming.

One dazzling, sun-drenched morning, I hear distinct laughter, familiar, as it echoes through pure, fragrant breezes. My perfect attention, drawn across a verdant, impossibly lush valley, spies a picnic table overflowing with exquisite fruits, cheeses, wine, and joy. The table, by design, is shaded under a towering, ancient tree so laden with fruit that its bowed branches bring to mind the wings of an eagle. And there's my mom, surrounded by family and friends, sipping her unthickened sweet tea while playing an aggressive, vicious game of bingo. I hear laughter. It is coming from Jesus, who is calling out the numbers.

CONVERSATION STARTERS
FROM TERRY BAKER

Road trip! Terry and Nelda Alexander and I are known for our extravagant yet budget friendly road trips. Terry is always in charge of road snacks. We even have special cookies we call "Terry's cookies." She didn't make them, but still. Once, she even brought build-your-own trail mix. Our trips are spectacular. Others are sad they aren't us. Terry is so pretty.

1. When approaching a significant life event, do you prefer to experience it as it evolves or educate yourself so you can be armed with knowledge of what's to come?

2. As a child, what did you think happened to people who passed away?

3. What is your current belief about life after death?

4. What emotions rose up in you as you read the description of heaven that Randy Alcorn paints in his book?

5. Have you ever contemplated the prospect of joyously laughing with Jesus in heaven?

Halloween 2015

I KNEW I would have no trick-or-treaters since I live out in *The Blair Witch Project* and have seen only two monsters in the twenty-some years I've been out here.

That doesn't stop me from buying the obligatory bags of my favorite candies every year, just in case. I was halfway through both bags and one peanut butter cup away from a sugar coma, when I decided to tackle a long-overdue job: changing the dead lightbulb in my refrigerator. I couldn't remember when it had gone out—obviously quite a while ago.

Once the fridge's dark recesses finally had illumination, I noticed a plastic container in the far back right corner, on the bottom shelf, just above the veggie-crisper drawer.

I don't know what possessed me to open it, but I did. I felt sure I'd chanced onto a possible cure for some new locker-room disease called shibola, a hybrid of shingles and Ebola. I wonder if the Centers for Disease Control and Prevention has researched the curative power of green peas from the 1980s.

On the off chance I would not, in fact, be awarded a Nobel Prize in medicine, I immediately carried the noxious container out to the burn pile, away from the house, to keep the dogs from finding it.

Later that night, when I took the dogs out for their evening constitutional, I couldn't find Scout for a few minutes. We can't figure out what kind of dog he is. He's a fifty-pound, skinny, long-legged solid-black tornado of teeth and toenails. He usually doesn't let me out of his sight. I eventually glanced over and saw him high atop the burn pile, perusing his kingdom, as if he'd just discovered a hidden kitty litter box. I screamed, "Scout!" He came running—the coolest kid on the playground.

I didn't know how much of the offending entree he'd scarfed down, but I knew I had to keep an eye on him.

Later on, as I was working on a lesson I was to give the next morning at the prison, I heard what sounded like a plunger in a commode and knew precisely what was happening. I raced into my bedroom and heard Scout under the bed. I kept trying to coddle him. "Come on out, little buddy."

But alas, it was too late. When I got the courage to look underneath, I saw total carnage. I was trying to think how I would ever be able to clean that much vomit out from under my bed without taking the whole thing apart, when Scout started up again.

I couldn't even try to coax him out. I just watched in horrified fascination as he projectile-vomited everything he'd eaten since he was born.

I thought, *Oh, look—more peas.*

He must have felt a little better, because he crawled out from under the bed and looked at me as if he'd hurled demons into a herd of pigs.

I took him outside for a while and watched him wander around as if he were in a daze. I was a little concerned and called him to me. He will usually run as fast as possible until he gets right to my legs and then come to a screeching halt; however, this time, he came at me, tilted his head to the right, and plowed right into my knees, causing hyperextension and considerable, unnecessary pain.

He was stumbling and weaving. I was horrified. I carried him into the house and called Cliff Peck, one of the top-five vets in the universe. I screamed, "I've killed Scout!"

When I told him what had happened, he laughed and said, "Dude, he's drunk."

"What? He ate moldy—something with peas in it."

Cliff said, "Yep. Some molds are intoxicants. He's just drunk. Watch him for a while. Give him Pepto-Bismol if you have any, and keep an eye on him. Don't let him eat tomorrow."

So I squirted some PB down Scout's throat and made him lie down in his bed so I could continue to work on my prison sermon.

Scout just sat there looking at me. He leaned his head away from me and glared at me from the corner of his eye. He held a paw up to me as if he were trying to figure out which one was really me. All of a sudden, he was channeling Gloria Swanson in *Sunset Boulevard*. I kept waiting for him to say, "I'm ready for my close-up, Mr. DeMille."

Suddenly, without any warning, he vomited again. I was just able to maneuver his head over the edge of the couch before he wretched all over me. I went cold when I looked down and saw red in the vomit—and peas. "Oh no! He's bleeding internally! He's dying! Oh, wait. Pepto-Bismol."

At that moment, I remembered the mess under the bed and decided I needed to go clean that up before—

Oh no.

I grabbed paper towels and a plastic grocery bag and ran to my room. I threw myself onto my belly and looked under the bed. There was nothing.

Just as I was thinking, *What in the world?* Chester, my brown-and-tan beagle-Catahoula mix, who is typically fairly adroit at jumping up onto the bed, slammed into the side of it and glanced over at me with his tongue hanging out the side of his snout. With his eyes squarely focused on mine, Chester slowly slid down the edge of the bed and onto his back haunches.

He just sat there panting and staring, desperately trying to focus on me. It reminded me of someone watching the old game Pong on a primordial computer monitor. Back and forth, side to side.

Obviously, Chester felt it his responsibility to help Scout live up to Proverbs 26:11.

I was getting a little nauseated at that point. Even telling the story is making me a bit woozy. I don't want to say the word *vomit* again. I'm going to change it to something a tad bit more palatable. Since I had a few similar experiences as my dogs in my younger days, I'm going to use the word *vermouth*, a botanically induced wine.

At that point, Chester peered sideways at me, got up, and began turning in awkward circles. I knew what was coming. I grabbed his collar to pull him outside. He got away from me, jumped up onto the couch, and vermouthed—a lot. There were peas.

At that juncture, I had two dogs vermouthing simultaneously. At the same time, I screamed at Falkor, my black Labasset, who had jumped up onto the back of the couch, ready to high-dive into the vermouth. He was perched like a vulture on a telephone wire looking down at roadkill. "Falkor, get outa here!" He was crushed. As if I'd kicked a homeless person away from a twenty-five-foot-long smorgasbord. *Whatever.* "Get out!"

Finally, at about midnight, the dogs seemed to calm down. I went outside and buried what was left of the demon casserole from Dante's third level of hell. Something straight out of a Stephen King novel.

It seemed I hadn't buried it deep enough. The next night, I was doing laundry, and Gawa, my little rat terrier, who is almost completely blind but apparently has a keen sense of smell, was out by the burn pile, high-stepping like a drum major. She was missing only the baton.

Good gravy. Is there no half-life to this stuff? The only things that will survive a nuclear holocaust are cockroaches and peas that have been vermouthed.

CONVERSATION STARTERS FROM JIMMY AND MARNA MONAGHAN

These are incredible people. I cry every time we see each other. Parenting seven beautiful children keeps them hopping. They're great leaders devoted to the ministry God calls them to pursue. They're fun-loving, life-giving adventure seekers. I will never catch up with them on tattoos. But I'll make a valiant attempt.

1. Is there something in your life who reminds you of toxic peas?

2. What's the nasty vermouth you keep returning to?

3. What is hidden in the back of the refrigerator of your life that needs God's light to see?

4. Did Tim say he was going back to prison?

5. If a fool returns to his folly as a dog returns to its vermouth, what's your folly? What's your vermouth?

6. If your metaphorical fridge light came on, what would you need to take to the burn pile of life?

I Hate Having to Be the One to Tell You, but "Takes One to Know One" Isn't in the Bible

I'M ALWAYS SURPRISED when I hear someone misquote a scripture, use a verse out of context, or use a supposed Bible verse that just isn't found in the Bible. I can't decide if I want to laugh and let it pass or try to find a gentle way to adjust the person's error. I don't know exactly how to correct someone without it seeming as if I'm trying to be superior and make him or her feel stupid.

I'm not saying I always know if I'm using a scripture correctly. But I'm reasonably sure I never claim a phrase is biblical if I don't know for sure that it's in the Bible. Here are just a few popular phrases that may or may not actually be found in scripture.

- "Cleanliness is next to godliness."
  No. The Old Testament contains a lot of scripture teaching ritual cleanliness, but this phrase

is nowhere to be found in the Bible. And I'm grateful.

- "Be in the world but not of the world."
  Nope. There are some scriptures that imply this thought (e.g., John 15:19 and John 17:14–16), but this particular phrase is not there.

- "This too shall pass."
  No one is positive where this one originated. The day after Mike Ditka was fired from the Chicago Bears, he tearfully said, "Scripture tells you that all things shall pass." In fact, over the next couple of days, he said it a couple more times. It ain't in there.

- "The lion shall lie down with the lamb."
  This one surprised me. I love pictures I see of a lion cuddling with a lamb. Isaiah 11:6 (MSG) says, "The wolf will romp with the lamb, the leopard sleep with the kid. Calf and lion will eat from the same trough, and a little child will tend them." Isaiah 65:25 (MSG) almost announces it: "Wolf and lamb will graze the same meadow, lion and ox eat straw from the same trough, but snakes—they'll get a diet of dirt!" But there is no verse saying a lion will cuddle with a lamb, unfortunately.

I've noticed that some people tend to use Bible verses to emphasize or prove their beliefs or opinions. And most people, because they don't want to question someone who seems to know what he or she is talking about, accept the nonscripture at face value.

But here's some good news: I have the Holy Spirit living inside me. Ephesians 1:17–20 (NIV) says,

> I keep asking that the God of our Lord Jesus Christ, the glorious Father, may give you the Spirit of wisdom and revelation, so that you may know him better. I pray also that the eyes of your heart may be enlightened in order that you may know the hope to which he has called you, the riches of his glorious inheritance in the saints, and his incomparably great power for us who believe. That power is like the working of his mighty strength, which he exerted in Christ when he raised him from the dead and seated him at his right hand in the heavenly realms.

When someone says something to me that doesn't ring true, I have the freedom to know it might be the Holy Spirit nudging me and warning me of spiritual manipulation. Or it could be an innocent mistake.

During the 2016 election season, I was discussing the pros and cons of several candidates with a friend. She is very resolved on which side of the aisle she stands. At one point during our discussion, she loudly proclaimed, "Even Jesus said, 'Give a man a fish, and he'll eat for a day, but …'"

Wait! What?

I kept waiting for her to finish the quote, but apparently, she couldn't remember the rest. She works hard to understand the Word and takes Bible study classes regularly, so I decided not to correct her. I prayed she would go home and Google that specific alleged scripture so she could remember the next time she chose to use it and, in so doing, find that it was not a scripture at all.

We have to be careful on two fronts. First, when we choose to use scripture to uphold our belief system, we'd better know that it is, in fact, in the Bible. Second, we need to have a basic idea of where it's found in the Bible and know that we're using it in the correct context. Here's a third thought: we need to be confident we are teaching not doctrine but theology. Doctrine is a set of beliefs, usually dependent on a specific denomination. Theology focuses more on the study of God and faith rather than religion. Sometimes the differences may be foggy, and the methods may be different, but the message should always be valid. Often, we get a cosmic nudge from the Holy Spirit when something doesn't ring of truth consistent with God's Word.

Recently, my friend Jan told me about a meeting she'd experienced with a mutual supervisor in a faith-based ministry in which we both volunteer. Apparently, the conversation had become heated, and the leader had told Jan, "I'm going to tear your flesh."

When Jan recounted the story to me, I said, "Whoa, whoa. Tear your flesh? What does that even mean?"

My feeling was that it was some scripture the leader had used to intimidate Jan and leave her fearful. But I wasn't sure where it was in the Bible, and the Holy Spirit was speaking to me right then, telling me this was being used not as exhortation but as punishment.

After Jan and I finished our conversation, I began to research that phrase: "Tear your flesh." After a couple of hours, I called Jan to tell her what I'd discovered.

"Jan, there have been times in my life when people have, whether intentionally or unintentionally, used scripture to throw me off balance and leave me feeling unstable in the confrontation. It's a ploy to get the upper hand. You have to learn to hear with better ears, especially when someone uses scripture to undermine you. This person used a scripture that left you feeling vulnerable. It's a scripture that he probably heard a pastor use and thought would be a great dart to throw. Or he was the victim of someone else's ignorance and knew he could use that phrase to his advantage. When you told me what he said, I immediately felt something wasn't right about it. I decided to listen to the tug of the Spirit's prompting. Here's what I found.

"There is a scripture that speaks of 'tearing of the flesh.' It's in Micah 3:1–4 (NIV). Micah says, 'Listen, you leaders of Jacob, you rulers of Israel. Should you not embrace justice, you who hate good and love evil; who tear the skin from my people and the flesh from their bones; who eat my people's flesh, strip off their skin and break their bones in pieces; who chop them up like meat for the pan, like flesh for the pot? Then they will cry out to the Lord, but he will not answer them. At that time he will hide his face from them because of the evil they have done.'

"So what he's saying to you—if he is, in fact, the flesh tearer—is that he tortures and abuses the people entrusted to him and, more importantly, hates what is good and loves what is evil. When he cries out to God, God's not going to hear him, because of the evil he's done. That's what he's saying about himself because he's ignorant of how he's misquoting and misusing scripture."

Jan said, "Ooh. Should I call him out on that?"

I chuckled. "No, probably not. He will more than likely use it again. Then remind him, according to scripture, what he's inferring about himself."

There've been times in my life when I've been victimized by people who know how to use scripture or other phrases to throw me off track of the immediate issue. That way, they can feel they have the footing to bear down on me and come in for the kill.

I was once in a meeting with several people. One of the attendees was dissatisfied and disheartened by the way the ministry was moving. He voiced his opinion, and the ministry leader said, "You don't have permission to do my inventory for me." We all, about ten of us, just sat there and stared at the leader. The proclamation he'd broadcast was entirely off base with the concerns being addressed.

At some point, one of the other attendees said, "What does that have to do with what we're talking about? No one here has any desire to do your inventory for you." Although the leader said little for the rest of the meeting, we all felt the die had been cast. It wasn't long before the team was dismantled. That leader destroyed a vibrant, soul-mending, God-honoring ministry, thanks to his own arrogance and selfish ambition. Second Timothy 2:15 (NIV) says, "Do your best to present yourself to God as one approved, a worker who does not need to be ashamed and who correctly handles the word of truth."

It's a command. We're called to correctly handle the Word of truth. That doesn't only mean we must be sure of how we administer the Word. It also means being sensitive to the Spirit of God and listening for the elbow nudge when someone uses scripture to incorrectly uphold his or her beliefs.

If something (or Someone) in you is telling you the statement isn't ringing true, it's probably not true. The best way I've found to get a good layout of scripture is, shockingly, by reading it. Yes, I read Bible studies, watch video series, and listen to Christian audiobooks, but the way to know and have a basic understanding of specific scripture locations is by reading. I have no agenda other than asking God to help me remember something, even one thing, I'm reading and, just as important, where it is in the Bible.

I ask him to reveal to me only what I need to know during that time. Occasionally, when someone asks where a verse is, I can at least remember the cadence or character of a specific biblical writer. It helps me discern when I feel something is being misused.

And again, I always make sure I keep my mouth shut if I'm not sure I'm using a verse correctly. I try to remember Romans 8:11 (NIV): "And if the Spirit of Him who raised Jesus from the dead is living in you, He who raised Christ from the dead will also give life to your mortal bodies because of His Spirit who lives in you."

The Spirit lives in us. We can listen to his whisper when we need discernment. We can trust him to tell us when something ain't right.

Whether it's cleanliness and godliness or lions and lambs, I want to use scripture correctly. In fact, whenever possible, I think it's crucial to insert my own favorite verse since I'm left-handed: "Thus sayeth the Lord, Everyone is born left-handed until they commit their first sin" (3 Timothy 7:11).

CONVERSATION STARTERS FROM DR. PATRICIA A. KNOTT

Author of *The Search for Kum Ba Ya*, *The Parent Trap*, and *9 Things Kaylan Should Know*, my dear friend Pat serves on our church's board of directors. She's the perfect choice for the position. She's a wise and gifted writer, she's able to broach potentially difficult situations with a God-filled heart of unity and love, and she's really fun to hang out with. And she's so pretty.

1. Has there been a time when you used a supposed scripture only to find out it wasn't in the Bible? How did it change your behavior regarding scriptural quotes?

2. Do you use a method to memorize scriptures? If you have a method that has helped you tremendously, consider sharing it with others.

3. How does it make you feel when someone uses scripture against you or to manipulate you? Have you found yourself doing it to others? Have you asked for the Spirit's help to always use God's Word with the right heart and the right motive?

CONVERSATION STARTERS FROM BONNIE KEEN

Founding member of the critically acclaimed recording trio First Call, Bonnie is an actor, writer, and speaker. She's a deep thinker. She's a wife and mother. She's fiercely in love with Jesus. My sweet friend is tall and blonde and a beauty inside and out.

1. Important primary question to settle: Do you believe the Word is accurate? Do scriptures need to be sifted, taken out of context, or amended? This has to be a settled question between each of us and God. Every other question in your life falls under this answer.

2. Jesus claimed to be the living Word. When he bled, he quoted scripture. How then do we view the importance of being biblically literate in our shoes and time?

3. Even Satan knew scripture and twisted it with a spirit of manipulation. When we study, it is to be articulate, knowledgeable, and used by God's gentle Spirit to bring the good news of Christ to a world of broken friends. Are you willing to be loving and truthful in the process of study? Will you dare to believe God will use even the tiniest moment of searching his Word for good?

It's Not Your Time Yet

I REMEMBER A line from *Pretty Woman* when Julia Roberts's character says, "The bad stuff is so much easier to believe." It makes sense that Satan would use the bad stuff about us to keep us feeling less than what the Lord has planned for us to be. The Enemy has done a masterful job of convincing us through media that we are not, and can never be, the ideals that our culture has set up as symbols of success.

We read Bible verses that tell us we can give God thanks because we are fearfully and wonderfully made, we are the light of the world, we are a city on a hill that cannot be hidden, and we will shine like stars in the sky. We can read the blessings from the best book ever written. We can even believe them for others. But sometimes it's hard to conceive that these verses were meant for us. Why? Maybe because we tend to see ourselves through eyes of betrayal, hurt, and rejection, which forces us to believe that striving for approval and perfection is the answer.

A while back, I ran into a guy I hadn't seen in a few years. We talked for a few minutes, and he said, "You know what I remember most about you?"

My mind began to race. What had I said to this guy that was rude or unkind?

He said, "Once, you asked me if I would run the media program for the lyrics at church. I was scared to do it. And instead of forcing me to do it by insisting I was capable and could do it, you said, 'Ya know, you do have permission to say no.' That has freed me up on many occasions to not be bound by my need to always say yes."

What a small, insignificant thing I'd said. It had become a blessing for that man.

We have no idea how one small word of affirmation can change a life permanently. Interestingly, in an unrelated incident, a worship pastor said I'd once told him the same thing. It set him free to not feel responsible to say yes to everything.

Blessings are obviously a big deal in the Bible. When Jacob wrestled with God, he refused to let God go until God blessed him.

> Do not repay evil with evil or insult with insult. On
> the contrary, repay evil with blessing, because to this
> you were called so that you may inherit a blessing.
> —1 Peter 3:9 NIV

I wonder if there is neutral ground between curse and blessing or if everything is either a blessing or a curse in varying degrees of power.

I may be walking down a street and see children clutching their parents' hands and feel a prompting from the Holy Spirit to pray for those children. I quickly, quietly pray the Lord will bless them and place them in places where they will rise up to be world-changers for his glory. I may pass an acre of ground and pray the Lord will bless that place and consecrate it for his glory. Sometimes we may give a blessing to someone that is a direct word from God that will set that person's life on a path straight into a relationship with the Lord.

I serve as a volunteer mentor at a prison. One of my guys there is Mark. He's in prison for murder. Although the death was an accident, he was strung out on drugs and alcohol during his interrogation. His lies and deceit after the accident sealed his conviction. Mark wrote out his inventory when he went through a Celebrate Recovery step-study several years ago. It was 320 pages long. He gave me permission to write his story in novel form. One of the chapters is hard. I believe the Lord spoke directly to what Mark needed to hear the most.

> It's all still pretty surreal to me, looking back. Within my first week in county jail, I was placed in isolation for observation because of my history of suicide attempts. This was all too much for me to withstand. I made another attempt at taking my own life.
>
> This is the one that changed my life forever. Why would you ever put someone on suicide watch and provide the means necessary to kill himself?
>
> When I was locked down, I was provided with all the amenities that the standard inmate is provided upon intake. This included a towel, a mat, a blanket, and a uniform. An inmate on suicide watch is provided none of those things. The suicide smock and a hard concrete bed are as good as it gets.
>
> I was on my third day of lockdown. I decided that I honestly couldn't take the horror my life had become. I previously told you about two other serious attempts on my own life, which were by hanging. And both failed miserably. I'm not sure why I chose hanging. Maybe it

was all I could think of besides blowing my brains out.

By the time I made my first attempt on my own life, I had lost my pistols due to incidents like running into people's houses and brandishing a weapon like some sort of cowboy. Plus, have you ever seen an attempted suicide by gunshot go wrong? I have. And Lord knows that's no way to live.

Maybe on some subconscious level, I felt an overwhelming kinship to Judas Iscariot. No loyalties to anyone except myself. And that in itself became too much to withstand. My literary style might lead you to believe that I am making a joke of the situation. Granted, some of the predicaments I have been in are worthy of being made a laughingstock. However, suicide attempts are taboo.

Without this particular incident, though, I'm not sure I would have come to recognize God's actual existence. I am like doubting Thomas. I thought I believed at one point in my life. Those days were long behind me. It was going to take me seeing God face-to-face before I truly believed.

And that is just what God had in store for me.

I don't remember a lot about the incident. Just tying the knot in the blanket. The guards left the food slot on the door open. I tied off one end of the blanket through the food slot to the handle on the outside of my cell door. I tied the other end of the blanket around my neck and sat down on the floor.

Strangulation is an unpleasant way to go. But once unconsciousness comes and darkness slips over you, it is peaceful. It's the period up to the blacking out that is unpleasant. The knowledge you are choking, that your body is starved for oxygen. That's the hard part. I almost made it. I slipped off into that long good night, that beautiful darkness, only to come to, surrounded by two deputies performing first aid.

The next thing I really remember is the ambulance pulling into the ER and being rolled through the front door on a stretcher. My reality started truly caving in on me when I realized that the ER technicians were putting me in the exact same room where I faced my crime ten days earlier. The same room. Even the same bed.

That's when the collapse of all things temporal happened. I lost my bearings and began to sob hysterically at my recognition of this place. It felt like some sick joke being played on me. Honestly, it felt like I had entered the first circle of hell. The one Dante forgot to mention. Hell on earth.

In my panic attack, I came to notice several nurses walking in and out of the room. The other patient in the room with me was moved to another location. My police escort and I were the only ones left in this room. All these nurses I noticed were huddled up outside the nurses' station, which was right outside my room, all talking and pointing in my direction.

Of course, they knew who I was. For a week, I was front-page headlines, every local news broadcast. The fact is, in a small town, news spreads like wildfire. And it burns out slowly. My crisis of faith began, my deus ex machina.

A short, portly man walked into the room, and it was obvious he was the doctor. You can always pick a doctor out from a crowd of nurses. They display a certain take-charge demeanor that gives them away.

This doctor had a very unpleasant look on his face. It was not a look of anger or even resentment. I couldn't place the emotion, but it was obvious discomfort. I believe it was a form of fear. The fear of facing a monster. The fear Ananias had when God instructed him to go to the apostle Paul and heal his blindness. Even with God on his side, Ananias was afraid of a blind, helpless Paul because his reputation had obviously preceded him.

Such was the case with me. I lay handcuffed to this bed under the supervision of an armed police escort. This doctor knew there was something definitely not right. But he proceeded anyway.

What he said to me changed my life forever.

Now, listen closely. I'm not going to get all "I had a revelation from God" or whatever. But that night, I had myself a good old-fashioned come-to-Jesus meeting in its purest form.

I laugh at Old Testament stories and the misconceptions that movies like *The Ten Commandments* make about God's voice. It's not some booming voice that comes over the intercom like an elementary school principal reading your daily lunch menu and saying the Pledge of Allegiance every morning. Not saying he can't or he won't go that route. But I have come to understand, for me, God prefers more subtle ways of communicating, because that is the most effective.

I believe God sends messages through people just like you and just like me.

So this doctor calmly walked up to my bed and looked down on me. He said, "Look, son. I know who you are. And I need you to understand: it's not your time to go yet. God is not ready for you yet. He has some sort of plan for you. I don't know what this plan entails. But it's obvious it does not consist of your dying yet."

He also informed me that he went to church with the victim's family and that more people than I could conceive were praying for me specifically. To me, that was as good as showing me the holes in Jesus's hands and the wound in His side.

I know you probably expected some tunnel with bright lights and a booming James Earl Jones–type voice. And if you were, I'm sorry my encounter with my God has let you down. It was not Wizard of Oz theatrics.

I believe in my heart's depths that my personal Savior knew precisely what I needed for me to believe. It was Him.

Mark is now a senior counselor for the substance abuse program at the prison and basically the leader over four barracks of inmates. He has completed eight Celebrate Recovery step-studies since I've known him and has never, in those eight years, missed one single class.

His dream is to finish college, even in prison, and then pursue his master's in substance abuse.

I don't know why the bad stuff is so much easier to believe. It's not from God. It's not what he feels about us, and it's not the truth. If we believe his Word, then we have to arrive in a place of healing. He makes no mistakes. We are created with a purpose, with specific gifts. No one can uniquely do for God what he has planned for us to do. No one!

CONVERSATION STARTERS
FROM VICKI BURNETT

Vicki is a former Miss Congeniality winner in the Miss Arkansas pageant. The next year, she made top ten in the Miss Arkansas pageant. The next year, she came back and sang at the Miss Arkansas pageant. For the life of me, I can't figure out why she didn't win. She thinks it was the swimsuit thing. I wasn't there to judge, so I don't know. Vicki is truly a lovely lady inside and out, so I get the congeniality thing. And she has a beautiful voice.

1. What are some of the lies you have allowed to become part of your narrative?

2. What are three things you can read in God's Word that give you a glimpse into what he really thinks about you?

3. What is an excellent first step toward renewing your thought process whenever a toxic thought tries to take root?

Cupcakes and a Chupacabra

JUNE 1977. *ANNIE* won a Tony for best musical. Stevie Wonder sang "Sir Duke," and KC and the Sunshine Band released "I'm Your Boogie Man." *Herbie Goes to Monte Carlo* and *For the Love of Benji* beat out *MacArthur* at the box office. Friends in college and I spent most of our time quoting almost every line from *Young Frankenstein*, which had hit theaters a couple of years earlier. I was in a college traveling musical group called Belles and Beaux.

We were about to begin our cross-country summer tour, going through Texas and west to California, swinging around through Colorado, and making our way back to beautiful downtown Searcy, Arkansas.

I loved traveling with that group. It was a kind of recruiting group for the university. We would go to churches, auditoriums, and all sorts of different venues, wearing our bumblebee-yellow costumes, and do a concert of popular tunes of the day. I usually ended up with a Barry Manilow ballad or a song like Neal Sedaka's "Breaking Up Is Hard to Do." We stayed with church families along the way, who fed us well and often gave us food for our trip. Homemade cookies and cupcakes were particularly popular.

Before we left on the first morning of our two-week adventure, Cliff Ganus, the director, and I went to pick up a U-Haul trailer, which connected to the back of the van by a hitch and two chains and carried our costumes, musical instruments, and sound equipment. I talked with Cliff about our options. Could we put everything in the van and forget the U-Haul? We decided to use the two-wheeler anyway, to give ourselves more legroom in the van. We hooked the chains and the hitch to the back of the van, loaded up, and headed out on our adventure.

The van, which was an off brand called Superior, had been donated to us from an old department store chain called Gibson's Discount Center. It was supposed to have an exceptionally sturdy frame. It was covered—floor, walls, and ceiling—with red carpet. Two separate seats were at the front of the van: one for the driver and one passenger seat, separated by a console. When you opened the back door on the right side, there was a labeled *Quickie-Step* that was, theoretically, supposed to mechanically appear from under the van and jut out and downward so you could step up comfortably onto the van. It never worked. So even for six-foot-three me, it was like stepping onto a moving train, jumping what seemed like two feet to get aboard.

When you were finally able to get into the van, to your left, you would see three rows of seats that could hold maybe seven or eight people. Well, not seats exactly—more like cushioned pews, so we could lie down to sleep if we wanted to. If you turned right, you would see two benches facing each other, attached to opposite sides of the van, with an aisle between them. We all claimed our spots for the trip and took off.

About midday, my friend Barbara Wright complained that her eyes were burning. I had natural, soothing eye drops made of rose petals. I didn't think to tell Barbara the drops were made from a flowering shrub since in that decade, we had no idea of the healing properties of essential oils. We put a couple of drops in each of her eyes, and she settled down for a nap. Evidently, unbeknownst to us, Barbara was allergic to roses. When she woke up, she looked at me, and I stifled a startled gasp, as if the Elephant Man had just crossed my path. "How do your eyes feel?" I choked out.

"Oh, wow. They feel so much better."

In truth, she looked uncannily like Marty Feldman. I felt as if I were watching a tree frog startled into bug-eyed awareness that a hoot owl was diving down to devour it. I spent the rest of the day keeping her away from anything remotely resembling a mirror.

The second day out, we were driving through Texas, about forty-five minutes from Seguin. The temperature could have melted metal, which melts in the neighborhood of 2,500 degrees Fahrenheit. Barbara, her eyes back to normal, sat in the driver's seat with Cliff beside her up front. I stretched out on the floor in the aisle between the two pews facing each other, sobbing while reading the last two pages of *Where the Red Fern Grows*. Being a true Arkansan, I was barefoot.

Barbara, driving the van, was trying to open her window to shoo an annoying fly. The window wouldn't budge. She wrestled with the clasp. Meanwhile, the van began to drift. It drifted more. It headed for the columns under an overpass. Cliff's wife, Debbie, sitting somewhere above me, said, "We're going to do something." I closed my book and laid it on my chest, oddly annoyed that I was only one page from the end.

Suddenly, the road was gone, and we were careening through a field. Cliff yelled, "Turn the wheels to the right! Turn them to the right!"

Then the weirdest thing happened. There was no noise. No sound. The van's wheels left the gravel and scalding dirt of a Texas flatland. The van rolled with a thud onto its side and then over again, settling on the roof. Everyone and everything was thrown around as if we were in a clothes dryer. My first memory after we landed was that I was still holding my book.

The silence continued for a few seconds.

We all began to stir around, obviously in shock. I had seen none of the wreck; one minute, I'd been on the floor, looking at the ceiling, and the next, I'd face-planted into the same ceiling. I jumped up and heard someone yelling out to see if Chuck was okay. Chuck, one of our group, sometimes had trouble walking. I realized he could have been hurt most, and I too yelled out for him. As fate had it, he'd landed at my feet, and he yelled that he was okay. So I stepped on him and plowed toward the door.

I threw the door open once I figured out where the handle was in its new upside-down position. My senses were firing on all cylinders, and I noticed several things simultaneously. One, when I opened the door, the *Quickie-Step* magically began to operate and slid into place, up toward the sky. To this day, I still think it was just waiting for the right time to show its abnormal, unhealthy sense of humor.

The second thing I noticed was that the U-Haul had not become unattached. Somehow, it had detached from the hitch, but the chains had kept it from running away or flipping over with the van.

At that moment, an unbearable stench met intense heat emitting from the sandy terrain. Shoeless, I jumped from the van, and my feet sank into something that recently had died in the very spot where we'd flipped the van. To be honest, to this day, the emotional trauma of that singular event eclipses the entire wreck experience. I am relatively certain it was a roadkill chupacabra.

Someone still in the bowels of the doomed vehicle behind me screamed, "Could this thing explode?"

Instantaneously, a herd of humanity piled out of the van into the blistering heat.

Miraculously, no one was severely hurt. We had only bumps and cuts. However, when keyboardist Jan stepped out, her face was covered with tiny white flecks of skin. It was apparent she had slid face-first on the carpet-lined wall up onto the carpet-lined ceiling. She wasn't reacting to the fact that she looked like an extra in *Night of the Living Dead*. I stood transfixed, waiting for her to start shrieking when her brain finally registered pain.

Then I noticed the same particles of skin on the front of her shirt. I chose not to think about it. It was too much to process. Besides, I just kept thinking, *I stepped in something really bad.*

Semis and cars pulled off the road, and their occupants ran to check on us. Nobody had cell phones back then, so one of the truck drivers got on his Convoy CB and called for a tow.

The van was eventually turned right side up again. The tow truck showed up. We all climbed aboard, which seemed more than a little dangerous, and were hauled to a cantina on the outskirts of a small town.

I looked around at our stuff scattered across the floor, wondering where my shoes had ended up. I noticed a cardboard box that once had been filled with white-frosted cupcakes, which now had what could well have been a face print in them. I glanced back at flake-covered Jan and burst into hysterical laughter.

"What?" She seemed unreasonably offended that I was laughing at her since no one had informed her she was covered in cupcake icing. At the same time, I was bizarrely upset that all those heavenly cupcakes were ruined.

Half an hour later, while the others tried to relax at tables in the tiny cantina, talking about the experience, I headed straight to the bathroom. I had my foot hanging precariously over the sink, trying to wash off the dead chupacabra, when one of the other guys walked in and leaned against the wall in the corner, glancing sheepishly at me, apparently channeling Boo Radley. Finally, he leaned toward me and said, "That was really scary, wasn't it?" I raised my eyebrows and nodded. He leaned really close to me and almost whispered, "Tim, did you have an accident?"

It took a few seconds for me to wrap my brain around his concerned expression. Finally, with my foot in the sink, I hollered, "No! I stepped in something really bad!"

When we got back to the tables, I sat down in just enough time to hear Debbie say, "It's a good thing we had a Superior body."

I thought, *Wow, yeah. I didn't even stop to consider how we were protected. It is only by the mercy of God that we're all sitting here okay.* We all solemnly nodded. I think I actually clasped my hands together in an attitude of reflective, grateful prayer.

Debbie continued. "'Cause if we'd been in a Winnebago, we'd all be dead right now."

I casually unfolded my hands and began playing with the salt and pepper shakers.

We all made collect calls from the pay phone to let our families know we were alive.

Then we joined in a group discussion and decided to be strong and resilient, rent a van, and continue our tour. The new van was decidedly better appointed than the old one. The new rig had beds for napping and even a bathroom. We chained the U-Haul to the van and forged ahead.

It's my personal opinion that the U-Haul somehow felt it was not being afforded the due attention it deserved after the accident. It, after all, never had lost its footing and had kept our clothes, speakers, and microphones safe.

About halfway into our two-week tour, Mr. U-Haul decided to have a flat tire. I can't remember if we changed it, if someone came and changed it, or even if there was a spare tire; I just remember having to unload the trailer on the side of the highway so it could be jacked up and then reloaded after the new tire was installed.

A few more days passed, when the same tire blew out again. Nobody was happy about having to unload the trailer, change the tire, and reload again, which added to the anxiety of rushing to get to the next venue.

But somewhere in Colorado, probably close to Castle Rock, while lounging on one of the beds, looking out the window as the sun set in breathtaking, dazzling fashion over the mountains, I thought how the drive was finally serene and peaceful.

Suddenly, out of the corner of my eye, I noticed something yellow rolling at breakneck speed across the field to my left, toward the purple mountain majesties. On further eye-squinting investigation, I realized it was Mr. U-Haul, seemingly still upset over being snubbed at the wreckage site. In his nomadic escape, blatantly snapping the chains that confined him, he appeared to say, "I can't take it anymore."

I watched in fascination, waiting for him to make his last effort for recognition by finally rolling over. But it never happened. I watched him, farther in the distance behind us now, do a half turn in the dust and settle back, as if pointing his trailer-hitch nose to the sky in a defiant "So there" attitude, before I turned my head toward the front of the van and calmly said, "Uh, Cliff?"

CONVERSATION STARTERS
FROM RYK TATUM

Ryk will tell you all about his life struggles. He will tell you because his life is a clear picture of how a life can be restored and become a beacon for hope. He is a big believer in giving all glory and honor to God. He's a good guy to be around.

1. Nearly everyone has a "How did I survive that?" story. What is your favorite "I almost died" experience? Share it with someone.

2. *Young Frankenstein, Forrest Gump, The Color Purple*—what movies do you know seemingly line for line? What is your favorite line from those movies? Why does that line resonate with you?

3. The U-Haul was destined to have its moment of glory (or diva-ism). Whom in your life do you think most resembles the attitude displayed by the U-Haul? Why?

The Catch

I HAVE TRAVELED to New Zealand four times for work. I paid for nothing while I was there (yes, please feel free to experience a scintilla of jealousy right about now!). Two coworkers and I decided to take an escorted Jeep trip down a canyon trail. We would savor a relaxed lunch at the bottom, hang out, enjoy nature, and then travel back to the top. It sounded rugged and almost expedition-like—an adventure for us city folk.

We started at a sustainable amount of excitement. The gently used utility vehicle sported no doors, had a canvas roof, and sat ten people—very safari-like. Of course, I landed in one of the seats near a gap where a closed door should've been—so close that if I moved my foot a few inches to the left, it would drag along the dirt road.

We all joked about being early pioneers in a new, undiscovered land. I didn't realize at that moment how close we would come to being the skeletons of primitive cave dwellers.

As we continued the forty-five-minute descent along the side of the canyon, the jovial conversation slowly ground to a terrified halt as the road became more and more narrow. We also noted that as the width of the path became more restricted, the speed of the dented dirt-brown vehicle did not. Although we probably never traveled faster than twenty miles an hour, we were going down the sheer side of a cliff with unlimited, anfractuous, blind turns and twists. I unwisely looked out the open space where a closed door should have been and saw that for the most part, we were never more than a foot from the edge of the precipice. I could actually see the drop of several hundred feet and birds flying below us. Flying below us! I'm sure they were vultures.

Although the driver and escort appeared totally at peace with the vehicle careening down the hill at what seemed to the rest of us like NASCAR speed, everything in me screamed, "For the love of all things holy, slow down!"

But for some reason, there was a catch in my throat, and I couldn't get the words out. We've all felt those moments before, when our emotions can rise only so high, keeping us safe from exploding or imploding. At that particular moment, I realized no one was yelling. I glanced around to see everyone else with the same pasty-white, no-blood-to-the-brain, mouths-agape-in-a-silent-scream, terror-filled, frozen expression, likely wondering, *Did I tell everyone I love them before I left?*

Everyone in the duct-taped jalopy was desperately peering at me. In retrospect, I assume they were looking at me because I was closest to the open space where a door should've been but wasn't and, therefore, should've been the one to activate an inflatable slide in the event of an emergency landing. I frantically prayed I would pass out before we hit the bottom of the canyon. I also prayed we didn't have a homicidal maniac as a tour guide.

Then it started to rain. Just a small drizzle, really, but those drops of water might as well have been a monsoon to those of us in mortal jeopardy.

Amazingly and miraculously, the rain stopped as quickly as it had begun. The tour guide, driving with one hand and holding a microphone with his other, gleefully told us something about something—maybe the history of the flora in the area. I don't know. I defy any person in that group to remember or care the slightest bit about what he was saying. Like telling a skydiver whose parachute failed to open that a bird had just pooped on his head.

Just as all hope for survival was lost, we rounded a bend, and I heard an audible gasp from every person in that doom-clunker.

The canyon opened up onto the most incredible view I had ever seen. A lush, verdant green vista spread out before us in every direction. Still well above the tree line, we saw nothing human-made for miles. Rising from one end of the horizon, blazing across the azure sky, and nestling on the other end of the horizon, framing the life-filled valley, was a dazzling, perfect double rainbow. The view was vast and breathtaking; we experienced the pure beginning of the bands of color from one end of the valley to the perfectly pristine other end. The spectrum of colors was immaculate. No fuzzy lines. A finished prism of light.

Only one sound irritated the moment: the grinding of tires over gravel as we continued down the compressed path. I can't remember how long I held my breath, but I recognized the holiness of the moment. I understood that catch in my chest, where the emotional impact seemed to settle and then move into tears. I couldn't physically fully express my unadulterated emotion at that moment. I had no choice in the presence of such a miracle. I slid off the seat I'd been holding with a death grip just thirty seconds before and silently lifted my praise and thankfulness to the Lord. He'd created that spectacular display of power, and I marveled at his creative genius. I thanked him for reminding me in that reverent moment that he was still on his throne, and he was still in control.

When I got back into my seat, I noticed that once again, the other passengers were all staring at me. But this time, I didn't care.

There are countless other times I've experienced the catch. Moments and snapshots of the Holy Spirit nudging me forward when it might have been painful at first.

One night, at the prison where I lead Celebrate Recovery step-studies, I was talking to an inmate. He believed in Jesus, but he had yet to become a follower. He knew everything he needed to know to become a Christian, but he couldn't make the leap for some reason.

As we talked, I asked Brad about his family. He paused and then said, "I've never told anyone this. But my father beat me. When I was a kid, I wasn't afraid or ashamed to cry or show emotion or hug. My father said it was a sign of weakness. So he was going to, in his words, force me to be a man. He would then proceed to beat me and tell me he was going to keep hitting me until I stopped crying."

My heart leaped into my throat. The anger, betrayal, and abandonment Brad must have experienced tugged at me until my own tears came. "Brad, that's why you have such a hard time trusting the Lord. You're scared to death he will hurt you if you trust him."

Brad looked intently at me. But he didn't cry. The bar for his catch had been set extremely high. I had total faith it would happen. He would surrender. I never pushed him. But I told him he needed to hurry up and give his heart to Jesus. I needed to move him from the accept-Jesus column on my prayer list over to the plans-for-Brad's-life column.

Another time, my friend Jack and I were exchanging catch experiences. He described a messy event that preceded a catch moment that stemmed from an agonizing encounter. Thanks to a stressful job, Jack usually left work every day anxious and frustrated, as did most of the other employees. He needed to know if it was the management or his attitude that was way off.

Jack asked the Lord to help him understand where the problems originated.

Jack attended a business networking lunch along with the owner of the establishment he worked for—the person he felt was causing a great deal of grief and discord. As part of the networking for the business, Jack attended weekly meetings with that particular group. The secretary for the crowd had been away on vacation for a couple of weeks. Because Jack was not yet a member, his contact information hadn't been entered into their computer system as quickly as the owner thought it should have been.

After the meeting, the owner walked up to the secretary. He began to verbally annihilate her because she'd failed to get Jack's email set up for correspondence. The man was a churchgoing self-proclaimed follower of Jesus.

Once she was close to tears, the owner berated her for poor math skills. She'd announced in the meeting that 90 percent of the group members had attended—twenty-five of thirty. He made sure she understood that twenty-five was not 90 percent of thirty and wondered why she would make such a statement.

The president of the chapter heard the aggression and moved over, as did the incoming president, to intervene. Within a matter of minutes, the temperature in the room became intense.

Jack stood back, dumbfounded that a follower of Jesus Christ would ever treat someone so horribly. He deliberately positioned himself behind the owner and mouthed, "I am so sorry," to the secretary.

She said, "It's okay." Then she left the room.

Jack wanted to explode. The catch was there. It stopped him for once. But I'm confident it was only because of Jack's need of job security.

Then, in the car on the way back to work, the owner announced that at the prior week's meeting, one of the guys—a member of

XYZ church—had made an off-color remark. Apparently, the statement was supposed to justify the owner's reckless display of rage. At least he didn't say anything "off-color."

Jack's heart grieved for the rest of the day. He held himself together for the last three hours of work, but the minute he sat down in his car, he began to shake. He tried to come up with any possible scenario in which the action in the meeting could have been justified. There wasn't one. Jack kept thinking of the poor lady trying to defend herself against someone who was, in every respect, a bully.

My eyes brimmed with tears as Jack detailed how the Lord healed his heart that afternoon.

It rained that day. It seemed another narrow, twisting, winding, anfractuous path lay in front of Jack. The heartache and bitterness were getting to a specific point and pausing just there, a nebulous area he was unable to navigate. He prayed, *Okay, Holy Spirit, interpret my groaning.* Just as he reached the top of the hill, about a mile from his house, Jack glanced to his right, and there it was—the catch.

The sun was setting. A brilliant display of bright yellow, dusty orange, burgundy, and bluish purple—a God-sent eye feast. Seriously, who besides God could put orange and purple together and make it look good? It never even worked for Howard Johnson.

God was right there. Jack pulled into his driveway, turned the car around, and sat in the silence. He felt the glory of Psalm 65:8 (MSG) as the tears began to flow: "Far and wide they'll come to a stop, they'll stare in awe, in wonder. Dawn and dusk take turns calling, 'Come and worship.'" So Jack did.

The next day, he sent an email to the secretary and apologized.

> I'm so sorry for the bullying you had to face yesterday. I don't believe you were treated with

integrity. Nor do I believe you were shown much respect. I need you to know that I am a follower of Jesus Christ. And I don't believe that when we face eternity, God will care one bit about when you set up my email or what percentage of enrolled members attended the meeting. What he will remember is if or how we shared the glory of his precious Son, Jesus.

All we can do in these bodies is throw our arms up in praise and worship; wonder and awe; and even pain, grief, and fear, because we're incapable of fully expressing the depth of love, joy, and need we feel.

But there is soon coming a time when the catch will no longer be part of our makeup. The quick intake of breath, that gasp of wonder and amazement because our senses are accosted with something breathtakingly magnificent, will be normal and will finally be our home.

There will come a time when these frail, time-sensitive bodies will be different. I believe God has placed the catch in us as a taste of what's to come to keep us yearning for our future home. Graveclothes dropped and veil lifted, we will see Jesus face-to-face. We will finally know the beauty that he alone saw in us at Calvary. Our bodies will be metamorphosed and made responsive to an entirely new, fresh atmosphere. We will be fully released to express the limitless, eternal, inexhaustible thankfulness we have always desired to lay at his feet.

Psalm 56:8 (NLT) says, "You keep track of all my sorrows. You have collected all my tears in your bottle. You have recorded each one in your book."

It's a balm to me, a comfort, to know it's okay to have days when I want my praise to rise higher. When the worship I want to express is not as full, complete, loud, or finished as my heart longs for it to be and can only be expressed in grateful tears. One day Jesus will show me a bottle in which he's saved every catch, every tear he has caught, I'll know just how cherished and precious they are to him.

Finally, unrestrained and unfettered by earthly barriers, I will proclaim and shout from without what he has made me from within: "Holy, holy, holy is the Lord God Almighty."

CONVERSATION STARTERS FROM
GREG AND JULIE HILLEGAS

You know the Creative Living Connection class I'm always raving about? Julie came up with the name. Because that's kinda who she is: creative. And really pretty. Greg loves to connect with people in meaningful ways. He's not as pretty as Julie, but that's okay. He's cool.

1. When and where have you experienced a catch from God?

2. Share a time when you were challenged or questioned in a personal or group setting. How did you respond?

3. Explain a time in your life when you truly feared for your safety.

Pies in Chapel

ONE OF THE quirky perks about attending a small Christian college in a small southern town in the mid-1970s was that there were many unconventional, creative, and, yes, sometimes questionable ways to have fun. Following are some examples.

Chapel, which all students were required to attend daily, was held in the vast auditorium in the main administration building. On one occasion, dozens of hymnals, resting peacefully in racks nailed to the backs of dozens of seats, mysteriously disappeared. Days or maybe weeks later, the filched books were located. The culprits had crawled into the dark recesses of the ceiling and dropped the songbooks down fifty feet into a previously undiscovered space between the outside and inside walls, never to be recovered. As unbelievable as it may seem, I had nothing to do with that crime.

Another time, other innocent songbooks, which had also rested unassumingly in seat racks, were pilfered, collected into boxes, and relocated to the women's restroom in the lobby, near the auditorium entrance. Somehow, those boxes allegedly managed to balance themselves atop toilet seats. At the same time, shoes were set at the foot of each commode. The perpetrators, from the inside, locked the stalls and then crawled under the doors.

For the next two weeks, any janitors assigned bathroom cleaning glanced modestly under the stall doors and, seeing shoes, assumed the area was occupied and moved to the next empty stall. Eventually, one of the janitors figured out that several female students were either dead or simultaneously suffering from the most grievous case of digestive stress known to mankind. Again, I had nothing to do with that crime.

But my time was coming.

The typical agenda for chapel remained relatively unchanged for years. Students poured into the auditorium and took their primitive wooden-and-metal assigned seats. The bell rang, followed by a prayer, a hymn, various announcements, a few more songs, and then a speaker or maybe a special event, usually a speaker.

I didn't mind chapel. I can't say I remember a single speaker, but occasionally, announcement time allowed memorable proof of the creative genius of the students.

The Cheerbillies, being the perfect illustration, were a lively group of button-pushing students who demonstrated time and again the originality we commoners could only aspire to emulate. Students actually chose to attend chapel if the Cheerbillies were rumored to be making an announcement for various groups or departments.

When members of the Cheerbillies graduated, they carefully chose underclassmen to replace them. In my junior year, I got the invitation. Thrilled, I immediately began searching for a way to set myself a standard of button-pushing that would surprise even myself. I watched and waited.

One Monday, after the final hymn, Ray Winters, one of the original Cheerbillies, walked to the lectern to introduce the speaker, an American studies speaker.

In those days, an American studies speaker meant less than entertaining and nowhere near compelling. An immediate shroud of drowsiness fell across the auditorium like a wet blanket of week-old gravy. The boredom factor became almost palpable. Maybe it was a tiny bit audible. Students searched the stack of books in their laps for something—anything—to read or do. Reading newspapers, finishing nearly late homework, scratching initials into the armrests, mentally planning a hostile takeover of the student center—anything.

However, the students were not expecting that particular speaker. The Cheerbillies had prepared an announcement that, unbeknownst to them, became a call to solidarity, railing against the deplorable practice of American-studies-speaker-induced torture.

Ray came onstage and gave a blatantly fake introduction for the speaker, touting his many varied accomplishments. Meanwhile, Cheerbilly Wayne Kinney, who should have been nominated for a Tony award, portrayed the fake oil magnate. He sat uncomfortably straight-backed in an even straighter-backed chair, with horn-rimmed glasses, a glossy brown briefcase on the floor by his side, hair oiled back, and legs crossed. His crossed pant leg, pulled slightly up, revealed a good swath of skin between the top of his black nylon sock and the bottom of his pant leg. The perfect representation of all things uninspiring.

With Ray's intro finished, Wayne walked to the lectern and began spouting weird statistics and futures and stock stuff. He delivered the colorless data as though the info comprised the most fascinating and thought-provoking knowledge since the discovery of the Dead Sea Scrolls.

Just when the lack of cohesiveness and impossible-to-understand facts reached a fever pitch, two Cheerbillies ran from opposite sides of the stage and hurled shaving-cream pies directly into Wayne's face.

The crowd went wild.

The rest of the chapel service went without a hitch. The following week, unfortunately for him, an authentically monotonous, energy-sucking American studies speaker, an expert on China, was scheduled. Several of us rabble-rousers secretly gathered for a clandestine meeting to discuss.

"Wouldn't it be funny if ...?"

Perfect. Here was my chance. I volunteered myself and, by extension, my roommate, Rick Cook. Everyone agreed that once we all had approved and finalized our covert plans, Rick and I became, for all practical purposes, unknown special operatives. No other humans were aware of our existence or carried knowledge of the upcoming event. For some insane reason, I was cool with that.

Friday arrived. Two identical chapel assemblies, one right after the other, afforded me the opportunity to scope out the situation. I managed to find an empty seat during first chapel to watch and ascertain the perfect moment for our bomb drop. No detail could be overlooked.

After songs and announcements, the expert on China walked to the lectern. He began his talk with a couple of well-planned but nonetheless dreary jokes. Of course, no one laughed. In part, that particular audience was a challenge to impress, but more importantly, the jokes weren't funny.

I knew immediately how the swiftly approaching adventure would play out.

Between chapel assemblies, Rick and I met behind the administration building, which housed the auditorium. After entering an unused back door, we climbed the backstage stairs and moved with precision and masterful stealth across the dark, empty stage. Cautiously scrutinizing the immediate area for any perilous movement, such as intrusive student stage managers, we spied a small storage room fortuitously located on the far side of the stage. We bolted into the small empty closet and slammed the wooden door behind us. We listened, sitting in pitch black with two pie pans and a full can of shaving cream, as the clamor of incoming students filled the auditorium.

More than likely, fear and adrenaline brought on the insane urge to laugh, and unfortunately, we couldn't stop. Raucous laughter at that moment became our downfall. The closet door creaked open. Horrified, Rick and I caught our breath, as if that action alone would somehow render us invisible. Unfortunately, we recognized the silhouette of Mark Fisk, resident stage manager, with a confused, quizzical expression. He squinted into the dark room.

To be transparent, I feel relatively certain that had I been in his position, I too would've registered the same expression of confusion if I'd walked across a barren stage, heard raucous laughter coming from a storage room, and opened the door to discover a couple of guys sitting in the dark while holding pie plates and a can of shaving cream.

My response to the unfortunate intrusion only added to the discomfort: "Mark, just close the door, and walk away. You saw nothing." He did.

The first hymn of the assembly began, announcing our cue to fill the pie plates. In the dark. We cracked the door open to let in what essentially resulted in almost no light at all. However, we hit the targets pretty much, filling the pie plates as high as we could manage while keeping wandering shaving cream from splattering all over the floor. I'm sure we left evidence behind but not much.

Again, we couldn't stop laughing. I informed Rick that the expert on China would tell two jokes. We would commit our expulsion-worthy infraction between the two.

A red velvet curtain (known as the "grand drape" for those of you who aren't part of the thespian community) covered the length of the massive stage. Still, it allowed enough space in front for the speaker, chairs, and other people associated with the program. The grand drape provided a barrier between the audience and the rest of the stage—vital for me and Rick to get into position. The curtain, made of two panels, opened from the center of the stage. Having observed the area during my first chapel stakeout, I knew the lectern was positioned directly in front of the point where the curtains joined. Rick and I would be able to pull the curtain apart just far enough for our arms to be in clear view of the entire audience without the rest of us being seen.

Chapel continued with songs, a prayer, and announcements. The expert on China was introduced. Less-than-enthusiastic applause erupted. I might have heard a moan or two.

Showtime.

The China expert told his first unfunny joke. No one laughed, of course. Three long seconds passed. With perfect precision, Rick and I pulled our designated side of the curtain apart with one arm. We each threw our other arm out, displaying a shaving cream pie on either side of the expert on China's head.

The guest to our campus never knew what was transpiring a mere foot behind him. He stood in front of a red velvet curtain, in front of a thousand students who desperately wanted lunch. Understandably shocked at the slow response to his dismal attempt at humor, he had no clue that shaving cream pies framed his noggin like a fluffy marshmallow cloud.

The crowd went wild.

The expert on China waited a full minute for the whistles, howling laughter, and applause to subside before he observed, remembering the slight but uncomfortable three-second pause, "Does it always take you people that long to get a joke?"

Unbridled hilarity ensued. The expert on China realized he had the students in the palm of his hand. Believing the assembly was responding to his pitiful jokes, he sadly—but, to his audience, hilariously—continued delivering them. Horrible, not even slightly funny jokes. He was on a roll. He was a certified hit.

Rick and I never found out how the assembly ended. We withdrew our pies and flew out the back door, running faster than green grass through a goose. We threw the damning evidence into a nearby trash can and then miraculously, magically morphed into two ordinary, unassuming guys leisurely meandering toward the school cafeteria.

Rick and I were heroes. Ace adventurers. Anonymous celebrities.

Within an hour, the exhilaration of a game well played subsided, only to be replaced by an increasingly apprehensive sense of panic. We were covert superstars. I couldn't understand where the gnawing sense of dread was coming from, but it was definitely there. Real. A dark cloud of nagging doom hovered heavy in the air, and I couldn't shake it.

Later that afternoon, our dorm room phone rang.

The weekend was a greasy fog for me. I honestly don't remember the caller on the other end of the line. It didn't matter. My first cognizant recollection occurred the following Monday as Rick and I walked across campus to the vice president's office with five equally guilt-ridden guys, condemned to whatever godless suffering Billy Ray Cox chose to inflict on us. Justice would most certainly be exacted. Administration—with thorough, exhaustive investigation as their superpower—had determined, more than likely through agonizing torture, waterboarding, or perhaps the terror of calling someone's mother, who exactly had perpetrated the despicable, contemptible chapel desecration.

Upon dismally slinking into Dr. Billy Ray Cox's office, we sank into surprisingly comfortable chairs and valiantly attempted to feign grievous sorrow and remorse for our infantile behavior.

Disastrously for me, at that moment, the deranged, uncontrollable compulsion to laugh unnaturally reared its grotesque mug again. My fatal flaw. A couple of mutant synapses deeply entombed in a never-before-discovered neuromuscular junction took their opportunity and came alive, soaring through my stunned nerve endings. Why couldn't it have been a sneeze? Even a belch would have been more appropriate. I'm not sure how well my feeble attempt at converting the clearly noticeable snort into a reasonable facsimile of a cough worked.

Apparently, we were waiting for Ted Altman, dean of students, to join the party. Dr. Cox attempted small talk to fill the space between as he segued between Christian fellowship and impending annihilation.

Billy Ray's telephone rang. He picked up the receiver and said, "Hello? Oh, hi, Ted. Yes, everyone is here. We're just waiting for you. Oh, you are? Okay. That's not a problem. I'll take care of it. Yes, everyone is here. Well, Ray Winters, Wayne Reed, Rick Cook, Tim Holder, Wayne K—yes, Tim Holder. Can you believe it?"

Snort. I fearlessly clenched every muscle in my jaw to keep the imminent chortle from erupting.

Dr. Cox ended the phone conversation with a sad nod. "Yes, Ted, after all the times Tim has been on the Harding stage. After all Harding has done for Tim."

The tears streaming down my cheeks and the quivering chin were an outright lie.

"Okay, no problem. Thanks for calling." Billy Ray ended the phone conversation and relayed Dr. Altman's message: because of a longer-than-scheduled meeting, Ted wouldn't be attending our punishment by guillotine. Dr. Cox placed his hands on the edge of his desk. Burgundy leather groaned as he leaned back in his overstuffed reclining armchair. He reached up and rubbed his temples in a circle with his index fingers.

After berating our repugnant, juvenile behavior for a respectable amount of time, Dr. Cox summarily made quick work of our immediate future. We were to write apology letters to the expert on China, the college president, and the *Bison* newspaper. He then looked at each of us in turn as he made the last pronouncement: "And one of you will need to make a public apology in both chapels." Somehow, his last word lingered in the air as his eyes clamped on mine. Then he smiled.

As much as I desperately wanted to inspect my belly button, I couldn't look away. After a few seconds of near-catatonic fear, I glanced to my left and found the other guys staring at me just as intently. I'm sure they were attempting to mentally convey that my freakish fit of uncontrollable chortling would be way out of line right then.

I slowly raised my hand, my white flag, indicating my surrender. "I'd be happy to make that announcement."

The next morning, I made my way to the front of the auditorium before first chapel and nabbed a seat close to the steps leading up to the stage. Students and faculty streamed slowly into the building and took their appointed places. The bell rang, signaling time for the program to begin. Adding insult to injury, President Ganus himself climbed the steps to the stage, apparently planning to preside over my funereal ceremony.

At the appointed time, Dr. Ganus announced, "Tim Holder would like to address the assembly."

Suddenly, there was dead silence. As I climbed, I heard every creak in every single step echo throughout the auditorium. I stood behind the lectern and read my prepared apology. Nobody moved. Nobody coughed. Nobody shifted in the obnoxiously loud seats, which notoriously echoed off every wall in the building. I apologized for embarrassing the faculty and students, Dr. Ganus and Billy Ray Cox, and the expert on China and for shaming everyone's parents who were working tirelessly to pay tuitions, the founding fathers of our great institution, the glorious saints who'd gone on before us, all creatures great and small, and, of course, God.

Then I said, "Thank you."

I felt it necessary to exit the stage in great haste from the fear that I might at any moment bust out in an abnormal, irreverent round of belly laughing.

But as I reached the bottom step, I looked up and realized everyone in the assembly was on his or her feet, screaming, shouting, and applauding. They offered their own standard of vindication.

I squelched the irrational urge to climb back up the steps with fists pounding the air to do the Rocky-on-the-steps-of-the-Philadelphia-Museum-of-Art dance. I stood stoically at my seat while Dr. Ganus waited patiently for everyone to regain composure and return to his or her seat.

Dr. Ganus generously thanked all of us involved for having the courage to own our mistake and acknowledge that it had been an unwise action. A half hour later, I, by then emboldened, met the same reception during second chapel.

Back then, I became known for being the rogue perpetrator of dastardly antics. Even now as I type, this particular flashback gives me an odd sense of accomplishment. A small circle of adventure seekers attained a semblance of triumph, a priceless endeavor, a unique grandeur that has become a favorite memory for many who sat in those hallowed, time-worn, arthritic wooden chairs.

It was worth it.

By the way, if you think Billy Ray Cox didn't have a sense of humor, you are wrong. The afternoon of our meeting, he ate lunch at my mom and dad's small restaurant just off campus. Later that night, Mom informed me that Billy Ray had told her the whole story. He'd admitted he thought it a great stunt and funny. But consequences had to be exacted.

Years later, I ran into Billy Ray unexpectedly at a restaurant in Dallas. After we visited for a bit, he reminded me of the pies in chapel. I was warmed when he told me that stunt had gone down as one of his favorite Harding memories.

I'm not sure what the moral to this tale should be. So make one up. For me, the most imperative is this: never give me information that's the slightest bit serious. More than likely, it won't be channeled in an empathetic display of shared anguish or heartache. But rest assured, as is the case in most experiences, it will one day make for a great story.

And if you ever see me walking through the church lobby with a pie plate and a can of shaving cream, it would probably be advisable to contact security.

CONVERSATION STARTERS FROM RANDY GRANDERSON

Randy is one of four wonderful leaders and teachers in our Creative Living class. He is a retired school principal. His wife is Janet. Janet is a retired band director. However, Janet doesn't look nearly old enough to be retired. Janet is much prettier than Randy.

1. Who or what let the dogs out? Seriously!
2. What difference has pie made in your life? How do you like your pie?
3. What animal, if utilized that day in chapel, would have made the story even more hilarious?

Explain that to the dean.

SUPPLEMENTARY QUESTIONS FROM RANDY FOR REFLECTIVE THINKERS

1. Should all parents keep their children away from Tim? Why or why not?
2. Is there even a hint of hypocrisy in this story? Will Tim go to hell?
3. Choose carefully one word (keep it clean) that defines Tim, based on what you just read.

Explain.

The Real Third Commandment

ONE OF MY faults, and this would fall under the column of faults that begin with a *T,* is that I tend to trust people far too easily. My unspoken motto has been "Trust people until they prove they are not trustworthy."

I realize this is not necessarily scriptural if you take into account scriptures like Jeremiah 17:5 (ESV), which says, "Cursed is the man who trusts in man and makes flesh his strength."

Ouch!

It's not usually a conscious choice on my part. I just lean toward giving others the benefit of the doubt. Maybe it's because I want to live as someone who can be a trustworthy and faithful friend.

I don't trust the Lord less than I should. That's not what I mean. I do, however, believe people are more reliable if they have a relationship with Jesus Christ. That's probably why hurt and betrayal seem to sting more acutely when they come from someone I should be able to trust freely.

As I've grown a bit older, hopefully a bit wiser, and definitely closer to the Lord, I've begun to make the deliberate choice of looking for him in every situation. If he's not there, then it's not for me. The Holy Spirit is good at giving me a nudge when I need to know.

Even when—especially when—it concerns relationships with other believers. If I firmly see that their walk is not matching the Word and that they speak words that don't bring life, I will adjust the relationship accordingly. As impossible as it may feel at the time and as rarely as it happens, I have ended relationships that proved to be drastically unhealthy.

I grew up believing that breaking the Third Commandment included phrases like "Gosh," "Gee whiz," "Golly," "Oh my God," and a slew of far worse interjections. I learned at an early age which words and euphemisms for God or Jesus were unacceptable, and it still catches my attention when I hear someone use them. But I've also learned there are other possibly more insidious ways to take the Lord's name in vain.

An individual in my life, over the span of a few years, three times, gave me the same message: "The Lord told me you are holding on to something you're not letting go of. I don't know what it is. He didn't tell me that. But you're holding on to something, and you need to let go of it."

"The Lord told me …"

The first two times she said it, I went home in shame and failure. I asked the Lord to tell me what I was holding on to that I wasn't surrendering to him. There was no response. The Lord knows I'm willing to work on anything that keeps me from being totally his man.

Eventually, the discouraging feelings passed, only to be resurrected when the person repeated the message.

"The Lord told me …"

Finally, in a meeting in front of others, she said the Lord had given her messages for everyone in the room. She proceeded around the room, telling everyone what the Lord told her about each person. The messages, filled with encouraging words, made the ones receiving them feel valued.

However, although the words spoken were valid and affirming, they didn't reveal fresh revelation or new direction. Anyone in the room could've delivered the messages. Although the words were important to hear, they weren't from God.

When she came to me, she repeated the same message she'd delivered twice before: "The Lord told me you're holding on to something, and you need to let it go. He didn't tell me what it is. That's between you and him."

This time, I noticed she couldn't look me in the eye when she said it, and once it left her lips, she quickly moved to the next person, giving me no room to respond. *Interesting.*

However, as soon as she made the pronouncement "The Lord said …," the guilt- and shame-invoking statement, I began to feel the same pressure and angst I'd experienced two times before.

Suddenly, the Lord gave me clarity: *The Holy Spirit is a Spirit not of confusion but of unity. Yes, you do hold on to something. But so does she. So does every person in this room. Whether it's anger, bitterness, resentment, lack of forgiveness, or pride, whatever the particular sin looks like, everyone holds on to something. If they didn't, Jesus would never have needed to come die for them.*

I felt immediate peace and freedom. I didn't need to carry guilt and shame with me again. Other unnecessary, unkind encounters soon followed. I prayerfully and deliberately made the choice to separate myself from the wounded, broken person, and I haven't looked back.

There is one who speaks rashly like the thrusts of a
sword. But the tongue of the wise brings healing.

—Proverbs 12:18 NASB

I realized that guilt, if it is from God, always leads to a resolution. The shame and guilt deliberately used to gaslight me were not from God. Those emotions threatened to fill me with fear and feelings of failure. But through his gentle whisper, I peeled back layers of doubt and recognized that all those negative emotions rang only in my head and nowhere else in the universe. No one on this planet other than the broken one who willingly manipulated my emotions believed the painful nontruth ascribed to me, and the Lord certainly did not.

From that moment forward, I decided my response to someone breaking the Third Commandment would be "Thank you for that word. I will pray about it and wait for the Lord to reveal to me if that is, in fact, a word from him. And I will act on it accordingly."

People tend to justify their desires, their sin, and their disobedience by saying, "God told me." People attempt to gain power, influence, or their chance to speak by saying, "God told me."

My pastor, Rod Loy, wisely once said, "Be careful when you say, 'God told me.' Or 'I have a word from the Lord.' If you try to communicate what God wants or thinks, if you do that in a selfish way or a trivial way, ascribing your desire to God's name, you're violating the Third Commandment. When someone says, 'The Lord told me that you're supposed to do this,' doubt it. Most of the time, the Lord will tell you what you're supposed to do, not reveal to you what somebody else is supposed to do. Don't be fooled by people who try to manipulate you into doing their wishes by using the name of the Lord. The Lord will only reveal through someone else to you what you already know."

Part of my relationship with Jesus during these aggravating trials is to look for blessings. They are always there. They are sometimes excruciatingly obvious and other times torturously hidden but always there. The key is to look for them.

Soon after the meeting, when I felt a shift in my spirit to take action, I received a message from Blake, a friend I haven't talked to in quite a while. He lives in Texas. He said, "Brother, I just wanted you to know I love you. Someday soon, I'll come hug your neck."

Proverbs 17:17 (ESV) says, "A friend loves at all times. And a brother is born for adversity." I'm sure it was, for Blake, a simple reminder of friendship. But at that precise, perfect moment, it was a gift from the Lord, providing me not only the courage to move forward but also the deep knowledge that God is in the blessing business. His heart is to make sure we, his children, know that we are cherished and that he loves to remind us we can profoundly, eternally trust him. He will send blessings. Just look for them.

The world teaches that the Lord should bless in proportion to our circumstances. We get what we give. But in God's economy, that particular axiom couldn't be further from the truth. Most blessings, on the surface, would be sweet but not necessarily earth-bending. But strategically placed in time by the star-breathing Creator of the universe, they are perfect. No loose ends. No hanging chads. Finished. Pure expressions of acceptance from hands that were nailed to a cross and bled for us. Hands that applaud us and a voice that sings over us.

> So don't fear, for I am with you. Do not be dismayed,
> for I am Your God. I will strengthen you and help
> you; I will uphold you with my righteous right hand.
> —Isaiah 41:10 NIV

Look for the blessing. It's there. Sometimes you have to dig for it, but it's there. The diamond is there. It might be a text, a phone call, a note, a falling red oak leaf, the smile of a grandbaby, a couple of dogs jumping all over you, or a great ribeye with melted butter (and a loaded baked potato—overloaded). Maybe it's finding a ten-dollar bill on the church pew and feeling the Spirit's prompt to hand it across the aisle to someone who is watching and might need it just as much as you. Maybe your profound, abiding blessing is in the delight of blessing someone else.

Just look.

Commit to listening to the prompting of the Spirit. He's there to let us know when a word is correct or not. Above all, he is trustworthy.

> May God give you heaven's dew and earth's richness—an abundance of grain and new wine. May nations serve you and peoples bow down to you. May those who curse you be cursed and those who bless you be blessed.
>
> —Genesis 27:28 NIV

Now, that's a blessing. The Lord told me!

CONVERSATION STARTERS
FROM JIMMY MONAGHAN

I remember the first time I heard Jimmy and Marna give their testimony. They had great tatts. They were way too cool to ever be friends with me. Jimmy is my sponsor.

1. Where do you see God's blessing in your life?
2. Whom do you need to stop listening to for validations?
3. How can you feel like you let God down, when the scriptures say he holds you up? Love strong!

CONVERSATION STARTERS
FROM MARNA MONAGHAN

Marna is an amazing mom and wife and a lover of Jesus. She's a lot like Jimmy, only prettier.

1. Where in your life are you listening to the wrong voice?
2. How do you handle guilt and shame when it creeps up?
3. How has noticing God's blessings given you comfort?

Epitaph

IN BIBLICAL TIMES, the practice in Israel was for all relatives of a conquered king to be killed. This tradition ensured the safety of the newly seated king and kept him from being assassinated by the descendants of previously dethroned royalty.

King David faced a dilemma. After several years of battling neighboring nations and soundly defeating them, he finally took time to grieve the death of his beloved friend Jonathan, the son of King Saul. Earlier in their friendship, knowing that David would one day be king of Israel, Jonathan had asked David to promise that once he became king, David would take care of his descendants. Of course, David promised.

After Jonathan's death, David asked if any of Jonathan's family were still alive. His heart desired to show kindness to them. Mephibosheth, whose name meant "One who destroys shame," was hiding in Lodebar, a barren, dry, lonely brown village to the east of the Jordan River. He had lived there in fear and resentment for many years.

Mephibosheth's nurse had fled with him after the death of his father and grandfather, fearing the new king would kill him. In her haste, she'd dropped him, rendering him lame for life.

Imagine his horror when King David's soldiers showed up at the home of Machir, where Mephibosheth was living. Now in his thirties, the lame man must've felt the tightening grip of a decades-long fear.

Taken to the very throne room where he'd spent his childhood, Mephibosheth concluded that one of the possible outcomes for his eventual death was about to come to fruition. How many times had he practiced his death in his dreams? How many ways had he imagined he would be found out by the king? And here it was. Mephibosheth had recognized from an early age that this moment was not only possible but imminent.

When David entered, Mephibosheth fell facedown on the floor of the throne room.

Seeing Jonathan's prostrate son, David must have felt a surge of compassion. He said, "Mephibosheth."

How David's heart must have broken when Mephibosheth looked up and said, "Yes, sir."

David surely saw the resemblance of his dearest, most trusted, covenanted friend, Jonathan, in the eyes of this panicked, confused young man.

Then David said words that Mephibosheth never, in all his imaginings of that moment, had allowed to enter his consciousness. Instead of watching the sword fall in his last moments on earth, Mephibosheth heard the one who held the continuance of his days in his hands say, "Mephibosheth, don't be afraid."

I'm not even sure the relief of his life handed back to him was the first thing that registered in Mephibosheth's brain. All the years of knowing he would die by the king's sword were mercifully exorcised from his imagined scenarios.

His first words demonstrated disbelief rather than gratitude. He stuttered and stammered, "Who am I that you would pay attention to a stray dog like me?" Almost as if he were admitting, "Wait a minute. You're supposed to kill me."

But David chose words of life instead of the words of death that Mephibosheth expected, like many of us expect, to hear. I can't even begin to comprehend Mephibosheth's response when David returned to him all the land and everything that had belonged to his father and even his grandfather, King Saul.

When David ended the moment by telling Mephibosheth that he would eat at the king's table for the rest of his life, he must have felt like a dog with two tails.

Proverbs 18:21 (MSG) reads, "Words kill, words give life; they're either poison or fruit—you choose."

There is no neutral ground here. No disengaged, disinterested, noncommittal, isolated rock to stand on. This scripture says words bring either life or death. If I'm honest, I can't say I spend the majority of any day deliberately choosing to disperse life over death.

That's not to say that everything I dish out has to start with "Jesus loves you" or that I have to end each phone call by saying, "In accordance with prophecy." I don't have to announce to anyone that I am uberspiritual by saying, "Have a blessed day."

What it does mean is to give life, which, in this instance, is the word *zoe*, the Greek word for eternal life, God's life.

Jesus's death and resurrection have secured our forever life, our zoe life, so it just makes sense we should be speaking with an ongoing eternal mindset. Our words to others should be seasoned with that mindset.

I am amazed that many times, when I give people encouragement or a word of hope, they respond as though they don't deserve it. Or they feel guilty about receiving a blessing. I can even recall incidents when certain people were on the giving end of a compliment but seemed uncomfortable, almost as though my offering a kind word left them weak and vulnerable.

Recently, I talked with someone who recounted a conversation he'd had with an employee. He had gotten frustrated with the employee for not doing a project the way he would have done it.

First, I asked if the employee had gotten specific directions. He said no. Then I wondered if the employee had finished the project. He nodded. Finally, I asked him how the employee had taken the criticism. "Not well," he said. He then asked, "What would you have done in my place?"

I told him, "I have been thinking a lot about my legacy. I'm not talking about at my memorial service. But even now. The legacy I leave on a daily basis. I would have told that person, 'Good job. You finished the project. Thank you for getting it done.'"

Doing something my way is just another way, not the only way, and what I might think is a better way is still not the only way. It's just my way. If the project gets done, it's done, no matter whose way it gets done. Doing it my way will not make either of us a better person. But man, what gratification I get when I can tell someone, "Well done. Great job."

So what does our living legacy look like? Are we dispensing zoe (eternal) life? Or death?

Everything we say will make a difference. Everything. We will either ride the popular wave of uplifting ourselves or disrupt the status quo. Most people won't get it. We will leave them feeling uncomfortable but uplifted, confused but questioning. Some will feel vulnerable without having to strike a defensive pose.

I want to live out the process of feeding life instead of death into people's lives on a far more regular basis. I believe we are chiseling our epitaph every moment of our life. It doesn't matter what is actually etched on our monument. What we pour into people's lives—even the lives of strangers—is what will be read on the tombstone that ultimately matters.

I muddled through one of those moments a while back, but that day, I specifically asked for it. It was a rainy Sunday morning. A very rainy Sunday morning. I was singing a solo that morning at church. I accidentally woke up a little past two o'clock in the morning and found my electricity out. I decided if it was still out when my phone alarm went off, I would pack everything in the car and go to the vet clinic where I worked, take a shower, and head to church.

When the alarm went off at 5:00 a.m., the electricity was still out, so I turned on my phone flashlight and gathered everything. I took the dogs out in pouring rain. I gathered my clothes and toiletries and made three trips to the car. It was like taking a shower every time I walked outside.

With everything loaded, I jumped into the car. Just as I turned the key in the ignition, the porch light came on. I sat there in a short-lived state of postal before I got out of the car and made three more rain-soaking trips into the house. I took a shower, which at that point seemed a bit redundant; dressed; and ran to the car.

Finally, on the way to church, I attempted to settle down, asking the Lord to help me not be a distraction that day. I asked him to give me the chance to bring life to someone with my words. In my thoughts. I was referring to my song at church.

When I entered the worship center, I felt God's calming in my soul. I sang and soaked up my pastor's message.

Afterward, I decided I would stop at the local grocery to get some stuff for lunch.

There's a streetlight at the corner before you turn right into the parking lot of the grocery store. That particular day, the red light was blinking. I assumed it was because the power had been out the night before. I was relieved to see plenty of cars in the parking lot, which let me know the store was open, so I pulled in.

I walked into the store, grabbed a handbasket, and spent about thirty minutes gathering avocados and supplies to make guac—I was having a hankering.

Going down one aisle, I ran into a young man, obviously doing family shopping, with a cart full of groceries. I needed to get past him and asked him to excuse me, which he graciously did.

A few minutes later, as I approached the self-check aisle, the same guy was ahead of me, and I heard him say, "No way. Are you kidding me?"

The register assistant tiredly said, "No. I'm not."

He replied, "Well, what am I supposed to do?"

She said, "You can go to the customer service desk."

I glanced up and saw a fairly long line of brow-furrowed people at the service desk. I jokingly said to the guy, "Are you giving her a hard time?"

He looked at me, trying to hide frustration, and said, "I hope you have cash."

"Why?"

"Because every credit card machine in the store is down."

I had no cash. My first reaction was to get my back up like a spitting cat. But then I remembered the prayer.

It was not fair. I wanted to be mad. But I noticed the other guy refrained from exhibiting frustration. He must have shopped for at least an hour. He asked, "Why didn't they announce it over the intercom?"

She said they had. But I'd never heard it while I was in the store. The other guy said, "What should I do with all this stuff?" She told him to just leave it, and someone else would take care of it.

He left, and then she turned her weary eyes toward me. She had her shoulders squared, ready to be defensive. I looked at her and said, "I feel so bad that someone is going to have to return all this stuff to the shelves. But I know it's not your fault. So don't think I'm going to be one of the people who try to make it your fault."

Her shoulders drooped as she said, "Thank you."

Then I drove to the closest discount center and bought all the same stuff cheaper.

The next day, I was recounting what had happened to a friend, and she said, "Well, you were a lot nicer than I would have been. I would have told her they wasted a half hour of my life. And there should have been notes on the door in big red letters. And there should have been people standing at the door to tell people the credit card machines were down."

I said, "Yeah, that may be right. But the bottom line for me is that I know if that lady remembers that moment, I may have been the only chance of her seeing Jesus that day. And if she saw something different from the rest of the crowd, then that's to God's credit." I want that to be my legacy. Besides, it just felt good. I didn't walk away feeling like I needed to be justified, stand up for my rights, or have a "Guess I showed them" moment. It may have taken thirty minutes, but I learned something, so it was worth the time.

That's what I want my life to look like.

Today what will my legacy be? My days and weeks can prove stressful, especially after a torrential downpour and power outage. Will I speak words of death? Or will I choose to leave others with words of life?

Have you been given the opportunity today to treat someone with undeserved respect? Or will you avoid another's eyes as you insist on having something done your way? My challenge for you and me is to feed words of life to someone today. We may not see the chance, because we are so used to reacting without thinking instead of responding.

First Peter 3:10 (NIV) says, "For whoever would love life and see good days must keep their tongue from evil and their lips from deceitful speech."

There's no neutral, drab, or flat color to it. Words either bring vibrant, active responses that resonate eternity or are passionless, monotonous, indifferent platitudes that blend in with the rest of the world. If you pray for the chance to give life today, you'll get it.

Old Testament giants, such as King David, knew the value of life-affirming words. So did Mephibosheth when he received them. That's the kind of legacy I want.

Popular culture will answer with "Cheese and pepperoni." But the eternal maxim still stands: "What do you want on your tombstone?"

CONVERSATION STARTERS
FROM ANDY HOLDER

Andy is my younger brother but only by three years—not really that much in light of eternity. He's a great husband to Kerry, a dad to two amazing kids, and now a crazy person about his grandkids. He's a hard worker and, like the rest of us, loves to find humor in pretty much everything.

1. Do you live your life in fear like Mephibosheth? Or do you believe there is no place for fear because of Christ's sacrificial gift? Take a moment to write down what holds you back from surrendering all fear at the foot of the cross.

2. A wonderful author by the name of Lois A. Cheney, in her book *God Is No Fool*, wrote that we are made up of bits and pieces of everyone we come in contact with. When you think of your interactions with others, is what you leave with them a positive or negative bit or piece? Think of your most recent personal interaction. Write down what legacy you left with that person.

Merry Christmas, Sarah Ann

JESUS IS THE Son of God. He was with God from the beginning.

John 1:1 (MSG) says, "The Word was first, the Word present to God, God present to the Word. The Word was God, in readiness for God from day one."

I have wondered at what point in his life Jesus's mother, Mary, understood his mission on this little ball of water and dirt that Jesus himself made from nothing. What were the points in Jesus's life when different aspects of his mission became clear to Mary?

I have to believe Jesus always knew. The fully human part of him learned how to walk, talk, and eat independently, just as the rest of us do. He learned a trade by using his earthly father's carpentry tools. At the same time, the fully divine part of him was always aware of who he was and is. Always. He is, after all, God.

> Have this attitude in yourselves which was also
> in Christ Jesus, who, although he existed in the
> form of God, did not regard equality with God a
> thing to be grasped, but emptied himself, taking
> the form of a bond-servant, and being made in the

likeness of men. Being found in appearance as a
man, he humbled himself by becoming obedient
to the point of death, even death on a cross.

—Philippians 2:5–8 NASB

I don't believe deity and divinity are attributes one would or even could lay down. The idea of Jesus leaving the face of his beloved Father; leaving the love and affection of his Father's home; and discussing and deciding in the great halls of eternity to come down to this tiny, time-inhibitive, gravity-grinding planet is incredibly claustrophobic to me.

First, in willingly walking away from his Father and coming to this tiny speck of dust in the universe, not to mention knowing ahead of time that he would be completely cognizant while deliberately floating in amniotic fluid for several months, Jesus understood that he was wrapping himself in the very dirt he'd created.

I can't imagine the sacrifice of his Father, by design and with foreknowledge of what was to come, as he let the hand of his Boy go so he could leave home for a while and go away to fulfill a mission that would ultimately be rejected by many.

The one lesson I can carry away from all of it is service. Giving. The simple definition of *sacrifice* is "the act of giving up something or enduring the loss of something you want to keep, especially in order to get or do something else or to help someone."

It's easy for me to think of the sacrifice of Abba in relation to Jesus coming to earth to help us, teach us about God, and serve. But I equally love the idea that he sent Jesus to earth to get me. It tells me there is nothing he wouldn't do and no opportunity he wouldn't present to ensure I'm with him forever, and in fact, he made the most significant sacrifice by giving up his Son for a season.

I have, obviously, not seen Jesus, my Buddy, face-to-face yet. Though Jesus's human existence was just thirty-three Earth years, it breaks my heart for Abba. He willingly went without the physical presence of his most precious possession, the One who knew him best; the One who was always with him; and the One who, for all of eternity up to that point, had lavished his love on his Dad.

But God and Jesus were willing and did it for us. Abba Father let go of that mighty, perfect hand, the hand that had created the universe, knowing that it would one day come back but would never look the same again. That hand would become, for a while, small and fragile, reaching up to be supported and held by parents and relatives. Those fingerprints would grow to heal the sick, hurt, and broken and even hearts. That wounded hand would one day become the symbol of my salvation. That wounded hand would, figuratively, never heal. The blood from that all-powerful hand still flows. It has covered me and saved me.

How can I, knowing the absolute reality of that love and sacrifice, not raise my own hand to reach up to such perfect devotion? I give such a small token as I hold on to the mystery and the hope of Jesus's birth.

A few days before Christmas, even at the Christian bookstore where I worked, the stress was palpable. I could taste the anxiety in the demeanor of the guests I checked out. Every morning, I prayed before I walked through the front door that I wouldn't let them get to me. Although 90 percent of the people I checked out were excellent, those remaining 10 percent pulled me down. A couple of times, I seriously wanted to just stop, look them in the eye, and say, "Tell me something. If I were not a follower of Jesus, what is it about your attitude right now that would ever make me want to say, 'Wow, whatever you've got, I want it'?" Seriously, it was getting bad.

One day, after standing at the register nonstop for five hours, I looked up and saw a lady walking into my line. Just behind her, I saw a couple of my friends smiling and heading toward my queue. I couldn't wait to connect with them. I knew they would make everything okay with a smile and a hug. If I could just get through this one lady first.

I looked down at the tiny woman. Her head was slightly bowed, as if she hoped I wouldn't notice the tears streaming steadily down her face. I froze. I'm not talking about a few tears. She was silently sobbing; her body was discernibly racked with the pain of sorrow and terrible loss.

All I could do was respond. I leaned toward her. "What's wrong?"

She shook her head and said, "I'm okay."

"No, you're not okay. If you want me to check you out, you're gonna tell me what's wrong."

With tears still streaming down her face, she sobbed, and her voice trembled. "My son died three months ago."

I leaned closer. "Oh my. What was his name?"

"Aaron."

"This is your first Christmas without your boy. I'm so sorry. I'm so very sorry. How did he die?"

"Meningitis."

"How old was he?"

"Thirteen."

"What is your name?"

"Sarah Ann."

"Well, Sarah Ann, would it be okay if I prayed for you?"

She nodded.

I looked at my friends behind her, who'd heard the whole conversation. I motioned for them to move to the next checker. They nodded with full understanding and moved to the next queue. I put up my "We would be happy to check you out at another register" sign.

Sarah Ann and I moved past the busyness of holiday shopping to the children's section. I took both her hands in mine.

At that moment, a miracle happened.

Remember the precursor to a miracle: there has to be a problem first. It is that moment when we give the Holy Spirit permission to move in and build a vacuum, an invisible yet palpable fortress, around us. The Enemy can't penetrate the holiness of that place, no matter how hard he may try. Grief was the problem here, and in that moment, I physically felt the presence of the One who breathes out stars into the universe, understands grief, and is fiercely engaged in the next breath we take.

I began to pray. I prayed to a Parent who perfectly understood the specific emotion Sarah Ann was feeling—the excruciating loneliness—and was acutely acquainted with the impossible horror of experiencing the death of his own beloved Son.

I said it made no sense, from our vantage point, for this boy to die. But even if we couldn't understand the experience, we could trust his heart.

I prayed for Sarah Ann. I asked the Lord to wrap his strong arms around her. I prayed that God would hold her so tightly she would have no doubt he was right there with her. I prayed that he would cover her with his feathers and that under his wings, she would find refuge. His faithfulness would be her safe hiding place. I prayed he would send angels to stand in strategic places around her so she would find a peace that the darts of the Enemy could never penetrate. I prayed he would hold her son's hand and tell Aaron his mom missed him very much, loved him, and couldn't wait to see him again one day. I told Jesus and Sarah Ann that I looked forward to Sarah Ann introducing me to Aaron one day. Then I said, "Amen."

Sarah Ann turned toward me and wrapped her arms around my neck. We stood there for many seconds with her heart-wrenching tears falling into a deep ocean of loss.

I held her there, a pretty shabby life jacket, beaten and weather-worn, held afloat only by the buoyancy of grace.

Finally, Sarah Ann was able to stand on her own. She looked up at me with tears pooling in her exhausted eyes. I couldn't help but, in that moment, see Jesus's mother and think about how Mary must have grieved when she realized her Boy was gone. The searing emptiness. Confusion over what the future would hold for her Son. Lost hope.

But what that pivotal moment must have been like, and how glorious for Mary, when she finally reached out her tiny hand and once again wrapped her fingers around the warm, wounded hand of her resurrected Son.

I'm certain that somehow, someday, even in light of this inconsolable loss, Sarah Ann and Aaron will reach for each other's hand, and there will be absolute joy in the reunion.

For the first time that season, there was only one thing I could say to Sarah Ann, and I genuinely meant it: "Merry Christmas. Merry Christmas, Sarah Ann."

CONVERSATION STARTERS
FROM DEBBIE SISK

Debbie is the owner at rosebriardining.com. She's a college buddy. She's adorable and pretty. She's a hilarious, fun entrepreneur and is married to Rick, whom I tortured when he lived next door to me in Harbin Hall. Great folks.

1. We don't know the future of our loved ones, as God did his Son's. How can we take advantage of our time on earth with others to really form deep relationships?

2. As a parent, what is the hardest part of raising children today, in the hope they will follow the Lord?

3. What examples did Jesus give us about family love?

Mr. Pancake

I HAVE GREAT memories of my time as a server at Dalt's American Grill on White Bridge Road in Nashville, Tennessee. Back in the mid-1980s, the eatery enjoyed a quick acceleration from infancy to heyday. Golden days, I thought. We employees were family, and to this day, as many as we can find stay in close contact with one another.

Working at Dalt's was always an adventure. I could write a book on just the time I was there. I went in thinking I would be there for, at most, only a couple of years. I remember one of the first shift meetings after the extraordinarily strenuous schedule of two full weeks of training behind other more seasoned servers and taking countless tests. We were required to remember every ingredient of every dish offered on a *War and Peace*–sized menu.

During that shift meeting, Kitty, one of my good buddies, got her red three-year 50-percent-off-everything card. I thought, *I'll never be here that long. Surely I'll be well on my way to an Academy Award by then.* However, I was saying the same thing when I got my gold ten-year appreciation ring.

One of my favorite memories at Dalt's occurred when a nearby elementary school held a fair. The president of the PTA came to Dalt's, hoping we'd come to their recess yard with giveaways and coupons. Fortunately, we were rolling out our brand-new weekend brunch menu, and we were supplied with incredible Disneyesque costumes for street advertising.

An egg costume consisted of a cracked egg with the two halves held together by a stream of bright yellow yolk in the middle. The top half featured a broad face complete with a huge, happy grin. One of my best friends, Ann Estelle Stanley, wore that costume.

The obligatory bacon costume, which was, well, a slice of bacon, again with a bright, happy, huge-eyed, smiling face, was worn by Ann Green.

Mr. Pancake was the fattest, bulkiest, most hulking, most awkward costume of them all. That costume, that creature, became my alter ego. Mr. Pancake was round. Big, round, and heavy. His infrastructure was, I'm sure, made of two-by-fours. His humongous golden-brown body had two holes in the front. The wearer of said costume slid his or her arms through the holes on either side of the splat of butter in the middle, which also contained the enormous eyes and demented smile of a Steven King character. The eyes were not functional. A small patch of matching yellow mesh just below the joyful eyes was where the occupant could actually see through—a little.

The frames for the costumes were not made of fabric. Perhaps double-walled steel. Galvanized chain mail maybe. They were like the characters one might see at a theme park: solid and equipped to handle the onslaught of childhood misconduct.

We drove into the school parking lot, far enough away from the entrance to put on the costumes without the students watching. Ann Estelle and Ann Green slid into their costumes fairly easily on their own.

Mr. Pancake was laid on the ground with his deranged face to the clouds so I could lie on my back and slither backward into the dark chasm. Then Burt, the restaurant manager, stood behind me and, with brute strength, deadlifted me into a standing position.

Wearing brown costume footwear the size of small kayaks, I rested the weight of the costume on my shoulders by two metal straps with padding that was not much thicker than 2-ply toilet paper. With that, we began the trek toward the school entrance. We knew we would find the fair behind the school, on their recess field.

We turned left toward the front entrance. I glanced to our right, and through my mesh peephole, I noticed a big, long, happy banner announcing the merry event. The banner, held in place by a rope stretching through the top of the banner, ran across the front drive of the school, all the way from a tree across the drive to a flagpole outside the front of the building. *Very impressive.*

We walked in hot and sticky Nashville humidity in late May. That meant I quickly got the impression I should have been sizzling on a well-oiled griddle.

From the get-go, all three of us characters asked how long we were required to be at the event. Could we possibly endure? Without an answer and only a shoulder shrug from our intrepid leader, we courageously moved through the halls and out the back door.

The minute we stepped onto the field, kids thronged around us. Burt handed out balloons and coupons as boys and girls squealed over Mr. Pancake, Miss Egg, and Miss Bacon. We waved, blew kisses, and shook hands. Miss Egg and Miss Bacon gave hugs because they could slightly bend over. It was so much fun—for all of four minutes and forty-seven seconds.

We were sweltering, feeling like the Parker Solar Probe must have felt traveling 430,000 miles per hour toward the surface of the sun. The more our maniacal, smiling faces growled at Burt to get us out of there, the more he said between a forced smile and clinched teeth, "Just another few minutes."

Burt, believing it was in his best interest, I'm sure, led us to the back of the brick building so we could at least lean against a wall. But even that was in the thick of booths, parents and kids, and a kitchen of activity. Kids were running everywhere. We just stood and waved with our outward heartwarming smiles and our less-than-cartoon attitudes.

Then came Fred, a sweet-looking little kid with a Popsicle in his hand. Fred walked up to us and smiled and waved, and we waved back. I slightly attempted the pirate dance but stopped short of bending my knees too far, out of fear of collapsing. No one enjoys a crimped up pancake. Mr. Pancake weighed 89.5 pounds, and the metal shoulder straps with toilet-paper padding were digging into my shoulders like a backpack filled with cinder blocks.

For some unfortunate reason, I kept Fred's attention longer than I should've. Fred looked around to make sure his mom was nowhere in sight and then walked straight up to Mr. Pancake and kicked him in the shin. Mr. Pancake was not happy. When Mr. Pancake felt as if he'd just come out of a frying pan, it was unwise to slap him with the spatula.

Mr. Pancake, still trying to convey the same spirit as his animated face, whispered, "No, no."

Precious little Fred stepped forward and planted his foot again into Mr. Pancake's shin.

"Be nice to Mr. Pancake now."

Fred, perhaps feeling the slightest pang of guilt, walked away for a couple of minutes. However, when he returned, he again made sure no one was looking before he, with a vengeance, stepped up and struck Mr. Pancake's leg with his offending Kangaroo tennis shoe.

At that point, oppressive, glass-fogging humidity and brutal shin pain joined together to override any logical cognitive brain activity. Mr. Pancake shook a bit as he hissed, "It's not nice to kick Mr. Pancake." With perhaps a bit more Pennywise demeanor than intended, he added, "And it's dangerous."

For some unexplainable reason, all three of Mr. Pancake's comrades were facing other directions when Fred came in for the kill. He sauntered up to Mr. Pancake, looked around with a heinous grin, and just as he threw his leg back for the fatal blow, Mr. Pancake raised his own leg.

I want to believe it was only to protect himself. However, and I'm sure it was totally accidental, Mr. Pancake's foot came in contact with Fred's chest. Mr. Pancake's foot was only raised. It was not moving. Fred did, in fact, run into Mr. Pancake's kayak.

I also want to believe it was purely unintentional that the toe end of Mr. Pancake's shoe slightly pulsed forward as Fred came in contact with Mr. Pancake's happy footwear.

Whatever the case, darling little Fred went sprawling backward. As there was a small downward slope behind him, he rolled a couple of times. Just a couple. Nothing serious. He stood up and stared at Mr. Pancake with eyes, I'm confident, as big as the breakfast character's, except Fred's chin was quivering in disbelief. He looked as though Mickey Mouse had attacked him with a spinning teacup. As he ran off bellowing into the distance, Burt, sensing trouble ahead, proclaimed, "Okay, time to go."

Because of where we were standing, because too many people were pouring out of the doors we originally had come out of, and because Burt was horrified we might run into Fred and his mother, he chose to lead us all the way around the school and across the front drive. By then, sweat was pouring off my body in buckets, and I imagined the two Anns must've felt equally tired and sticky.

When we got back outside the front of the building, all I could think of was getting that convection oven off my body. Unbelievably, with a wild burst of energy, Mr. Pancake started galloping. Indeed, he sprinted straight down the front drive toward the parking lot when he saw the big, lovely, happy banner announcing the merry event strung across the asphalt.

I knew it was held up by a rope at the top, and I was aware that as I ran, I would hit the banner, and it would flap away as I galloped under it. I could not, at that moment, have cared less. All I could think about was getting out of Mr. Pancake and perhaps rolling him like an old tire into a lake.

I didn't realize at that pivotal moment, however, that another rope held the bottom of the aforementioned banner in place as securely as the top.

Imagine, if you will, a vertical trampoline.

One second, Mr. Pancake could see an oasis in front of him. In the next, he was flying backward through the air as if a skeet shooter had just yelled, "Pull!"

I vaguely remember lying on the 400-degree concrete, as flat as a—never mind. Too easy. I was staring through yellow mesh directly into the sun. After a moment of silence, my companions checked to see if I was conscious.

Then I heard Miss Egg. I was able to see just far enough out of my yellow mesh to observe her motionless egg face, every bit like one of those bizarre mechanical clown mannequins outside a carnival funhouse, laughing its head off.

The whole thing felt surreal. Burt swarmed around me, asking if I was all right. Miss Bacon stood there wondering, I'm sure, if she was about to live up to her namesake and start sizzling. Miss Egg was still belly-laughing. I managed to crawl out of my costume the opposite of the way I'd crawled in, looking and feeling as if I'd just stepped out of a sauna. I stood up, glared at all of them, rubbed my sore shoulders, and said, "Okay, who's ready for some brunch?"

So next time you decide to eat pancakes, remember: don't mess with Mr. Pancake. He's dangerous.

CONVERSATION STARTERS
FROM CAROL SKIBA

Carol is my dear, sweet, funny cohort in Creative Living class. Encouraging, joyful, and beautiful, she carefully balances her school-principal professionalism with her unsurpassed love for the kids entrusted to her care. I'm glad I know her. She's a blessing. She's so pretty.

1. Think back to a time when you worked in a place where you were close with your colleagues. How did you live out your faith or share Jesus with them?

2. Tim was in a pancake costume that concealed his identity. What masks do you wear that conceal the real you?

3. Remember, don't mess with Mr. Pancake. He's dangerous! Are there any areas in your life that you know are dangerous to your walk with God? How do you refrain from messing with that area?

One Sentence

I HAVE ALWAYS loved the idea of a father running to meet his runaway boy. I imagine it this way: not only did he sprint to meet him, but he waited for him, watched for him, grieved for him, worried about him, lost sleep, and aged, thinking about the trouble his son might have been in.

After waking up one morning and seeing the waste and ruin of his life, the younger son came home. His speech, prepared ahead of time, based on what he perceived his father's reception would be, convicted him. The prodigal deserved condemnation and judgment. After all, his father had no idea where he had been or what he had done. So he tried to spare his father the details and hide the life he'd lived, ashamed, simply saying, "I have sinned against heaven and you."

But when his father reached him, the boy barely even got that first sentence out before his father began to bark orders—not at the son but toward the servants. "Bring a robe. Let's party. We need food and lots of it." It only took that small confession to get the party started.

I notice that the father was interested in a contrite heart and a humble spirit. He was far less interested in the sin. Graham Cooke, founder of Brilliant Perspectives, says in *The Way of the Warrior*, "When the Father looks at you, He doesn't see anything wrong. He's not obsessed by sin; He's not like us. He is consumed by life! God is relentlessly kind. He is never going to quit on you."

Does our Father want us to be aware of and confess sin? Absolutely. But does he want to end there? No, absolutely not. He wants us to throw a party. In Luke 15:7 (MSG), Jesus begins these parables with the moral. In the parable of the lost sheep, he says, "Count on it—there's more joy in heaven over one sinner's rescued life than over ninety-nine good people in no need of rescue." I believe we need to build a vertical avenue of celebration between earth and heaven when a renegade comes home and throw a blowout bash horizontally. We do it for birthdays and weddings, and we even have memorial services and going-home celebrations. What better reason could there be for a cake, burgers, joy, and applause than one who was lost but now is found?

In a small way, I experienced one of these parties a few years ago. I regularly go to a prison where I lead Celebrate Recovery step-studies. In step four, we are to do a fearless and honest inventory of our lives, which means taking responsibility for the pain we have caused others and also acknowledging the pain that was inflicted on us—even by ourselves. It's imperative that we speak our inventory out loud to someone we trust.

One guy asked me to be the one to hear his story. We stood outside the prison chapel one bright, unusually hot, sunny day in February. I leaned against the wall as he paced back and forth and courageously, in brokenness, confessed his past and how he ultimately had ended up in prison. He'd been born into what became a broken home and shuffled back and forth from his father and stepmother, who hated him, to his biological mother, who stopped physically abusing him as he got older and started using emotional and verbal abuse.

He would occasionally land with his grandparents, whom he adored. But they would tell him he needed to work on his relationship with his parents.

The cycle would begin again: back and back to parents who didn't want him and then to grandparents who thought he needed to be responsible at too young an age for gaining his parents' approval. He was abandoned and alone.

Growing up, he loved music, the arts, and writing. It was the only time he felt alive. But he made unwise choices and began using drugs and alcohol to cover his loneliness and self-hatred. He was consumed with fear of being abandoned.

He fathered a child with a woman he wasn't married to. He sabotaged all relationships with drugs and alcohol. Drug-driven fear drove him to cover lies with more lies, suicide attempts, crime, and, finally, murder, which ultimately cost him his freedom.

He began a descent into deep depression, guilt, and shame.

That man, large, physically strong, and ridiculously gifted by God, hung his head down to his chest, heartbroken by his failure. No one had ever said to him the one thing he needed to hear.

Once he finished his inventory, it was time for us to go into the step-study session. During that hour-and-a-half class, I noticed him watching me. I knew without a doubt he was sizing me up, sure I would turn my back on him like everyone else now that I knew him to be a miserable horror of a human being. He was sure I would find him worthless and not worthy of love.

As for me, the whole time, the Holy Spirit was working on me. He was, even before I was aware of it, forming the words in my heart that would pierce the fear of that wounded child of his and open him up to allow the truth of God to course through his heart, veins, mind, and soul.

First of all, of course I wouldn't do all those things he feared. Of course I would continue that journey with him. His story broke my heart for him, just as it broke God's.

Yes, hearing his life story was brutal. I was exhausted while driving home that night. But I believe what God said: we are to bear one another's burdens. Confession sets us free. Or I can walk away from a burden, relieved, because it's just not a happy feeling.

His life experience told him what he had learned, and as he peered at me during class, he thought, *No one is trustworthy.*

After class, I pulled him aside. "Listen, I need to tell you two things. No, actually, three—I just thought of a third. First, you in no way have any responsibility for the abuse you endured at the hand of your mother. Zero! Nada! You were nine years old, for crying out loud. You were just a kid. No one deserves that. You are not guilty!"

He said, "Yeah, but—"

I furrowed my brow. "No *but*s. There are no *but*s here—except the people who abused you."

He said, "I know, but—"

"No *but*s! Period! You have no responsibility there. It's time to be free of that guilt. It has brought you nothing but undeserved pain your whole life."

I wasn't going to let him out of that truth. He smiled and said, "Okay, I hear you. I believe you. I'll work on it."

I surprised him with another nugget of truth. "I believe you feel guilt and shame over your love to sing and write."

He hung his head. "Yes. I guess I feel like I should have done something else."

I said, "Dude, you were given those gifts by God. Yes, you chose to use them in unhealthy ways. Hear me clearly: God's plan for you, in whatever way he chooses, includes those gifts. Even though your unhealthy choices landed you here, his plan hasn't changed for you. He will still use you if you stay surrendered to him and seek him. Do you get that?"

"Yes."

He tried to read me, as if he felt it was impossible to believe that his life could matter and that God had ever had a plan for him. I saw it in his eyes. They said, "I believe what you're saying. But it can't be true for me. How could God ever stick with me after all I've done?"

Then the Holy Spirit nudged me. I spoke the words that man had waited his whole life to hear and had probably never heard. I took a deep breath. "One more thing. And you're not going to want to believe it, so I need you to let go of everything you have known your whole life and, even if only for a few seconds, hear me and trust me. Can you do that? For just a few seconds?"

"Okay. Yes, I'll try my best."

"Unless the Lord comes back or calls me home, I am never going to abandon you. I will not leave you. I will walk this journey with you as long as you need me. Do you hear me? I will never abandon you."

The spiritual implications became physical. For approximately thirty seconds—an eternity—our eyes stayed locked on each other.

Then, slowly, his shoulders relaxed. For another thirty seconds, our eyes remained locked on each other. I became acutely aware that my jaws were firmly sealed, resolved. The bones in my cheeks clenched and unclenched over and over. My brow was furrowed. I do that when I make my mind up about something and take a resolute stand.

His chin began to quiver. He corrected himself for a few seconds and pulled himself into the tough-guy stance again. Then he took two steps back; his eyes filled with tears; and, broken, he said, "You have no idea what that means to me."

I said, "Oh yeah, I think I do."

He ran forward and grabbed me. Remember, he was not a small guy. He was a runner who lifted weights, all muscle.

I couldn't breathe. That so-called hardened criminal held me in a bear hug, with both of us crying and me not breathing, until I was able to squeak out, "I need air."

Now, don't think I was being altruistic. As the words I spoke were coming out of my mouth, I was thinking, *What are you saying? Do you realize the implications? The responsibility you're putting on yourself?*

If I had listened with human ears, I probably would have never said it.

I like my aloneness. I like giving to those guys once a week and then coming home to my quiet house and my pooches. No real responsibility. No real need to be vulnerable.

But for once, I listened to the Spirit of God, and I obeyed.

One sentence. One statement of acceptance. One moment when I willingly allowed the Holy Spirit to work through his small, feeble fallen son. Is that all it took? Yes!

That was ten years ago. We are still walking the journey together. I'm more observant now. I listen better. I pray I will be an instrument of God's grace and mercy, which he has generously poured out onto me.

I pray I will hear the plea of a hurting heart and will be able to, with a party, celebrate a homecoming; legitimize the wounds; bear witness to the truth that God's grace is sufficient, even for the prodigal; and lead them to a clear understanding that they are not alone. Lead them to truly know and believe they are uniquely made and dearly, eternally loved by the One who hung the stars in the heavens. I pray they will live a life knowing that God willingly sent his Son to earth to bear their sins on a cross and that by believing in him, they have not only become his kids but also been given all rights as heirs.

I want them to know that God created the entire universe to sing his praises and that they know—they truly know—at the core of who he is, his desire and plan for them has always been that they be part of the great symphony.

CONVERSATION STARTERS
FROM BONNIE KEEN

Bonnie is the author of *A Ladder out of Depression*, *God Loves Messy People*, *Blessed Are the Desperate, for They Will Find Hope*, and *Women Who Dare to Believe* (coauthored with Nan Gurley). She's very pretty.

1. Is it difficult to imagine God's love would include throwing a party? To imagine a God who laughs and swings us around like a child coming home to music, dance, and the best food and wine? How can this imagery broaden our acceptance of his love?

2. What circumstances or people in your past framed the sin and shame choices over which you had no responsibility? How can you release those influencers to the overwhelming grace of God?

3. Are you afraid of being the arms of Jesus to a hurting friend? Does it feel like too much? Can you imagine a crushing bear hug of gratitude?

Find My iPad

IT WAS A hot and sticky day. A humid, sleepy, sticky day. That summed up my last sixteen hours in the fireworks tent. Tired, I struggled to stay awake and spent time alternating among packing up the last of the fireworks, burning boxes, petting my dog Falkor, and dozing. At one point, I heard someone say, "Hey!" I woke up to find a family looking for deals on leftover pyrotechnics.

Later in the afternoon, I got a text from my high school buddy Jimmy Campbell, owner of the stand. He said he would be at my location in thirty minutes. He was bringing his big rig to load up the last of the fireworks and tent. I burned empty boxes behind the fireworks tent, picked up tidbits of trash, and decided to grab my iPad for a little *Candy Crush Saga*.

I glanced over the counter where my iPad should have rested, but I didn't find it. I looked around the tables and under papers and bags. It wasn't there.

I panicked. More than just a tool, my iPad had come from a friend. He'd believed in me and chosen to affirm me by giving me something he knew I needed. I could get another tablet, but I couldn't replace the sacrifice it represented.

When Jimmy showed up, I told him my iPad might have been stolen.

I immediately pulled up Find My iPad on my phone. I couldn't believe the app would actually work, but when I activated the app, it showed my iPad a few miles away, near a shopping mall.

Trying to act calm, I talked to Jimmy about the fireworks business. Jimmy, always the steady one, stopped me midsentence and said, "If you know where your iPad is, you need to go find it."

So I took Falkor, my Labasset, who does not travel well due to severe motion sickness, and jumped into the car.

On the way to the mall, I called the North Little Rock police, who told me to call them when I was a block from the location, and they'd send a car. Upon reaching the site, I used the tracker again and found my iPad had moved from North Little Rock to downtown Little Rock.

I was beginning to get a bit miffed at that point. I couldn't believe some loser had taken my iPad, and the farther I traveled, the madder I got. I called the North Little Rock police. They informed me I would have to call the Little Rock police since it was now in a different city.

I got to 1000 West Third Street in Little Rock and called the police. They said they would have a car there in a few minutes.

My sense of justice in full throttle, I visualized every possible scenario as to how I was going to love watching the police handcuff the scumbag. I imagined the satisfaction I would feel in seeing the thieves hauled off to jail while I stood smiling in the background. The gratification of being responsible for saving the world from a degenerate criminal.

While waiting for the police, I decided to update the location. The app said my iPad was just around the corner. I decided to run around and take a look. That didn't work. I saw nothing more than a corporate office building and not a soul anywhere. I drove back to the parking lot and waited for the police.

I updated it again. This time, the app said my iPad was back in North Little Rock, just off JFK. So I headed back across I-30 toward North Little Rock. I called the police again and told them where I was headed.

At that point, Falkor was exhibiting critical signs of travel distress. I knew exactly what to expect. All things come from the earth, and all things return to the earth. Falkor returned much at that time.

Holding the steering wheel with one hand, I used the other to spread out a hoodie on the passenger side so Falkor's lunch wouldn't get on the floorboard. Then, using the same hand, I grabbed his snout and held it over the floorboard so he wouldn't puke on the seat.

My frustration was mounting. I couldn't believe the stress—all thanks to one thieving slimeball. I couldn't wait to nail the reprobate to the wall. I had a pocketknife, and I wasn't afraid to use it.

Just as I crossed the river into North Little Rock, driving with one hand while attempting in vain to keep Falkor from fulfilling Proverbs 26:11, I heard a voice as clean as a glass of cold, fresh water. The voice of my Father in heaven said, "How much have you been forgiven?"

I love the way God chooses flawless words to make his perfect point. I have no scriptural precedent for this, but looking back and processing, I believe if he'd said, "How much have I forgiven you?" I would have felt guilt, shame, and self-condemnation. I didn't realize from the beginning how I should have been feeling about the person who'd wronged me.

But because he said, "How much have *you* been forgiven?" my body instantly relaxed. A supernatural calm and understanding came over me. I felt forgiven. He gave me the gift of peace, love, and affirmation that can only come from knowing I am totally, unconditionally forgiven. My eyes filled with tears as I whispered, "Lord, so much more than I could ever begin to pay back, much less understand."

I knew then that no matter what the law might do, no matter the consequences that might await the individual, my job was to show forgiveness and mercy. I thought of what Jesus said in Luke 6:35–36 (NIV): "Love your enemies, do good to them, and lend to them without expecting to get anything back. Then your reward will be great, and you will be children of the Most High, because he is kind to the ungrateful and wicked. Be merciful, just as your Father is merciful."

At that moment, my phone rang. Jimmy was calling from the tent. I was sure he wondered why I'd been gone for more than an hour.

When I answered, Jimmy said, "Someone is here, and he wants to talk to you."

Jimmy handed the phone over to the someone, who said, "My name is Alex. My brother stole your iPad for drug money and sold it to me. I have it here, and I want to give it back to you."

Incredible! I said, "I'm on my way back there now. Can you wait ten minutes?"

He said, "I'll wait here all night if I need to."

When I arrived at the tent, I let a grateful Falkor out of the car. Sighing deeply, I glanced at my hoodie on the floorboard, thankful it was washable. *Deal with that later.* I saw a young man and lady waiting. Walking toward them, I could see the fear and anxiety on his face. Immediately, I calmed him by saying I wasn't going to involve the police. I told him what had happened over the last hour and how the Lord had sweetly dealt with my attitude and changed my heart. I also told him exactly where he lived. He asked how I knew. With a calm resolve, I answered, "That's the address where the police and I were going to meet."

He then informed me, "I've recently been released from prison, and I'm trying to do the right things. My brother told me the iPad belonged to a friend of his who needed money and said he could sell it for sixty dollars." Alex bought it, and his brother left. When Alex looked at the iPad screen, he could see tracking information. He knew immediately the thief would face prosecution.

Knowing that could cause big trouble for him, Alex called his brother and said, "What have you done? This iPad is someone else's." His brother hung up. Not deterred, Alex texted him and said, "I'm calling Mom."

That, to me, is far worse than threatening police action. I guess Alex's brother thought the same. He immediately called Alex and told him where he'd gotten the iPad. And Alex brought it back.

I asked Alex if he knew Jesus. He smiled and issued an emphatic "Yes!" I invited him and his wife to come to church with me sometime.

The consequences of sin might include whatever the wheels of justice and law deem appropriate. My job, as a follower of the One who paid the price for me, is to offer forgiveness.

Alex's brother needed mercy, not judgment. Just like me.

CONVERSATION STARTERS
FROM DAVID RICHARDS

Pastor Dave helps lead and teach Creative Living class, is a former choir director, and now serves as Latino ministry leader. He was one of the first people I met when I began my journey at First NLR. He helped me remember that I have worth and that God still has a plan.

1. Shouldn't someone have to pay a price for stealing? Or do you think the wrath of Mom would be sufficient?

2. Would you wear a hoodie after an animal unloaded its dinner on it?

3. If a dog is man's best friend, shouldn't Falkor have taken a motion sickness pill before going on a wild, raging car ride?

CONVERSATION STARTERS
FROM CHERYL RICHARDS

Cheryl leads the Latino ministry with Pastor Dave. She also helps lead Creative Living Connection class. She's an encourager who loves everyone she comes in contact with and freely shares her love for Jesus. And by the way, she looks exactly the same as she did when she and David got married. I've seen pictures. It's uncanny, like there must be a picture of Dorian Gray in her attic or something. Gorgeous.

1. "I have a knife, and I'm not afraid to use it." Isn't that a violation of one of the Ten Commandments?

2. How could Tim be so careless that he'd leave his iPad lying around, tempting someone to steal it?

3. Why would someone take his dog to a fireworks stand when the temperature is in the upper nineties in Arkansas, where the heat is unbearable? Isn't that dog abuse?

servers

A RECENT STUDY has shown that demanding jobs offering employees little control, such as serving weekend brunch at restaurants, are the most detrimental to mental and physical health. In fact, one study showed it's more stressful to be a server than a neurosurgeon.

It's easy to forget that even though we are paying customers, the human beings serving us work unsociable hours with almost no actual pay, not to mention exhausted feet and, in many cases, unwanted advances from drunk patrons.

I was a server for many years. I kid you not, the most dreaded shift to work was Sunday brunch. I don't know what happened between the altar call and the seating hostess, but it was as if the incoming patrons forgot that once you've swept your house clean, you have to put it in order, or seven other wicked spirits move in—to any given booth at any given restaurant.

There were some weeks when I deliberately took a Sunday brunch shift just so my nonchurchgoing friends didn't have to endure the onslaught of "goodwill" from obstinately tenacious laypeople.

However, I was occasionally able to come up with a subtle remark or two that went virtually unnoticed by the guests but made me feel snarky.

One Sunday, eight ladies came straight from a Sunday school class to have brunch together at our popular restaurant in Nashville. I was to be their ever-joyful, long-suffering, imperturbable server. They all but told me I was personally responsible for not carrying Earl Grey tea. I received a couple of raised eyebrows for not having crackers as a substitute for rolls in the breadbasket. I dealt with the lemon-or-no-lemon-in-the-glass-of-ice-water debacle. Then, in vain, I attempted to explain why a Caesar salad with Thousand Island dressing was no longer a Caesar salad. One lady placed her order for a Cobb salad. The lady who had previously ordered a club salad liked what the Cobb lady was getting better and changed her order to a Cobb salad, except with no bacon and adding extra broccoli. The second lady thought that variation sounded better, changed her order to match the first lady's, and had a myriad of other problems inherent with the menu.

I finally got all the orders, all with special instructions taken, and turned them in. The cooks glared at me through the kitchen window for the next fifteen minutes while I bit my nails to the quick, horrified that something would come out wrong. When everything got to the expediter station, I personally went and oversaw each dish to make sure every plate went to the table exactly as it had been ordered, down to the placement of every sprig of parsley. I dragged a couple of other servers over against their will and better judgment to help deliver the food to the table.

Once everything was set down, they all viciously examined the plates for any sign of missing or misplaced items. After approximately nine and a half seconds of total silence, I said, "Well, there ya go, ladies. Is anything okay?"

Another time, I could not get a single thing correct for a guy—even though I got him exactly what he asked for. His steak medallions were overcooked every time, even though I kept telling him they were thinly sliced cuts of beef and could not be cooked so they were pink in the middle, unless I served them raw. His beer wasn't cold enough, and there was, ironically, too much ice in his water glass. Finally, when I brought back his credit card and slip, I made the obligatory cordial statement that I was glad they had come in, hoped they had a great night, and hoped they would come back soon. He didn't even look up as he signed the receipt and said, "Well, I will have a good night. But I won't be coming back here. I'm tired of not getting what I ask for."

I responded in the most ingratiatingly pleasant tone possible, "Well, we here at Dalt's like to keep our customers happy and satisfied. So if it would make you happy to never come back here again, it would certainly make us happy."

His wife, who had been ominously quiet throughout the entire meal, laughed so hard she almost choked on her final sip of water.

The first thought that went through my head was *I'm about to get fired.*

But the lady just looked at him and said, "You totally asked for that."

I felt just a bit vindicated.

A couple of friends from my church in Nashville, Mike Nolan and Eve Sarrett, wrote a crazy book called *You Can't Curl Your Hair with Holy Rollers: An Insider's Guide to Church Life.* They sat down with me and asked what things drove me crazy about waiting tables on Sundays. They named that section in the book "How to Witness While Dining Out."

> Come directly to the restaurant from a church gathering with a large number of people—preferably too many to sit at one table. Bring as many children with you as possible, especially whiny babies and strong-willed toddlers who have been forced to be quiet for the past two hours and

will need to be loudly corrected. Ask to be seated together, saying, "We don't mind scrunching a little." Remember to complain later about how crowded you were at the table they gave you. When you arrive at your table, someone should inadvertently bring a Bible with him, which will take up much-needed table space. When the hostess asks if you are okay with sitting close to the bar, look appalled, and cite how drinking defiles the temple of God. Act as confused as possible about who sits where. Several people should swap seats a few times, especially after orders have been placed. When the server arrives, request as many separate checks as possible, or use zigzag patterns to indicate who should be included on a single check. At least one person should request only water and say to the server, "I'm just here for the fellowship." This person must consume as much water as possible, requiring multiple refills, and should scarf food from the plates of those who order the all-you-can-eat salad bar. When the food comes, reel off a long, confusing list of orders that are wrong and items that have been forgotten. The meals in place, join others in nervously looking around the table until someone asks what everyone is thinking, "Are we going to pray?" Wait the long, tenuous moment until someone surrenders and responds, "I'll do it." Fumble with the hold-hands/don't-hold-hands decision and bow your heads just as the server arrives with a heavy tray of additional stuff. Have a long prayer, including in it a brief summation of the sermon and a spirited call to action. Keep praying until the server's arms start to spasm. Young children should crush as many crackers as possible. When a toddler stands in his chair and refuses to sit down, the parent should say, "Santa Claus won't come to see you if you keep this up" or, "When you act this way, you make God cry." Eventually, the parent should drag the kicking and screaming child to the bathroom while reciting to the young reprobate Ephesians 6:1. "Children, obey your parents in the Lord, for this is right." When the checks are distributed, several people should find errors and complain loudly. Those who have not been charged for items they received should offer a silent prayer to God for His abundant provision. Each person should tip 5 percent or however many coins they have in their pockets—whichever is less. Someone should remember that change is needed to buy a newspaper and take the appropriate amount. Place coins under plates, believing that all giving—not just tithing—should be done in secret. Finally, someone should leave a card with the tip quoting Luke 9:25, "What does it profit a man if he gains the whole world yet lose his own soul?" Or Joshua 24:15, "Choose ye this day whom you will serve."

I remember a few moments when respect and thankfulness were shown in ways I'll never forget. An older gentleman and his wife came in almost every Sunday and sat in the same place, booth number sixty-three, just next to a window overlooking White Bridge Road. The dear couple were obviously sweethearts. It was a pleasure to have that section of tables and an honor to wait on them.

They didn't come in for a few weeks, and we worried about them. Then, one Sunday, she came in alone and told us her sweet husband had passed away a few weeks earlier, and she was finding it difficult to visit places they'd loved going together.

She became our grandmother. Every Sunday, she came back, knowing we saved booth number sixty-three for her, even when we were on a waitlist. She sat alone, and she ate alone, most Sundays fighting back tears. We fiercely protected her time with us and were devoted to looking after her.

Because she was so kind and gentle and made us feel our service was important and needed, we worked to make her feel like family. One of the other servers, Amy Strobel, and I found out where she lived and snuck over to her house and left gifts at her front door one Christmas morning. The next Sunday, she came in smiling, proudly sporting the antique brooch we had given her for Christmas. It was an honor to be her friend. I never felt like her server.

Those moments forged a system of checks and balances that has stayed with me my whole life.

When I go to supper with friends, I make it a specific priority that no matter where we go, our servers will be part of the group. If they're hungry, we offer some of our appetizer for them to sneak back to the kitchen and eat. We ask about their family. We get to know them. We don't think of them as servers; we treat them as valued friends.

There is no question as to whether or not we will pray for our meal. We pray and thank the Lord for our food.

One Friday night, our server was Marta. Before we got our food, we found out she was a single mom. Her kids were seven and four years old. She had just returned from helping train servers at a new restaurant in Kansas. She had to work doubles to pay rent. She hadn't seen much of her kids in more than three weeks. Her brother had been her babysitter, but he'd gotten a new job, so she had to find someone new to take care of her kids.

I told Marta we believed in the power of prayer and asked her what we could specifically pray for her. She looked at me as if I were surely kidding. She said, "No one has ever asked me that before." She asked that we pray for her to have peace and that her schedule would lighten up. I told her we would pray for those things. I told her we would also pray for her kids and that her job schedule would be easier for her so she could spend time with her babies.

Often, if our servers are there when we get ready to eat, we ask what we can specifically pray for them. They are always shocked and surprised. But many times, they give us real problems and real needs that our Father will surely hear.

What if that's the only time that day someone makes them feel important? What if I'm the only chance they have? For many, it probably will be the only time. What if it's the only time that day they will see Jesus?

Marta was, for an hour or so, part of our family. Before we left, we made sure she knew that we were there for her and that she mattered. As we left, I told her, "You can know for sure you will be prayed for this week. And thanks for working so hard to make our meal so great. You deserve every bit of that eight percent tip we left."

The expression on her face was priceless, a cross between "I'm sure he was kidding" and "Or was he?" I can assure you she was pleasantly surprised when she realized I was only kidding.

First John 3:18 (ESV) says, "Little children, let us not love in word or talk, but in deed and in truth."

Philippians 2:4 (ESV) says, "Let each of you look not only to his own interests, but also to the interests of others."

Everyone has a story. We don't meet others by accident.

CONVERSATION STARTERS FROM ANTHONY AND LAURA HENNEN

Anthony and I met in the early 1990s. He is one of my truest and dearest friends. We not only were servers at Dalt's in Burbank but also attended church together. Anthony introduced me to sushi. He sat silently by and watched with great joy and expectancy as I, thinking it was mushed avocado lying serenely on the plate, stuffed the whole wad of wasabi into my unsuspecting mouth. I actually saw my own nostrils. I'm thankful (and relieved) he married Laura. One of the best decisions he ever made. And Laura is so pretty.

1. Can you think of people you interact with whom you may or may not really see or notice?

2. Why do we not see or notice these folks? What are we allowing to consume our minds and lives when we cross paths with them?

3. How can we better prepare ourselves to avoid keeping someone who comes into our daily experience from being noticed and blessed by the simplest of gestures or words? What can we offer to bless his or her day?

Bookends

"DON'T BE AFRAID, you who are highly esteemed by God." This verse reads a bit differently, depending on the translation. Some say "greatly respected" or "greatly desired." Two of my favorites are from the New Living Translation, which reads, "'Don't be afraid,' he said, 'for you are very precious to God,'" and the English Standard Version, which says, "Oh man, greatly loved, fear not." But my very favorite is from the Holman Christian Standard Bible. It reads, "Oh man, you who are treasured by God, peace to you. Be strong." But no matter which translation of Daniel 10 you read, one statement remains distinctly consistent. Every translation says, "Don't be afraid."

For three weeks, Daniel had been mourning over Israel, eating really lousy food (no meat or wine), and neglecting to use lotions or oils on himself. So apparently, he experienced brutal gas and didn't smell great either.

Then an angel appeared and touched Daniel. I'm assuming he touched Daniel on the back of his head since Daniel was lying prone on the ground at that point. Gabriel's words of affirmation and his touch gave Daniel just enough strength to rise.

Even though he was still fearful and trembling, Daniel heard the words that we all long to hear: "You are loved. You are treasured. You are precious." Daniel must have realized at that moment how important he was to God. Gabriel began the story by making Daniel feel worthy, and Daniel was able to hear the vision that was about to be poured out to him.

A while back, Becca was involved in an intense dialogue with someone involving a ministry she'd been working with for more than twenty years. Becca used material created by the program consistently, as national leaders of the ministry had perfected the resources from year to year. She used the national team's material to write an orientation document outlining expectations for the group, the program, the participants, and the leaders.

After he opened the discussion with a prayer for unity and restoration, the first words out of the ministry leader's mouth were "I have to apologize. You have been involved in this ministry so long I thought you knew what you were doing. It was wrong of me to assume that."

Processing through the encounter, Becca recognized what a significant growth opportunity it would turn out to be for her. It wasn't pleasant in the moment, not by the wildest stretch of her imagination. I've learned it doesn't matter how much recovery and healing we have under our belts; it's far too easy for one statement to propel us backward emotionally.

Becca has worked hard over the years to be a woman of integrity and worthy of earned respect, but she heard one false statement about herself, and she was immediately reduced to that unworthy, unlovable person with few, if any, redeeming qualities. She told me she became defensive, angry, and scared, a cornered rat.

It was not a pleasant exchange. After almost walking out of the conversation, she calmed down, and so did he. They finished the dialogue in a somewhat decent compromise.

But even after the dust settled and an agreeable compromise was reached, he bookended the conversation by saying the same thing: "Again, I'm sorry I assumed you knew what you were doing."

Wisely, this time, Becca chose to keep silent and not react. But the fact remained that she felt shame and embarrassment. She felt all the work she had done for many years was worthless. However, instinctively, because of the intense work she'd done over the years, she knew there was no reason for her to feel those emotions. Becca knew she didn't deserve to own them.

On the drive home from the meeting, Becca decided she needed to seek wise counsel. One of the strong points of her recovery has been deliberately positioning herself with wisdom from people she trusts. It's the healthiest thing we can do. I know I seek wisdom from these people on everything now, almost down to which flavor of ice cream I should get. Or sprinkles. Should I get sprinkles?

She called three friends who are all well established in the same ministry. She asked them if she could send them the document and allow them to tell her if it contradicted in any way the standards set by the national program or if it provided, as she intended, guidelines and expectations founded in the resources and best practices of the national program.

One said there was nothing that went against the DNA of the program. One sent her a written response outlining the major points of Becca's document and how it coincided with the national procedures and policies. The third rep wouldn't even let her send it, stating, "You gave me that document several years ago. I still have it. I adapted it and have used it in my groups."

That was all the ammo Becca thought she needed.

But suddenly, that somehow didn't feel right. It didn't feel healthy. Becca called her sponsor, and her sponsor said, "What's your goal here? What's your endgame? To prove the guy wrong? To make him feel as worthless as he made you feel? To feel better than him? To show him that you do know what you're doing?"

None of those sounded healthy or ultimately fulfilling. The crux of the issue wasn't really even about the other person. While recounting the experience, Becca repeatedly affirmed the leader isn't a bad guy. He's actually a really great guy. The problem was that Becca had let her guard down. It was her, not him. Yes, what he said and did wasn't healthy, but the truth of the matter is that what someone uses in an attempt to gaslight us can't fly across the table and into us unless we let it. She forgot one of the basic tenets of Celebrate Recovery for those of us who have been at it for a while. She'd read this verse during every step-study she'd ever done: "Don't be so naive and self-confident. You're not exempt. You could fall flat on your face as easily as anyone else. Forget about self-confidence; it's useless. Cultivate God-confidence" (1 Corinthians 10:12 MSG).

Becca realized her endgame needed to be stronger and lead toward the eternal. She remembered Micah 6:8 (NIV): "He has shown you, O mortal, what is good. And what does the Lord require of you? To act justly and to love mercy and to walk humbly with your God."

She needed to use the moment to figure out how to walk with God more wholly and surely. She realized she now possessed the truth she needed. Becca did, in fact, know what she was doing. If she felt the need to prove that, then she was working out of a place of pride and a need for approval. She knew where her support ultimately came from.

She sought wise counsel and got it. That was all she needed. She decided to keep leading the program the way she'd always led. She knows it's right.

> Keep your eyes open, hold tight to your
> convictions, give it all you've got, be
> resolute, and love without stopping.
>
> —1 Corinthians 16:13 MSG

I've learned that if bookends are essential in a conversation, I want them to leave the ones who receive my words feeling and believing they are valid and loved. They should feel highly esteemed and precious. I want them to know they matter; they are significant; and, most importantly, the star-breathing Creator of the universe treasures them.

Daniel was able to stand before the angel, even when he was horrified, trembling, and feeling unworthy. When Gabriel bookended the beginning of his time with Daniel by saying, "Don't be afraid, you are treasured by God," and ending that time by saying the same thing, "Don't be afraid, you are treasured by God," he was making sure Daniel understood that he was worthy and ready to receive the prophecy of what was going to unfold in the future.

A bookend in writing sets up a scene so it can be satisfactorily repeated at the end of a larger scene. In life, it shows the character of the person who places the bookends in their respective positions. The narrative of any discussion should always lead to an eternal conclusion. Either we leave someone closer to God, or we don't.

Our bookends matter a great deal. Daniel stood after hearing, "Hey, you're important, and God is crazy in love with you." Gabriel's similar phrases at the beginning and the end of his time with Daniel gave the man the courage to hear what Gabriel was about to lay on him.

Here's the kicker for me. How treasured was Daniel? How precious, loved, worthy, esteemed, and desired? Gabriel was saying, "Daniel, don't be afraid. Let me affirm to you how important you are. From the moment you set your heart to gain understanding and to know your God, your words were heard. And I have come in response to them."

Gabriel was saying, "Hey, God knew about you before he spun the world into orbit. He knew you would be mourning and would be grieving for Israel. From the very beginning, he knew your heart would be turned toward him and this moment would come. Guess what? He heard you. And here I am."

Today you and I can know this. I'm here to tell you. God treasures you. He adores you. You are precious to him. You have worth, and he has a plan for you. From the moment you set your heart to gain understanding and to know your God, your words were heard. Before the world was established, he heard you.

Angels are on their way.

CONVERSATION STARTERS
BY JACQUI LEFLER

Jacqui is a business leader, a wife, a mother, an aunt, a hospitality beast, my precious sister, a vicious protector, and a Jesus lover. She's never met a stranger, was born to be Quiqui, the best grandmom in history. She looks a lot like our momma. So pretty.

1. Can words, just words, change the physical feelings of the recipient? Yes! What is the best way to defuse the physical and mental feeling when you feel backed into a corner?

2. In the business world I live in, trainings, studies, and the like, including supporting documents, are intended to focus on the needs of the end users, the recipients. Healthy, productive counsel from others is always a good thing. But prayer matters most. If you prayerfully develop a business or Christian training, should you be confident in your results?

3. How could the person who approached Becca have handled the situation better? (I can think of many ways.) If you would like to offer feedback or constructive ideas, what words would you use? There will come a time to offer support of a brother or sister. Be prepared!

A Garden for Momma

ON MOTHER'S DAY 1995, my sister, Jacqui, and I spent the day preparing a special gift for our mom. The condo she lived in was in a great part of town. A narrow neutral area of green space separating her row of condos from the ones behind her afforded limited lawn usage.

Jacqui and I gathered up two of her kids, TJ and Tad, and we went to the local garden store.

Mom's God-given giftedness covers a broad spectrum. Unfortunately, green is not a color found in her palette. Knowing her proclivity to kill anything green, we looked for plants that wouldn't take much work, plants she could occasionally water, sit back, and watch grow. We bought a hosta, which I'd admired in one of her neighbors' gardens, and a rosebush, along with a few other perennial, self-sustaining shrubs we hoped she would like.

We asked the garden specialists about supplies for a lasting garden. They gave us wise choices on how to proceed. We bought the right kind of ground cover to keep out weeds. After buying good soil, we put in a garden barrier to prevent erosion during lousy weather. We then spent the day not knowing exactly if we were doing the right things. We hoped we weren't destroying Mom's garden with good intentions.

We carefully installed the barrier in an elongated *U* shape, backed by Mom's deck. We laid out the black ground covering, cutting holes in places where we thought the plants would make the best appearance. Hostas love plenty of sunshine, so we planted ours in an area with the best potential for growth. We planted the rosebush close to the steps leading to the deck, so Mom would get a perfect view of the future flowers. We fertilized the soil and profusely watered all the plants.

We were tired, dirty, and sunburned a bit but proud of our accomplishment. Mom, of course, loved it.

Those plants did grow. Every couple of weeks, one of us would go over to make sure they were watered and weed-free. It was a team effort that paid off. The lush, healthy green hosta grew and spread over much of the immediate area. So did the rosebush. It produced many roses over the years. Mom cut them and set them in a small vase on her supper table.

We were proud of that garden. I was a bit concerned some fifteen years later when we moved Mom to a retirement village. You don't leave behind something in which you've invested so much time and energy without wanting to know it will be taken care of.

Mom owned the condo, so after she moved, she decided to rent it for a while. One of the renters was an older lady who loved the garden and took the time to tend to it. Several years went by, and when the garden was twenty years old, on Mother's Day, I took Mom by the condo, and we knocked on the door. I asked the lady if she would mind if I pulled up a bit of the hosta to take home to my house in Little Rock. She readily agreed. She noted that she hadn't planted it, but she enjoyed taking care of it.

The hosta was huge. Mom and I went out back, and I uprooted a few small pieces and brought them home to Little Rock, where I planted them in front of my house, under my big red-leafed maple tree.

They took root where I planted them, and they grew strong and healthy.

A few years later, on Labor Day, we moved Mom to Springdale, Arkansas, to a great retirement village where she would be closer to grandkids and great-grandkids. Five days before closing on Mom's old condo, I told Jacqui I wanted to get a few more cuttings of the hosta to plant in my yard—because one can never have too much hosta in his yard.

So before going to Mom's current apartment to help load her up, I went to the condo, which now sat empty. I walked to the back and froze in disbelief. The most recent occupants had moved out. They cared nothing about the little garden. They didn't know its history. They didn't see the work and love we'd invested or the years of care poured into the plants. To them, the garden was no more than a landfill.

Weeds filled the small garden, and the edges of the leaves of the once beautiful hosta were brown from lack of oxygen and nourishment.

I walked around to the other side and found creepers growing out of the cracked, dry ground and crawling up the back of the deck—vines wrapped around the old rosebush, choking the life out of it. Old food wrappers and plastic water bottles had been thrown everywhere without any thought for the garden.

My heart broke. But memories of what used to be triggered my resolve to do everything I could to make the plants healthy again. To give those precious, God-created expressions of God's glory a chance, I would have to move them to a healthier environment.

When I told Jacqui I was going to run by the condo to get a few more cuttings from the hosta, she said, "Just be careful to make it look like you didn't take any."

"Okay."

I dug up every last bit of that plant.

I found empty flowerpots filled with trash under the deck. I dumped the waste, filled them with hosta, and carried fifteen buckets to the back of the truck. I walked around to the old rosebush and dug it up as well. Would it even survive? One single branch showed any sign of life.

I remembered when we'd planted it in good soil. I hoped those first nurturing moments filled with love and expectancy would still be alive and kicking in there somewhere, wanting to survive as much as I wanted them to.

After loading the truck, I went to Mom's apartment. I helped my family pack up her belongings. I gave my sister-in-law a bucket of hosta. We all hugged and waved goodbye to each other as they rolled toward Springdale.

When I got back to Little Rock, I stopped at the Good Earth Garden Center and asked for wise counsel on how to best revive and take care of my plants.

One of the guys walked to the truck with me and looked at all the hosta containers. He told me if I wanted to save them, I would need to cut them all down four to six inches from the root. I needed to plant them just deep enough for the soil to cover the root. Winter was coming, and the plants were tender and would need added protection.

He said the soil would be critical right now. I needed supersoil—equal parts organic compost or new soil added to older soil and some Jump Start.

Then he looked at the old, gnarled rosebush. I could tell by his resigned expression he would say there was no hope for it. Years of neglect had strangled its delicate beauty.

And he almost did say that, but he wisely recognized the bush carried sentimental history. He advised me to cut away all the dried-up branches and leave only the one that still struggled to survive. "Cut away the dead ends of the root, exposing the meat inside, and hope for the best."

I took new knowledge and wisdom and went home. Of course, as much as we try to take care of plants, we don't ultimately know what the final result will be. We keep feeding them, watering them, and watching for signs of growth.

I cut the hostas, tore them apart, and planted them, buried in new soil, close to the other ones I'd planted a few years back. Within a week, they were all sprouting fresh leaves. Yes, they would lose them when winter approached, but those strong roots would flourish, and new leaves would sprout again in the spring.

I was worried about the old rose, though. After cutting off the old branches that were no longer useful, I trimmed the root system so new growth could occur. I planted the bush near the steps leading up to my front door. I watched and anxiously waited, remembering the joy of the family planting it together and how Momma had loved it.

But nothing happened.

Then, one morning several weeks later, I walked outside to check on all my new plants, and here is what I found:

Somewhere in that old branch was the memory of what sustained it as a small plant. It knew where it came from and couldn't deny what God planned for it to be. Maybe the Lord wanted me to be a small part in displaying his creation for his glory. He is the God of resurrection, after all.

Something I'd cared about in its infancy, which had been neglected by others out of my control, revived because I chose to make the first investment and then the second investment, not giving up and even praying.

I hated waiting and not knowing what the results would eventually be. But knowing there was even a 1 percent chance that investing time and getting my hands dirty might make a difference made the anticipation worth it.

I didn't know what would happen throughout the winter. But I knew I could trust God with the outcome. I'd invested my time and energy—twice. I had done the work of pruning and eliminating the dead and dying branches that would do more harm than good. I'd planted and nurtured the rosebush well, and I would continue to pour fresh water and nutrients into its roots.

I am confident anyone reading this will understand the lesson. My sister said, "It's just like us. God has to prune away all the dead leaves before real growth and life can take place."

Take time to invest in the plants the Lord places in your life. Invest as many times as it takes. Even when we're not sure of the outcome, it's our job only to plant and water. It's God's purpose to make things grow. It's a team effort: us, wise counsel, and God.

First Corinthians 3:6–8 (NIV) says, "I planted the seed, Apollos watered it, but God has been making it grow. So neither the one who plants nor the one who waters is anything, but only God, who makes things grow. The one who plants and the one who waters have one purpose, and they will each be rewarded according to their own labor."

I'll continue to plant, water, and anticipate and expect God to make that old rosebush grow as he desires. I'll continue to invest.

One sun-drenched spring morning, I leaned against the deck railing outside my front door and breathed in the musky aroma of freshly mowed grass. I glanced at a small area of my flower garden, where I recognized small shoots of emerald-green hosta waking up, peeking out from rich, rain-soaked soil. I ambled down the steps to get a closer look and found, just at the foot of my front steps, this:

CONVERSATION STARTERS FROM TRICIA WALKER (WWW.BIGFRONTPORCH.COM)

Tricia is a singer and award-winning songwriter with southern roots running deep and clear. Watching Tricia's fingers on guitar strings is like watching God's healing on a broken heart. We've traveled halfway around the world together. Read "That Time I Almost Got Sucked down a Blowhole." My beautiful, precious friend.

1. What are some practical ways you can nurture faith in your own heart and in the hearts of others when a situation seems hopeless? Momma's rosebush showed no visible signs of life, yet, with nurturing, it bloomed again.

2. How do you work through or lean into seasons of loss or change in your life? Momma's garden had been left unattended and uncared for, and there was no way to make it the way it had been in that particular place as a new chapter unfolded.

3. As you face each new day, what are some practices that cause you to have deep hope? Momma's garden was planted with love, sweat, and tears but no guarantee that it would grow. But with a strong advocate and tender care, it brought forth beauty in every leaf and blossom.

That Time Dad Almost Drowned a Woman

THE CHURCH I grew up in was a blessing. It was a great place to learn a lot about Jesus. I was raised memorizing the books of the Bible, the names of the twelve apostles, the Lord's Prayer, and the Twenty-Third Psalm. I can sling a slew of stand-alone verses that have remained cemented in my conscious and subconscious and rise to the surface when needed.

This church was also excruciatingly strict in its theology and practices. Baptism was essential, and the biblically accepted form of baptism was total and complete immersion. In a few ultraextreme, hard-hat, conventional congregations, it was believed that if any molecularly small part of the body was not completely submerged during that beautiful statement of faith, the baptism did not take.

Today watching baptisms is still one of the most emotional and magnificent experiences I sit through, whether it's in a church service, a swimming pool, a lake, or a stream. Although I'm not as legalistic as I was growing up, when I watch a baptism, I still lean to the right, doing my part to make sure the baptizer is shoving the baptizee as close to the bottom of the baptistery as humanly possible.

I once received the following note from my lovely, dear friend Cathie:

> Last Friday night was such a special night for me. My choice to be baptized was an act of worship for me and a moment of great joy in my walk with the Lord. I very much felt the solemnity of offering my life as a sacrifice to the One who has redeemed me with a price. My heart was feeling the grace of being led by the Spirit to make the choice to truly follow Jesus. As I stood in the baptismal pool, I looked out on the people who were gathered to witness, and I was struck by such an expression of tenderness in your eyes. Your eyes looked like you were gazing on the baptism as though it were something of great beauty. I felt as though God used your expression as a mirror to reflect his love that I was feeling in my heart. The decision to be baptized remains solid, but the actual event seems like a blur. I was thinking about it this morning, and the two things that I remember most are the way the water felt and the expression in your eyes. You gave me a gift that I'm sure you are not aware of, and I wanted to thank you.

Cathie was right; I hadn't been aware. I responded,

> Oh, Cathie, thank you. What a precious gift you've given me. And I promise to carry that memory with me forever. To be honest, I get very emotional every time I watch a baptism. I know that it's the single most profound public statement

that a person will make. So I watch always in amazement and wonder that the very God who hung the stars in the heavens looks down on us during that moment with even greater wonder and amazement. What love and joy and pride he, I'm certain, felt for you at that moment. When you, unafraid and unashamed, told everyone there that you belong to Jesus. My heart swells up to bursting every time I experience that. I love that over all these years of being a believer, watching someone being baptized is the one aspect of my walk with Jesus—well, that and communion— that never gets rote or trite or commonplace. Thanks for your note, Cathie. And thanks for letting me be a part of it. Just remember, God loves you right where you are right now. And I know he's very, very proud of you.

Cathie's baptism and our exchange of letters afterward remind me of the gift of blessing. How many times have I strolled down a sidewalk, sat across a conference or supper table, pushed a grocery cart, waited on the phone for a tech representative to pick up, accidentally run into someone who has hurt or wronged me, and been given a sacred chance to fearlessly bless someone, often without even knowing I did it?

Matthew 5:16 says, "In the same way, let your light shine before others so that they may see your good works and give glory to you and know that you're a good person."

Is that what it says?

No! It says, "In the same way, let your light shine before others so that they may see your good works and give glory to your Father who is in heaven" (Matthew 5:16 NIV).

One of my favorite traditions was given to me by Carol Skiba, who leads our Creative Living Sunday school class. I've never liked making New Year's resolutions. In fact, I read that every year, 87 percent of adults will make New Year's resolutions, and 50 percent of those resolution makers will fail by the end of January. So I used the idea I got from Carol, which she read from a book called *One Word That Will Change Your Life* by Jon Gordon.

Simple is best. Every year, I pick one word that will be my life word for the year.

As I sat and prayed and asked the Lord to give me my word for a recent year, I wasn't seeing a clear answer. I'd felt I would go with *giving* a couple of weeks before New Year's, but sparks began to ignite in my head and heart that it should be a different word.

A little more than a decade before that, just before Thanksgiving, I had become gravely ill. I went to several doctors, none of whom were able to pinpoint the problem. After five months of not knowing, I was scared. One Sunday morning smack dab in the middle of the not knowing, between church services, I was in the church gym. People swarmed in all directions. I ran into my friend Lisa Fischer. She smiled and yelled, "How you doing?"

Over the typical echoing din of a gym, I'm not sure why, but walking with a black rain cloud of fear and uncertainty ready to burst open at any second, I fought back tears and told her.

She listened and then said, "I'm praying right now."

Right there in the middle of total chaos, Lisa raised one hand to heaven and put the other on my shoulder. She blessed me with a precious petition to the Lord, asking him to ease my distress, anxiety, and fear of the unknown. She asked that he meet me in the middle of my anxiousness and that I would find supernatural peace while waiting.

I'll never forget that vacuum moment. The thing is, living fearlessly for the Lord is so second nature to her that Lisa has no memory of that moment.

A few years later, I ran into a friend of mine in Walmart a week before Christmas. I knew he was having some health issues, so I asked how he was doing. He told me a recent fall had caused him to have constant headaches. There was a slight bleed on his brain, and he was in continuous pain, with migraines more often than not. I suddenly recalled the holy moment with Lisa ten years earlier, and I heard the Lord say, "Remember Lisa's blessing."

Right there in the food-storage-container aisle, I raised one hand to heaven, put my other hand on Andrew's shoulder, and took him to the throne. He messaged me later and told me what a great blessing that was.

A few nights later, a friend I've known since childhood responded to one of my posts on social media. She said that several years earlier, I'd brought her back into a relationship with the Lord. She told me that critical moment for her had indeed been a blessing. I have no memory of what I said or did to encourage her to look again toward Jesus. But in that moment, the Lord clearly gave me my word for the year: *fearless*.

I don't know from day to day all the ramifications of how that one word will enhance, change, and enrich my life and my walk and relationship with Jesus, but I know it will.

As in past years, I've wondered where I'll see the opportunities to use my word. But I've learned it's like buying a new car. A few weeks ago, I got my mom's 2010 Nissan Rogue. (With nine thousand miles on it. Seriously, she was the old lady who only drove to church and the grocery store.) The thing is, I never really noticed them before. But now that I have one, I see Rogues everywhere.

My hope is that when I get to heaven, someone will come up to me and remind me of a moment when I fearlessly showed him or her Jesus, even if I don't remember it. My hope is that I will have more of those moments than someone walking up to me and reminding me of a time when I was angry, short, rude, or cruel. Since that won't happen in heaven, I think I'm safe. I want *fearless* to become a habit.

This year is my year of *fearless*. What is your word?

As I said, baptism was a matter of salvation for the denomination I was born into, and that salvation was, at best, questionable if every centimeter of flesh wasn't covered in the cleansing flood.

When my father started preaching, he went out many nights to hold what was then called a "cottage meeting." He would go to a home and teach the family about Jesus. If they chose to accept Jesus as Lord and Savior, they were taken immediately to the church and baptized. I loved going with Dad to the church on those special nights.

At one of his first cottage meetings, after Dad explained what salvation looked like, the wife said she would think about it and make a decision by Sunday morning. After retelling her the stories of the rich young ruler and Acts 26, in which Agrippa is almost persuaded, and still not getting the response he wanted, Dad came home, disappointed.

But sure enough, come Sunday morning, the lady went forward at the end of the sermon to be baptized. There was general excitement in the room, as this was to be Dad's first baptism as a preacher.

She was a formidably built woman and tall. She and Dad walked down the blue-painted steps into the blue water of the baptistery. The lady wore the angelic, flowing white baptismal garment. Dad had on his starched white shirt with sleeves rolled up and chest-high waders. Dad placed one hand over her mouth and held his free hand in the air as he announced the usual proclamation: "I now baptize you in the name of the Father and of the Son and of the Holy Spirit for the remission of your sins. Amen!" She pinched her nose shut with a handkerchief and leaned backward.

Unfortunately, she held her head up, keeping it from going under the water. Dad tried again to push her down, but she held her head just short of complete immersion each time—complete, total, full, soul-saving immersion.

Dad must have pushed her down five times. He put more and more muscle into each endeavor, possibly out of irritation. We learned later that the more he leaned, the more water trickled inside the front of his waders.

Everyone in the audience obliviously leaned harder and farther to the right. From the back pew, the entire congregation appeared to be in the middle of the ocean, in a small dinghy caught in the waves of a sudden white squall. Many of them were okay with "buried with Christ," but certainly, no one was comfortable with the "raised to walk in newness of life" part.

Filled with horror, Dad suddenly realized there was a light blue painted step about two inches below the surface of the water. The step was invisible, being pretty much the same color as the water. Basically, Dad was bludgeoning that poor tall woman half to death.

It would have been a shame for her to miss getting into heaven because her nose wasn't submerged. Or maybe everything but her nose would make it. Who knows? Maybe that's where grace comes in.

So what's your word for the year?

CONVERSATION STARTERS FROM MICHAEL NOLAN (MICHAELNOLANWRITES.COM)

Michael is genuinely one of the funniest, warmest, gentlest, kindest, most authentic men I know. I love spending time with him. I laugh and learn. He's Nancy's husband and Nate's dad. Nuff said.

1. Think of a calamitous incident you experienced. What's a word or phrase that describes it? Humor is totally acceptable.

2. Consider words that have been meaningful in the past— no need to be hyperspiritual. If *laughter* is one of your words, so be it. If something raw, such as *addicted* or *broken* rings true, go with it. Make a list of whatever comes to mind.

3. If you were to summarize the last six months or year of your life, what word would you choose?

4. If you don't have a eureka moment, no worries. Keep the question in the back of your mind until something speaks to you. Consider praying for God to give you insight.

Hope

AS I'VE READ stories from the Bible, I've found myself interested in my definition of the word *hope*. I don't think I'm speaking out of turn when I say most people in our culture don't understand the term. They equate hope with not much more than a characterless wish that some life experience will turn out for the best—or all life experiences will turn out for the best.

If *hope* is only a verb meaning "wanting something to happen or be the case," it seems passive. It's a sort of namby-pamby admission that although I believe God's promises are true, the best I can run toward is an uninvolved, apathetic sort of weak-kneed armchair faith. That kind of faith expects only a God who understands my limitations in the belief department and loves me anyway.

I hope heaven is real. I hope I get to spend eternity there. I hope the Lord is true to his promises.

For years, based on what I believed of hope, I couldn't connect with folks of faith in scripture who were inspired by the Holy Spirit and wrote about their hope. How could they have walked and talked with God and Jesus and had only hope (a wish) that they would finish the race in his presence?

Such a wimpy idea didn't work for me. It almost seemed disingenuous to say I *hoped* or *wished* for things I couldn't see. I knew they were real—as real as the iPad I'm writing on or the wrong-colored pants and shirt I wore today for choir. Even more so. There are times when I could almost explode from the reality of life unseen and promises yet to be unwrapped.

So how was I to reconcile what I knew to be real with what I thought was a correct definition of a single word?

One day the Lord clearly said to me, "Is *hope* only a verb?"

I immediately looked for scriptures with the word *hope*. When I read them with *hope* as a noun, the skies burst open, and blessing after blessing fell into my heart.

Hope isn't static. It's not flat, spiritless, or wavering. It's moving. It's unpredictable. It's a strong and confident expectation that what my heart knows is true and real will one day be seen with my eyes.

My hope is that heaven is real. My hope is that I will spend eternity there. My hope is in Jesus. It has made all the difference.

Although *hope* is a noun, it's incredibly active. It calls me to be alive in every moment. Hope is a land, a green tree, the place I pitch my tent. It's not a dream. Check the following verses out. Use the noun, not the verb.

> When life is heavy and hard to take, go
> off by yourself. Enter the silence—bow in
> prayer. Don't ask questions: Wait for hope to
> appear. Don't run from trouble. Take it full-
> face. The "worst" is never the worst.
>
> —Lamentations 3:28–30 MSG

Before you know it, his justice will triumph;
the mere sound of his name will signal
hope, even among far-off unbelievers.

—Matthew 11:21 MSG

People of all nations, celebrate God! All colors
and races, give hearty praise! And Isaiah's word:
There's the root of our ancestor Jesse, breaking
through the earth and growing tree tall, tall
enough for everyone everywhere to see and take
hope! Oh! May the God of green hope fill you
up with joy, fill you up with peace, so that your
believing lives, filled with the life-giving energy
of the Holy Spirit, will brim over with hope.

—Romans 15:12–13 MSG

The lines of purpose in your lives never
grow slack, tightly tied as they are to your
future in heaven, kept taut by hope.

—Colossians 1:5 MSG

We who have run for our very lives to God
have every reason to grab the promised
hope with both hands and never let go.

—Hebrews 6:18 MSG

At least there is hope for a tree: If it is cut down, it
will sprout again, and its new shoots will not fail.

—Job 14:7–9 NLT

And listen to this if you've only wished:

I saw God before me for all time. Nothing can shake
me; he's right by my side. I'm glad from the inside
out, ecstatic; I've pitched my tent in the land of hope.

—Acts 2:27–28 MSG

I believe the power of prayer cocoons us in safety as we individually or corporately petition God. I believe prayer is an energy field that repels the Enemy's darts from puncturing our faith, our passions, and even our dreams. It's one of the reasons I have dogs: I love walking around the house while talking to God, so if neighbors chance to see me dancing, singing, or just talking, they will think I'm playing with my pets.

I believe connection with our Father God and our best Friend, Jesus, should be the most natural, commonplace, normal thing we do.

So I asked the Lord to give me more opportunities to live out of my hope. The realness of hope, not just a wish.

Then a conversation happened at work, propelling me into one of the most normal adventures of my life.

I stood behind the cash register at work at a Christian bookstore. On a counter behind me, we'd displayed the book *Heaven Is for Real*, marked on sale. One day a tiny lady probably my age (young!) came through the line. I, as per protocol, asked, "Would you be interested in purchasing *Heaven Is for Real* for five dollars today?"

She looked up at me and smiled. "No, thank you." There was a slight pause, and then she said, "I know heaven is real."

What I'd learned earlier in the week was forefront in my mind. "Yes, ma'am. Me too."

She looked me square in the eyes. "I'm going to see it very soon."

Every energy synapse in my body began firing at warp speed. The air around crackled with electric, spiritual activity. I wanted to take my shoes off. My focus shifted immediately from what I thought was an unusual experience to a confident expectation of the genuinely natural. "Really? How can you be sure?"

She spoke quietly, as though she didn't want to cause anyone in hearing distance to be uncomfortable. "I have esophageal cancer. I have very little time left. I am moving into hospice next week."

I chose—surely prompted by the Holy Spirit—to live that moment in the secure assurance of hope. "Wow, you know what? I have a friend who died just a couple of months ago from that same thing. He's home now. His wife, one of my dear college friends, died several years ago too. I love knowing they are together now. And I love knowing I will see them again. When you get home, would you find Chris and Vicky Dell and tell them I said hey and can't wait to see them?"

She looked up at me, and tears filled her eyes. The reality of her bright future filled with a secure, real, substantial, tangible hope suddenly crystallized for her. She wasn't scared. She didn't have to be. She suddenly realized there was and always would be work for her to do. She was important.

I asked her if I could pray with her. She nodded. Walking her to the end of the counter, I took her hand. I thanked the Lord for the opportunity he'd given me to meet that precious lady I knew I would see again. I thanked him that his promises are true, and I thanked him for the hope of heaven.

When I finished, she looked up at me and said, "Chris and Vicky Dell, right?"

"Yes, ma'am. Chris and Vicky Dell."

"I will find them."

I watched as she walked out the doors into the sunlight.

The vacuum—the feeling that nothing else in the world was really real and that nothing was more significant than that single moment—slowly evaporated. But the sweet aroma of what it feels like to be in a position of real normalcy and the standard of how I should live my life overwhelmed me.

Suddenly, the curtain between the natural and what I always felt was the supernatural was far less defined. I felt as though that little lady's transformed body would soon merely walk around the corner to a cool, familiar restaurant where she'd not yet been. And I knew my friends would be there.

I was sure that when she got there, she'd find my buddies and say hey for me. I imagined the Master Chef preparing a fantastic meal at that cool little restaurant. I hear the Master Chef preparing the meal is impressive, far beyond five stars, since he is the One, after all, who created the entire star system.

I am confident I will see that precious lady again. That's what is normal. That's where I have pitched my tent. That is my hope.

Hope is feeling the grass of heaven beneath my earthbound feet.

CONVERSATION STARTERS
FROM JERROD PIKER

Jerrod is my scary-movie partner. We wear that bottomless bucket of popcorn out. Jerrod is the worshipper everyone wants to emulate. We all move directly into the throne room when he sings. I love my buddy Jerrod. He's married to Bethany. She's so pretty.

1. Think about a time when you hoped to receive a particular gift for Christmas or your birthday. What did it feel like while you were waiting for that day? If you ended up receiving that special gift, what went through your mind as you opened it? Now think about how much greater those emotions will be when you receive your heavenly gift of eternal life with the Father!

2. Hebrews 11:1 describes faith as "the substance of things hoped for." So faith is essentially putting wheels on hope and letting it take you somewhere. Can you think of a time when you knew for sure something you hoped for was going to happen, and it did? What made you so sure it would happen? How did that affect your faith?

3. Have you ever hoped for something so desperately that you could hardly focus on anything else? What if we could be that dedicated to the hope we have in Jesus? What if you asked God to give you that kind of desperation for him?

ShiRLeY TeMPLe and YeRtLe the TuRtLe

ALL MY LIFE, I've worked hard to understand attributes of God. I could sit here for hours and pour out a list of virtues and features of his character, each one colored slightly differently and with contrasting significance for us based on our personal experience with his infinitely deep, eternal love.

However, as hard as I look, I have never seen listed as one of his attributes the word *arrogant*. I know that he is a just God and a jealous God and that he is perfect, and I know that he knows that. Because, well, he just is. I believe it. I love that about him. I love that he can be perfect and still love someone like me.

But if he knows it, I know it, and I know he knows it, why in the world would he feel the need to create angelic beings who fly around him day and night whose primary duty is to forever proclaim, "Holy, holy, holy is the Lord God Almighty. The earth is filled with his glory"?

The closest I've ever come to deserving those phrases is having a Yes Man doll. When I simply pull a string, the goofy-looking doll tells me how great I am, saying, "I couldn't agree with you more completely," "Oh yeah! I'm behind you all the way," "I'm sure whatever you're thinking is correct," "Say, I wish I'd thought of that," and "What more can I say? When you're right, you're right."

Seraphim literally means "burning ones." Seraphim, whose name could also have derived from "ones of love," had six functional wings, according to Isaiah 6. They used two to fly all around and above the Lord, two to cover their feet, and two to cover their eyes, so they don't even get to see how amazing and perfect he is. All they can do is fly close enough to experience him—to feel him. More than likely, just like Moses, they couldn't bear seeing the face of the Creator of the universe without becoming charred Cheez-Its in a millisecond.

But they felt the same impossible energy that infused dead cells at an atomic level and resurrected the beloved Son of God. They were there when that same impossible energy brought back to life my own perishing heart. "Holy, holy, holy is the Lord God Almighty."

In Hebrew, using a word twice showed the importance of a person or object (e.g., "Verily, verily," "Moses, Moses," "Saul, Saul"). Definitely an attention-getter.

A word used three times meant off-the-chart perfection. So the seraphim, "the ones of love," are proclaiming God as totally and utterly perfect.

Bringing that down to a more human level, I have always thought Jesus asked Peter three times if Peter loved him to match the three times Peter denied Jesus. That might be partly true. But is it also possible Jesus used that moment to show Peter he would make something perfect out of Peter's failure? The third time Jesus asked broke Peter, who replied, "You know all things. You know that I love you." Could Jesus, in that perfect moment, have revealed this undeserved, unconditional love to Peter, and Peter finally believed it?

In my human mind, the whole seraphim thing sounded like a dull job at first—saying the same thing over and over throughout all eternity. I kept hoping, for the seraphim's sake, they at least had shifts they changed out every twelve hours or so. Or they could at least say, "Hey, can you please take over for a while? I've got to get some caffeine."

But then I read 1 Peter 5:7 (TLB): "Let him have all your worries and cares, for he is always thinking about you and watching everything that concerns you." Love in action. And the only response is to scream from the rooftops how stunning God is. If God is always thinking about me and watching everything that concerns me, he would be, by logic, doing the same thing for everyone. That would mean the seraphim are experiencing God's immediate love for each and every one of us each and every time they fly around his head.

In other words, they aren't saying, "Holy, holy, holy is the Lord," because it's just their job; they are reacting to a new facet of his love for all his children. They are so overcome by the sheer weight of his unfailing love for us and all he created that they have no other outlet than to scream out how perfectly magnificent he is. They have, as we do when we experience his bloodred grace, no one earthly word to express how blameless, faultless, and absolute his love is for us. So we along with the seraphim can only cry out, "Holy, holy, holy is the Lord God Almighty. The whole earth is filled with his glory."

The burning ones of heaven are constantly reminded of how the Lord puts love into action. He doesn't just make promises; he fulfills them.

If you pass me on the 67/167, sometimes you might see me and think I'm talking to myself. But what I'm really doing is joining with the angels in proclaiming how perfect the love of my Father is: "Holy, holy, holy is the Lord God Almighty."

First John 3:18–20 (MSG) paints a picture of how real love should look: "My dear children, let's not just talk about love; let's practice real love ... It's also the way to shut down debilitating self-criticism, even when there is something to it. For God is greater than our worried hearts and knows more about us than we do ourselves."

One day, at my former job, working register number one, I glanced up to see a long line of customers. Standing beside the lady next in line at the counter, I noticed a little girl who was maybe six years old. The child was a miniature Shirley Temple with brown hair. She had the curls and rosy cheeks. I waited for her to break into "On the *Good Ship Lollipop*." As I looked at her, though, I noticed that she stood very still and seemed to be fighting back tears. In one hand, she held a small book, *Yertle the Turtle*, and in the other, she held a pen that read, "Teachers are the heart of learning."

I assumed she belonged with the lady I was checking out. But when I finished with her, the lady left, and the little one walked to the center of the counter.

There were probably four people waiting in line behind her and a few more over at the imprinting station, all within earshot. I looked down at the precious little girl. Our eyes met as she looked up and laid the two items on the counter. She said something to me so softly I couldn't understand her. I looked at the next lady in line, hoping she was the child's mom. She shrugged and mouthed, "I don't know."

So I said, "I'm sorry, sweetie. What did you say?"

I leaned down closer so I could hear her. Her chin quivered as she whispered, "I wanted these. But I took them without paying for them."

I knew exactly what was going on. I really hoped all those in line would understand my taking a little extra time. I wanted us on a level playing field. I walked around the counter and got on my knees so we were eye to eye. I feigned extreme seriousness, furrowing my brow, and said, "Well, little one, how do you feel about it?"

"Bad."

"Are you sorry for taking those things without paying for them?"

The tiny head crowned with curls nodded. "Yes, sir."

"Are you ever going to do that again?"

Her voice was as broken as her heart. "No, sir."

"Well, I'll tell you what. I've done some pretty silly things in my life I sure wish I hadn't done. But you know what? I know Jesus forgave me for doing those dumb things. And I know he forgives you. So I forgive you too. I forgive you, little friend. Thank you for bringing these things back and being honest. That was the best thing you could have done. You're a very, very good girl."

She didn't seem convinced as she turned to leave. She got about four steps away from me, when I said, "Hey." She turned back. "Can I have a hug?"

There they were—the Shirley Temple dimples. She ran to me and buried her little head in my shoulder. As I held her close, I could feel her sobs and her tears hitting my neck.

I looked up to see a tall man, Dad, at the end of the counter with tears in his eyes and his lower lip quivering. He smiled and gave me a thumbs-up. I gently turned her around, facing her dad. As she walked away, he said, "Okay, come on. Let's go home."

Although I did the best I could at verbally conveying how much, despite her actions, God truly cared for her and loved her, the real breakthrough didn't occur until I put those words of love into action. The words may or may not have been adequate by themselves. But I hope she will remember the feeling of forgiveness and love from the hug, the action. There's something about the physical action of a hug that mere words just can't convey.

I stood up and turned to see about ten people wiping their eyes. We all stood there for a few minutes and discussed which Maxwell House Christmas commercial made us cry hardest.

When I got home and had time to process, I thought about the seraphim, ones of love, flying around God. We all shouted together, "Holy, holy, holy is the Lord God Almighty! The whole earth is full of his glory!"

CONVERSATION STARTERS
FROM CHERYL RICHARDS

When their kids were growing up, every night during suppertime, Cheryl would have a question prepared for her family to discuss. She compiled two hundred of the questions into a book called *Table Talk*. I love icebreaker games, and this book is divinely inspired. I've used it many times at parties and community groups. It is, unfortunately, out of print right now. I'm thinking this little affirmation will encourage Cheryl to get a few more printed. Cheryl is probably the single most organized human I've ever known. If she ever saw the inside of my house, she'd most likely have to be sedated and possibly institutionalized. But she's really pretty.

1. Our words simply cannot do justice to describe our Holy God. Still, God possesses many attributes that help us understand who he really is. Name and discuss some attributes of God.

2. List some ways we can practice real love. Can you share a personal example of love in action?

3. What is the importance of the holiness of God?

CONVERSATION STARTERS
FROM DAVID RICHARDS

David stays in line only because he's married to Cheryl. Cheryl is really pretty. David is one of the most approachable people I know. His love and care for others is a deep well. He lives his faith out in real time. His absolute trust in God is what draws others to chase after that same depth of faith. He teaches well. He leads well. I want to be like David when I grow up.

1. Have you ever wondered why God emphasized that we should worship him continually?

2. Does God really know what you're going through today?

3. We've all made many mistakes; does God really forgive all of them?

Spit and Bingo

PROVERBS 14:4 (NIV) says, "Where there are no oxen, the manger is empty, but from the strength of an ox come abundant harvests." Now, I'm not calling my friends oxen, although I could stand to lose a few pounds. This scripture jumped out at me as I wrote this essay.

Yesterday was a perfect day. A few childhood friends decided to get together to celebrate our sixtieth year of life. For at least forty-five of those years, we have known where we all were and kept up with each other's lives.

I moved back to Arkansas in 1994, and we have made it a point to be together as often as possible. I live in Little Rock and struggle with chronic fatigue, which forces me to slow down and rest—totally against my nature. Judy, who is retired, lives in Conway, where she led the band for thirty years. She has cataracts, which means that after surgery, she will never have to wear glasses again. Sherry works for the literacy program in Searcy and also facilitates adoptions for an agency there. Billy lives in Clarksville and is in the transport industry. Billy has no major maladies, as he hasn't turned sixty yet. We shall wait. We shall wait.

We ate cheeseburgers at Market Cafe in Bald Knob and recounted ancient tales of growing up in Searcy. All topics were, as always, open for discussion, except one. In high school, we vowed we would never be like our parents, so our one and only concrete rule was to never discuss bowel movements. Ever!

Because a few—not all but a few—of us grew up in excruciatingly dysfunctional homes, this group of friends was our safe place.

We were all in band together, so there were plenty of travel stories. In our junior year, we made a trip to Six Flags over Texas. Billy and I were in a long line for a roller coaster. We thought it would be hilarious to intentionally get into a heated, although completely fake, verbal argument. We also decided to have the disagreement in a foreign language. Neither of us speaks a foreign language. We held the surrounding group of complete strangers spellbound for about fifteen minutes as we spewed forth red-faced, nonsensical verbal assaults on each other.

Later in the day, we found ourselves in line for the Spindle Top, a big barrel of a ride in which people stand inside against a circular wall. The barrel starts spinning faster and faster. At some point, centrifugal force takes over. The floor drops out from under you, and you are plastered against the wall.

Bill told me he had ridden it before and knew a cool trick: "Work up a big mouthful of spit, and the moment the floor drops, let 'er fly. The wad of spit will shoot to the people on the opposite side of the barrel. They will be so concerned with the floor dropping out that they'll never know who did it."

As the door to the barrel closed, with probably thirty people against the circular wall, I began the job of collecting. I mean, this was going to be one epic spitball. As the barrel started to spin, my anticipation built. The dude straight across from me, probably twenty-five feet away, was going to be very surprised.

The floor dropped. I spit.

My face immediately metamorphosed into a slimy bowl of soup.

At first, I was so shocked I couldn't do anything but stare at the dude across from me and wonder how he could have been completely dry. Trying to raise my arms to wipe it all off was futile. The force caused me to slap my face rather than make the intended windshield-wiper action I intended.

There was nothing for it, in the end, but to weather it out for another forty-five seconds till the ride ended. I heard the people on either side of me emit a well-deserved gurgle of repulsion. "Ew!"

I glanced to my left and saw Bill, strategically positioned five people away from me, laughing hysterically and slapping himself in the face, vainly attempting to wipe tears from his eyes.

That's just one example of our shenanigans. Growing up in a small town, we learned how to be creative. I will save for later stories of the times Billy and I sneaked into the drive-in movie theater in someone's car trunk.

Years later, Billy, Judy, Sherry, and I could still laugh ourselves silly over that and many similar memories. Once we composed ourselves and finished our burgers, we decided to go to my mom's retirement village for a few minutes. Some of the friends she hadn't seen for forty-some years. What a blessing to watch her hug them and kiss them on the cheek. I took a heart picture. It was a joy to watch them all get caught up and spend time with one another.

I thought about heaven and all my friends and family who were already there. I knew that was a taste of what heaven would be like. To sit in one another's homes and get caught up on our lives and how we plan to spend the next few millennia hanging with each other and Jesus.

Closing our visit, Mom informed us it was time for her to go to bingo. We said our goodbyes, and she left, heading toward the cafeteria.

But we had one more stop to make. Another friend lived in the same retirement village as Mom: Fayetta Murray, our junior high English teacher.

We traipsed up to the third floor and got lost. We wandered through wings A through C and walked our cheeseburgers off while trying to find wing D.

We finally stood in front of her door. I knocked and heard her singsong voice: "Come in." I opened the door and saw Miss Fayetta propped up on her bed, reading. She looked up, laid her book in her lap, and smiled. "Tim Holder? In the flesh?"

I said, "Okay, we are not going to invade you. But I have a surprise for you."

She hopped up while I turned around and ushered everyone into the small living room. Mrs. Murray looked at them and said, "Bill Townsend. What a sweet face. Judy Lance and Sherry Treat." Of course, Judy and Sherry have different last names now.

I said, "We all got together to celebrate our sixtieth birthdays."

Mrs. Murray said, "Well, guess what? Yesterday I turned ninety-two."

Sherry smiled. "I turned sixty yesterday."

We sat down to talk for a bit. Mrs. Murray hadn't seen Billy, Judy, or Sherry in probably forty-five years. We were amazed she remembered that Billy had lived across from the football stadium. She then proceeded to remind Judy that her dad had worked for AP&L. We sat for a good while and told stories and laughed.

When it was time to leave, I looked across the room and saw a precious lady who I knew loved the Lord. I smiled and said, "Mrs. Murray, we're here because you made a difference in so many others' lives. We want you to know that you are important."

She smiled her humble, sweet smile and simply said, "Thank you."

I really wanted to see Mrs. Murray stand up and glide through the room while wistfully waving her arms up and down like a butterfly the way she used to do down the halls of our junior high school.

We took a group picture; held her sweet, brittle, fragile hands in ours for a few precious seconds; and left.

Realizing we'd forgotten to get a picture with Mom, we went to the cafeteria to find her. Apparently, bingo time in a retirement village is serious business. When we walked in, everyone's face was buried in a bingo card. I think I may have seen sweat on a couple of furrowed brows, even the ones with strikingly blue hair. Some used checkers chips as markers. Others used glistening red jewels as their markers, the kind of glass you find in the bottom of vases filled with plastic flowers.

We attempted to be quiet as we looked through a crowded room for Mom. She was in the exact center. I stealthily took the lead as the four of us traversed the chairs to get to her. More and more heads looked up to see the unwelcome intrusion. By then, I'd lost my nerve and dreaded the steps still needed to reach Mom. I reckon I would've felt the same if I had been at the White House and accidentally stumbled into the Situation Room during the Cuban missile crisis.

Two college-aged girls calling out the numbers picked out of a rolling cage looked at us with embarrassingly fake and condescending smiles. Not to be deterred, I knelt down next to Mom and said, "Sorry. We forgot to get a picture."

The guy at the next table yelled, "Bingo!" Mom shoved her card away. I thought she was mad. And she was—but not at the intrusion. She was mad because she'd lost. The guy at the next table began calling out his winning numbers, as though someone might have thought he'd lie just to win a pill separator or the ever-popular chip clip.

Mom grabbed my hand and pulled me down close. Bill, Sherry, and Judy all jumped in, and we got the picture. Just to be rebellious, the lady next to Mom said, "Hey, let me take one for ya." She snapped the photo, looked at it, puckered her lips, and said, "Not bad. Except"—she pointed to Sherry—"I chopped her head off."

Memories like that are what binds friendships. After seeing Mom and Mrs. Murray, we went back to Sherry's house and spent a little more time processing the day.

We haven't fully figured out what was so special about our group. Was it generational? Was it being in band together? Was it a small-town dynamic? Was it a combination of some or all of those things? One thing we do know for sure: it's definitely a God thing.

We are not oxen, but these friends are part of my herd. We know that the memories we build together today and the memories we've spent a lifetime building will never be lost. I'm thankful for technology and the terrific pictures I can take with my iPhone, but the most important, substantial pictures I take are heart pictures. I took plenty of those that day.

C. S. Lewis said in *The Four Loves*, "A friendship is born when one man says to another, 'What! You too? I thought I was the only one.'"

The four of us friends, and a few others who couldn't make it for our outing, are different in many ways. Somehow, when we were just kids, subconsciously on our parts but certainly not God's, we chose to look for similarities instead of differences. It brings home to me the truth that God never meant for us to travel this journey alone. He was deliberate in telling us that two are better than one.

Lewis also said,

In friendship, we think we have chosen our peers. In reality a few years' difference in the dates of our births, a few more miles between certain houses, the choice of one university instead of another, the accident of a topic being raised or not raised at a first meeting—any of these chances might have kept us apart. But, for a Christian, there are, strictly speaking, no chances. A secret master of ceremonies has been at work. Christ, who said to the disciples, "Ye have not chosen me, but I have chosen you," can truly say to every group of Christian friends, "Ye have not chosen one another but I have chosen you for one another." The friendship is not a reward for our discrimination and good taste in finding one another out. It is the instrument by which God reveals to each of us the beauties of others.

Think of your friends. Be deliberate. If you haven't already, start taking heart pictures, whether at the Spindle Top, a retired teacher's home, or a mother's bingo game. Those pictures are eternal.

By the way, later that day, I got a text from Mom: "Yay! Y'all brought me luck. I bingoed right after y'all left. Big ole package of bite-sized pretzels."

CONVERSATION STARTERS
FROM JANE HURLEY

I sit next to Jane every Sunday morning in Creative Living. Well, I sit in a chair close by. She sits behind the audiovisual setup, hoping no one has messed with the system and praying the mics have batteries. She takes it all in stride and handles each distraction one at a time. I watch and learn how to have a patient heart. Jane has the sweetest smile.

1. Suppose you and some friends from high school were playing bingo. List a few prizes that would be fun or funny to hand out (e.g., an eight-track tape of Earth, Wind, and Fire).

2. Tell a story about a teacher you had, funny, frustrating, or endearing.

3. Imagine starting a company where you could only hire your high school friends. What type of business would it be? (No limits.) Who would be in what roles?

4. Tell about a significant, spiritually defining experience, decision, or realization from your early years.

Jessie and Prissy

I DON'T GET to see my friend Jessie often, but she occasionally sends me a note. The following is an email from Jessie:

> Hey there, Tim! You are someone who has always inspired me with your relationship with God. I can admit that I yearn for that. As my life gets more chaotic, I feel doubt creeping into my heart. Not doubt that God exists, but doubt that he is involved in our everyday life. Doubt that he has a master plan for me. I seem to feel there is a person within me that God wants me to be, and the choices I make can help lead me to be that person.

> We were given free will so we could choose God and choose to be that person he wants us to be.

> Tim, I end up asking a lot of questions that I could never get answers to. Questions of his motives. Questions that have probably been asked since the beginning. Is there any advice you could provide to help me find peace with this doubt? I still feel

God's profound love within me. But sometimes I get so down on myself I cannot find it. Any prayers or advice you could give would be most appreciated.

My reply was as follows:

Well, first of all, let me tell you that I think about you and how we used to sit down in the catacombs of Doubletree Veterinary Clinic. I remember how I loved taking care of the pooches with you, even if our most common chore was cleaning kennels.

Never does a holiday go by when I don't think of the recipe you gave me as I prepare pumpkin-swirl cheesecake. Still a family tradition.

But believe it or not, my best memory of you is Prissy. Remember her? The little five-year-old Boston terrier we rescued who had been horribly abused and neglected. She had sustained a broken leg that Dr. Peck tried valiantly to mend. We never could get it to heal. Finally, we were forced to amputate. I wanted to change her name to Tripod. But we still called her Prissy.

I remember her eyes and nose with an angry infection, and we cleaned her up and put meds in those wounds several times a day.

I took her home, basically because I held her pretty much the whole time I was at work, carrying that precious girl everywhere. For two years, I was privileged to love on her, feed her, and let her curl up with me at night. She finally knew she was safe. I had an old sweater that she claimed and carried with her like Linus's blanket.

And I remember the day, after all that work and love, when I found a bump on her head. After x-rays, we learned she would not be with us much longer because of bone cancer. She made it another six months or so. I came home one night to find her gone, curled up on my old sweater.

I remember carrying her to the clinic the next morning, tears flowing, and laying her on the exam table, wrapped in that silly old sweater she loved so much.

Heartbroken, I questioned why God would allow her to endure so much suffering only to die just when she knew she was loved and safe and could feel secure enough to trust. She was nothing but a pile of love.

My most vivid memory of that day is walking downstairs to take care of other dogs that were boarding with us. You were already there, and when I told you Prissy was gone, you wrapped your arms around me and whispered, "No one could have loved Prissy the way you did."

Jessie, that was all I needed to move through the pain of losing that sweet dog.

When I read your note yesterday, of course I remembered that tender moment. Honestly, after all these years, I still don't think of it without getting misty-eyed.

I don't know that I have a one-size-fits-all answer to the question of doubt. We all have differing life experiences and come at and move toward our relationship with God from so many distinct and divergent train tracks. I can tell you how I think it works for me, though. Maybe it will help some.

I have always believed in God. Always. There's never been a doubt in my mind that he is the Creator of the universe, that he did everything he said he did, that Jesus is his Son and did everything he said he did, that he is all-powerful, that he is watching me and has a specific unique plan for me, and that he loves me.

But possibly, probably because I correlated my relationship with my heavenly Father with that of my earthly father, I was programmed not to trust God.

That was the big subconscious question: Is he reliable? Is he honest? If he is, why do I not feel like he's active in my life? I felt guilt for my futile attempt to find fault with him because I couldn't trust his motives. My head knew that he was never too good to be true. He is absolutely good and true.

My strongest desire was that I wanted my heart to follow. I finally figured out that I was waiting for him to prove he is trustworthy, when in fact, everything about life screams it.

I decided that if he is trustworthy, I needed to stop trying to understand his intentions on my own. Stop trying to control my definition of who he is supposed to be. Stop trying to create him in my image. I needed him to know that I will believe and practice trust, even when it seems counter to everything I think I need or want. It's not always a feel-good moment, since many of those are, at best, superficial satisfaction.

Jessie, it's a habit. I wake up every day and tell him that I will choose to trust him today. I purposefully memorize Bible verses that call for trust. And let me tell you, having a scripture or two close by has made an extraordinary difference. A couple of my favorites. Joshua 1:9 (NIV) says, "Have I not commanded you? Be strong and courageous. Do not be afraid; do not be discouraged, for the Lord your God will be with you wherever you go." What I love about this verse is that he doesn't ask or plead with us not to be afraid. He commands it. It's not a request; it's a proclamation, an imperative that demands trust. And trust is not something that comes naturally to us in a culture that breeds mistrust.

Again, it's a habit. And while God builds trust, I spend an abundance of time asking for patience while he perfects it in me. I find myself affirming my belief in his absolute good motives for my life on a daily basis. I trust his plan because I trust his love. I trust his love because I choose to give up control of my desires and what I think I need, even my dreams. Nothing in our society would teach us that this makes sense or is even appropriate.

Everything about my relationship is based on the idea that God is, in fact, the only trustworthy being in all of existence. Every person, every government, every idea, and even every religion will, in some way, disappoint. Only belief in the One dependable, honest, powerful God is worthy of our trust.

I read a book a long time ago with a chapter titled "The Adequacy of God." Again, our culture would see the word *adequacy* and define it as "just okay" or "barely up to par." But when I looked it up, I realized my definition of God needed to be more adequate: "as much or as good for some requirement or purpose; fully sufficient, suitable, or fit." For me, my trust in him, the habit of trusting him, is adequate. He is entirely sufficient. His trustworthiness is appropriate, as is his desire to be found trustworthy.

I find ways every day to tell him that I will choose to give up my control and trust him. When I drive to work, I tell him, "Today I will trust you." When I have to make hard decisions, I seek out community and, yes, trust, because I know where and from whom they build their confidence. Every time I tithe, I pray, "I trust you." When I catch myself trying to control my dreams and wants, I sit back, take a deep breath, and say, "I'm sorry. You take control. I trust you."

I wish I could tell you I have this down to a fine art. But I fall. And then I get up and give control back to him again. And the amazing thing I find is that the reason I desire to trust him more is because I desire a relationship with him more.

You don't develop trust with God and come out unscathed. I can't take time to think about how I feel or about my circumstances. I have to focus on his character, his motives. I don't ignore my pain or confusion. I just remember that he is adequate. He fits my environment. In that moment and in that experience, he is good. And it's easier to give him control because I can give him the glory. And I find great joy in that.

Jessie, his motives for you are not just loving and right and wise. They are pure. Here is another of my favorite verses: "What then shall we say to these things? If God is for us, who can be against us? He who did not spare His own Son but gave Him up for us all, how will He not also with Him, graciously give us all things? Who shall bring any charge against God's elect? It is God who justifies. Who is to condemn? Christ Jesus is the one who died—more than that, who was raised—who is at the right hand of God, who indeed is interceding for us. Who shall separate us from the love of Christ? Shall tribulation, or distress, or persecution, or famine, or nakedness, or danger, or sword? … No, in all these things, we are more than conquers through Him who loved us" (Romans 8:31–37 NKJV).

As hard as it may seem to us in the midst of the struggle, everything God does is wise and loving.

God is for you, Jessie. Don't attempt to trust him because it's the right thing to do. Trust him because he's God. Trust him because he loves you. Don't trust him expecting to understand his plan. Just believe that he has one. Trust that he is working it out with your best interest foremost in his mind. And believe that more often than not, that plan will be unveiled in a mind-blowing, ridiculously breathtaking, astonishing, anfractuous direction that you never expected. You will delight in the surprise of seeing your dreams and needs unfold in ways you couldn't have thought of on your own. You will breathe deep and nod with the satisfaction of knowing it was perfect for you. It's the only way it could happen to instill a gentle trust that leads to a more profound love and relationship with him.

He's good. He's so good. He longs for you to know it and fully live it. One last verse, and I'll leave you alone. This is one of my top-five verses. It's Zephaniah 3:17 (NIV): "The LORD your

God is with you, the mighty warrior who saves. He will take great delight in you, in His love He will no longer rebuke you, but will rejoice over you with singing."

You can trust him because he takes great delight in you. He doesn't yell at you. He believes in you. He is intimately interested in you and has great plans for you, even if you don't easily see them now.

You said there is a person in you that you think God wants you to be, and your choices will help determine who that person is supposed to be. Jessie, you are already that person. He used his vast imagination to make you unique from any other human who has ever lived. The only thing you need to do is—and here's the simple answer— live your life in relationship with him. It's similar to what you said to me a long time ago. No one could have loved you like he does.

Practice trust.

Practice trust, and listen for the song. He has one for you, you know. Your very own song sung by the One who breathes out stars into his ever-expanding universe.

I have no authoritative reference, but I'm relatively certain my tune is a hybrid of Dan Fogelberg; Donna Summer; and Earth, Wind, and Fire, with just a soupçon of Barry Manilow.

Jessie, that same God is singing your very own song over you right now. When that truth becomes more than a fleeting idea, you will walk without shame or fear, doubt or mistrust. Your days will be cool, God will be your friend, and you will experience a bit of heaven right here on earth.

The most precious discovery? It was never about you. It was all for his glory. He is rejoicing over you. If that alone is not worthy of our trust, I don't know what is.

Love you,

Tim

CONVERSATION STARTERS FROM RYK TATUM (RYKTATUM.BLOGSPOT.COM)

My twin brother from another mother, Ryk analyzes, dissects, and reconstructs thoughts into cohesive design and blueprints. Like me, he makes a lot of bullet points to get to a concrete plan. He's original and genuine and loves his wife, Alanna; his kids; and Jesus. If you ever meet Ryk, you will not leave without hearing, "I love you. And there's nothing you can do about it." Ryk is a good man.

1. Oftentimes, we have grandiose ideas of what our lives look like when God is working in our lives. What unrealistic visualizations do you have or have you had of God's work in your life? Have you learned to see him move in simple things? If so, how?

2. Praying for patience can be risky business. How do you exercise patience with God while waiting for God to produce patience in you?

3. Sometimes, as our stories unfold, we recognize that certain experiences we had were not about us but about bringing glory to God. Who in your life faces struggles similar to those you face but has less faith? How can you minister to them? How can ministering to them lead you in ministering to yourself?

Fearfully

PSALM 139:14 (MSG) says, "Oh yes, you shaped me first inside, then out; you formed me in my mother's womb. I thank you, High God—you're breathtaking! Body and soul, I am marvelously made!"

Other versions translate this verse as "I praise you for I am fearfully and wonderfully made. Your works are wonderful, I know that full well."

When I first read Psalm 139:14, I, of course, thought it great that I was "wonderfully" made, and it seems I spent all my time, when thinking about this verse, landing squarely on the phrase "wonderfully made."

If people are going through a tough time and I feel it's my responsibility to make them feel better—which, by the way, isn't usually healthy—this verse is a go-to. If I can help them, even for a moment, recognize that they are "wonderfully made," I've done a good thing.

They are incredible. The Lord put them together exactly the way he wanted them to be. I can go through a litany of phrases with anyone who feels self-image-shamed, filled with guilt over past mistakes, or fearful that the Lord or people have forgotten them. I can remind them, as I do myself, that we are "wonderfully made." That really is a good, sustainable concept. But I think it leaves out the single most pivotal point of the verse.

When I tell people they are "wonderfully made," if I leave that as a stand-alone thought, it could possibly lead to selfishness or a sense of entitlement, as if somehow we are owed some gift or merit awards because the Lord thinks we are off da hizzle.

The truth is, he does think we are wonderful. But why does he believe this? First and foremost, he showed us how wonderful we are by the sacrifice of Jesus on the cross.

And even that love leads to the most critical part of verse fourteen. There's a reason David began the verse with the word *fearfully*. He wanted us to understand that although we are wonderful, the goal was that the Lord God, the Creator of the entire universe, reverently and with the highest expectation and design put us together molecule by molecule, cell by cell, atom by atom.

The Hebrew meaning for *fearfully* in this verse means "reverential awe" or "worshipful respect." We were created by the Lord reverently and in worshipful awe. Not that we are worthy of worship. But we were created in wonder by the One who is worthy of worship. There is no assembly line. There are no prefab molds. There was only God; nothingness; and, most surprising, his imagination. A clean slate.

There was an intense, holy time when God fussed over you and me. A fervent anticipation of who he planned for us to be. Why did he give each person on this planet such deferential treatment? Because he is faithful and solemnly serious to see his plans fulfilled.

Ephesians 5:11–20 (MSG) says,

> Don't waste your time on useless work, mere busywork, the barren pursuits of darkness. Expose these things for the sham they are. It's a scandal

when people waste their lives on things they must do in the darkness where no one will see. Rip the cover off those frauds and see how attractive they look in the light of Christ ... Don't live carelessly, unthinkingly. Make sure you understand what the Master wants ... Drink the Spirit of God, huge droughts of him ... Sing songs from your heart to Christ. Sing praises over everything, any excuse for a song to God the Father in the name of our Master, Jesus Christ.

Why did God take on the self-imposed assignment of creating you? For his glory. God wants the world to see through you that he is good in every circumstance. He is reliable. He is faithful. He is unchanging in his mercy, wisdom, and holiness. He is not willing to waver in his devotion and interest in even the minutest aspects of your life.

Realize the exactness of who you are in him. Recognize and fully accept the bottomless implications of why the One who holds the universe in place would take the time to fuss over creating you. Those truths crystallize every application of every thought, every display of compassion, every song, every learned eccentricity, every choice, every time you think you chose intuition, the guiding of his Spirit, every judgment you hold captive, every meal you make, and every soul you lead to Jesus.

First Corinthians 12:12–31 (MSG) says,

You can easily enough see how this kind of thing works by looking no further than your own body. Your body has many parts—limbs, organs, cells—but no matter how many parts you can name, you're still one body. It's exactly the same with Christ. By means of his one Spirit, we all said good-bye to our partial and piecemeal lives. We each used to independently call our own shots, but then we entered into a large and integrated life in which he has the final say in everything ... Each of us is now a part of his resurrection body, refreshed and sustained at one fountain—his Spirit—where we all come to drink. I want you to think about how all this makes you more significant, not less ... But I also want you to think about how this keeps your significance from getting blown up into self-importance. For no matter how significant you are, it is only because of what you are a part of ... The way God designed our bodies is a model for understanding our lives together as a church: every part dependent on every other part ... You are Christ's body—that's who you are! You must never forget this. Only as you accept your part of that body does your "part" mean anything.

There is no one else in this room right now but you. So you can't say, "That's true for everyone here but me. It makes sense for them, not me." You are the only one here. I believe God is saying the following to you and to me:

I made you. I made you reverently. I thought about you. There's not a single soul on this planet who can do what I've made you to do. No one can—only you. I fearfully made you. So stop being afraid. You no longer have permission to think that you are a less important part of the body I specifically, carefully, and with great hope and dogged determination designed.

Seek wisdom from those who've been at it longer. Learn to be confident, adventurous, daring, courageous and unflinching with your faith, intrepid, and fearless and wholesome with your words.

Before I created the world, I chose you. And because of my Son, no matter what you think of yourself, I choose you to be holy and without fault before him. And I am calling you to travel together with the rest of the body. Stay together. I have given you gifts that no one else in the history of time can fulfill. Your gifts. Moses wouldn't be able to fulfill the plans I have for you. Not Abraham or Paul or any of the apostles. Not Lydia, Ruth, or Esther. My plans for you are unique in all the world.

Don't go along with the crowd. And don't believe their weak expectations of me or my love and my heart for your success. Trust me. I'm worth it. And above all, stick together. That's how the body will work. I knew you before "In the beginning" was written. And rest assured of this: I'll be with you day after day after day, right up to the end of the world.

CONVERSATION STARTERS
FROM BYRON SCHEIDER

Byron opens our Creative Living class every Sunday with prayer. I'm not talking about canned, prepared, cliché prayer. I'm talking about storming-the-gates-of-heaven, soul-and-body-healing prayer. I love him. Byron is healed. I love Sue, Byron's wife, as well. She's awesome. And she's pretty.

1. What would happen if you were to discover how unique you really are?

2. If you let yourself be aware of the awesome gifts God gave you, what fears awake in your heart about those gifts and your use of them?

3. Right now, how do you limit yourself in growing the gifts God has given you?

Fayetta

PSALM 139:13–16 (NIV) reads,

> For you created my inmost being; you knit me
> together in my mother's womb. I praise you
> because I am fearfully and wonderfully made;
> your works are wonderful, I know that full well.
> My frame was not hidden from you when I was
> made in the secret place, when I was woven
> together in the depths of the earth. Your eyes
> saw my unformed body; all the days ordained for
> me were written in your book before one of them
> came to be.

This has become one of the most comforting verses for my life. I realize I have, perhaps like many others, attempted to circumvent God's plan by inserting my own desires or, worse, misread how he wants to use the gifts he gave me to propel his kingdom forward.

I'm not sure my plans are important anyway. It's not that I don't think we should plan for our future. Of course we should. Should we dream big dreams? Of course we should. But we should pray for God's blessing that the aspirations we have coincide with his plans.

But more importantly, maybe my job is to simplify my life by being open to, recognizing, and responding to the next opportunity he puts in front of me to further his kingdom. Maybe that's always been his real plan.

My friend Greg Murtha called that "intentional living." Greg and I went years without speaking in person, but we stayed in contact with each other through social media. Greg went to heaven last year after a courageous battle with cancer. He went through more than seventy rounds of chemo. He posted almost daily about his journey, and his writings were perhaps some of the most compelling, God-honoring, joyous posts I've read. His focus didn't center on whether he would live or die. He believed our lives are an extension of heaven, and therefore, we should celebrate.

One of his last posts read,

> What were we celebrating? As I have shared before, one of the Murtha Family Values is to celebrate. We believe if you have something to celebrate, then you should do just that ... and you should do so today ... not tomorrow (we're not promised tomorrow). We also believe if you can go big with the celebration, then go big.

When Greg posted something, people responded with all the things you would think. Sweet and authentic words. Some were prayers. Some were sincere wishes for healing and health. I know they meant a lot to Greg.

I kept trying to think of original things to say when I read a post of Greg's. I wanted to say something that would make people stop and admire some pithy, catchy phrase I penned, which, thank

God, struck me as anything but authentic. My responses became less about my friend Greg and more self-serving.

So I began to respond to every post with nothing more than "I love you."

One day, when I was working at a package-shipping store, I was exhausted from staying up most of the night before with my pooch. Iggy had just endured emergency surgery from ingesting the stuffing from my comforter. I would have thought after one bite, he would've thought, *This doesn't taste nearly as much like cotton candy as I'd hoped*, and stopped eating. But apparently, he chose to make sure none of the other dogs got any of it. After that ordeal, all I wanted was to go home and get a good night's sleep.

All of a sudden, the front door of the store opened, and a guy walked in, talking on his phone and carrying a drop-off package. I heard him say, "Yeah, Greg. Hold on." He looked up at me and said, "Tim?" I didn't recognize him. "Greg, you're not going to believe this. I'm dropping off a return for Laura, and Tim Holder is working here." I clearly heard Greg scream through the phone. The guy in front of me said, "Tim, I'm Zach Murtha, Greg's brother."

Zach pressed the speaker button, and we were all yelling and catching up for a few minutes. Customers stared, and at the end of the conversation, Greg, as was Greg's style, said, "Tim, you are a great man."

I looked up to see Zach's eyes filled with tears, as were mine. I could barely speak as I said, "Greg Murtha, I love you."

The twists and turns, the anfractuousness of life, shouldn't surprise us. They happen every day, minute by minute. We either can be anxious about them and live in fear of what's around the next bend or we can recognize them for what God meant them to be: moments of pure affirmation that he is, in fact, in control. That specific moment was an opportunity for us to choose how we would respond before we were even born. It is not now, nor has it ever been about how much we can handle. It's about how we respond to every opportunity we are given to show his power and love.

A few years ago, I spent Thanksgiving Day with my precious mom and my brother-in-law and sister. We laughed a lot. We ate lunch with Mom at her retirement village, surrounded by quite a few people we had grown up around.

One of those lifelong friends was Fayetta Murray. She was ninety-one years old and as smart as a whip. She'd spent many years as an English and literature teacher at the junior high school I attended.

There have been a few teachers in my life whom I look back on and can emphatically say they made a significant impact on my life. Mrs. Murray is one of those teachers.

I was terrified when I moved to Searcy. But Mrs. Murray would smile her great big smile, and I wasn't afraid. She helped me know I wasn't weird or a nerd for loving books. She helped me trudge through and process *Great Expectations*. She marched our class three blocks to the Rialto Theater on the square in Searcy, catty-corner to the old courthouse, to watch *Romeo and Juliet*. I think of her when I pull out *Silas Marner* every few years to reread. She rode the bus with us to the high school to watch their theatrical production of *The Curious Savage*, in which her daughter, Peggy, had a notable character role. It was not uncommon to see Mrs. Murray floating through a crowded hallway lined with students and lockers with a sweet, serene smile on her face and a faraway gaze in her half-closed eyes, waving her bone-thin arms up and down as if she were a butterfly in flight.

One day in her literature class, she passed out the exams precisely and methodically, old wooden desk by old wooden desk. I'm assuming she could tell if someone was hiding cheat notes that she would be able to confiscate. One of the guys in class was wearing a necklace made entirely of bones. I don't remember if they were plastic or real bones, but they were definitely bones. Without missing a step, Mrs. Murray placed the test neatly on his desk, leaned down, and whispered, "Anyone we know?"

There was another day, however, when Mrs. Murray was hurt. On that particular day, Mrs. Murray was the duty teacher in the lunchroom. She made a decision to correct a student for behaving badly. That exchange infuriated the student, who began yelling horrible things toward Mrs. Murray. The insults hurled toward her were so painful that she ran from the lunchroom in tears.

It broke my heart. I sat down outside the band room and wrote a note to tell her that I was sorry she was hurt. I climbed the stairs to the second floor of the old school building, where we were strictly forbidden to go during lunchtime; sneaked into her classroom; and placed the note on her desk.

Honestly, I don't remember what I said in the note. I only remember that precious lady was wounded, and it wasn't right. I left the note on her desk and sneaked away.

In the years—decades—since then, there have been a few times when I was privileged enough to run into Mrs. Murray, even at the funeral of a classmate's mom, when she reminded me of that note.

I find it amazing that the smallest things, the slightest word of affirmation and comfort for a hurting heart, can make such an eternal impact. It's incredible that the anfractuosity of life—this catawampus, serpentine, winding, curving journey—can still give us moments of absolute clarity.

We often spend way too much time feeling guilty for all the hurtful things we've done or said, when in fact, there are moments when we get it right.

Today I'm thankful for this sweet, precious lady who took the time to invest in me. One of my many dreams for heaven is to sit with Fayetta Murray, C. S. Lewis, Greg Murtha, and Jesus and just hang for a while.

Psalm 136 (MSG) says,

> Thank God! He deserves your thanks.
> His love never quits.
> Thank the God of all gods,
> His love never quits.
> Thank the Lord of all lords,
> His love never quits.
> Thank the miracle-working God,
> His love never quits.
> The God whose skill formed the cosmos,
> His love never quits.
> The God who laid out earth on ocean foundations,
> His love never quits.
> The God who filled the skies with light,
> His love never quits.
> The sun to watch over the day,
> His love never quits.
> Moon and stars as guardians of the night,
> His love never quits.
> God remembered us when we were down,
> His love never quits.
> Rescued us from the trampling boot,
> His love never quits.
> Takes care of everyone in time of need.
> His love never quits.
> Thank God, who did it all!
> His love never quits!

I heard that Mrs. Murray, at the age of ninety-four, went home to see Jesus face-to-face. I love knowing she will be there to meet me when it's my turn.

Thank God for the opportunities and for the bends, curves, twists, and turns in this beautiful, anfractuous life that beckons us to respond to him and others. It's true. His love never quits.

You might write a note today that will be remembered forty-five years from now, making an eternal impact on a wounded friend. You might look at others, knowing nothing of their lives; speak a word of love and affirmation that will change the course of their journey; and not recognize the significance of that moment on this side of the veil.

Watch for the moments. They are there. Recognizing them and responding to them is our God-given job, right, and joyous privilege. In every exquisitely anfractuous moment of our lives, we are given another chance to say, "I love you."

CONVERSATION STARTERS
FROM BONNIE KEEN

She's so pretty. Bonnie is one of the first friends I met when I moved to Nashville. When I talk to Bonnie, she's focused and intent on listening—really hearing—what I want her to hear. I always feel like I'm the only person on the planet. What a gift that is. When I read one of her books, I feel the same, as if she wrote it just for me. I love when I see someone living out the clear vision, God's purpose and plan, for his or her life. Bonnie does that. The kingdom of God benefits because of her gifting. Lead on, young lady. Lead on!

1. Is the sovereignty of God comforting? How, and why?

2. Do you ever take time to think about God's intentionality in the everydayness of your life?

3. Who is your Fayetta?

4. In the Western cultural narrative, "Love wins" is posted with great abandon. Whose love wins? What love never quits? Why is this love the ultimate expression of God's character? How do we live out the authenticity of being in this love relationship?

The Veil was Pulled Back

IN THE THIRD installment of Peter Jackson's cinematic retelling of J. R. R. Tolkien's epic trilogy *The Lord of the Rings*, Minas Tirith, the fortified capital of Gondor, becomes the staging area between the forces of good and the evil armies of Mordor. All is seemingly lost as Mordor's onslaught rams through gate after gate of the city. Gandalf and Pippin find themselves trapped inside the citadel and believe their journeys are about to end in death. Pippin looks up to Gandalf and says, "I didn't think it would end this way."

> GANDALF: End? No, the journey doesn't end here. Death is just another path, one that we all must take. The gray rain curtain of this world rolls back, and all turns to silver glass, and then you see it.
>
> PIPPIN: What? Gandalf? See what?
>
> GANDALF: White shores and, beyond, a far green country under a swift sunrise.
>
> PIPPIN: Well, that isn't so bad.
>
> GANDALF: No. No, it isn't.

Back in 1997, a group of distinctively mismatched men—including myself—bonded and began a journey of friendship that has lasted almost a quarter of a century. Our travels have taken the three of us down different roads, and our individual stories have been rocky and sometimes obstructed by barbed thorns.

Tim Overby (called TO to avoid confusion) lives in Liberty, Missouri. He presently works for a home-improvement retailer. In order to be visible, TO usually stands in the front row when photos are taken. Although vertically challenged, TO is strong. Really strong. If he were put in a ring with a grizzly bear, I'm not sure where I'd place my bet.

Gene Nobles lives in Hot Springs, Arkansas, and is in an advanced stage of Parkinson's. His relationship with Abba has grown powerful and personal despite his diminished body. Gene is our biggest advocate and encourager. He dreams big. He listens for the voice of Abba and draws his strength from deliberately acting on cues, hints, and perfect intentions from the Holy Spirit.

I round out the posse of three. All I will say about myself is that I always think I'm thinner until I see pictures of myself. And for some insane reason, I think I have more hair until I see pictures of myself. I hate that.

There is a fourth member of our squad: Billy Borre. Billy was the youth pastor for the church we all attended. When Billy and his family moved from Little Rock to Nashville, he made it part of his mission to keep the other three of us together. He encouraged TO, Gene, and I to set up a weekly meeting to study books we loved, including *The Ragamuffin Gospel*, *Wild at Heart*, and *The Sacred Romance*.

We met early every Wednesday morning. We ate a lot of doughnuts. We continued to meet through life changes, holding each other up; encouraging each other; sometimes addressing hard, uncomfortable issues; and keeping each other accountable. And we ate a lot of doughnuts.

We loved each other through it all. We understood—whether spoken or not—that we would always be there for each other. There have been periods of silence, as happens in most relationships in which time and distance fight against endurance.

Billy suffered from diabetes, and over several years, ministrokes went undiagnosed. Once discovered, the damage to his brain was irreversible. He has vestibular dementia, which will only get worse and will eventually take his life.

The three amigos decided we would not let Billy leave this planet without us being with him. It was our way of telling Billy that he mattered and that he'd made a difference in our lives, an eternal difference. We needed him to know he'd made an impact that would far outlive all of us.

TO, Gene, and I met in Little Rock and made the five-hour journey to Nashville with little silence. Memories of shared times together and where life and the Lord had taken us made the trip seem short.

We decided to visit Billy in the nursing home before checking into the hotel. We weren't sure what Billy's condition would be when we saw him. I spoke with his brother, Bobby, who is a champion brother, Billy's biggest and most faithful advocate. He told us Billy had good days and bad days. His body had atrophied, with few core motor skills left. His mind, although intact, slipped almost daily. He remembered some things and people and not others. So we didn't know what we would find.

When we located the nursing home, we silently, apprehensively walked the hallway and into Billy's room. He was in his wheelchair, between two empty beds, with his head bowed to his chest. I was struck by how small and vulnerable he looked.

We stopped about five feet from him. I bent to eye level and waited. Billy opened his eyes and glanced toward us. He looked at me without recognition. I smiled and said, "What are you doin'?"

I will never, as long as I live, forget that moment.

Almost in slow motion, his eyes grew wide with recognition. He lifted his head and leaned forward as if he couldn't believe what he was seeing. He held out his arms. I raced to him and enveloped him in mine. He said, "I love you. I love you so much." He knew.

I smiled. "Hey, I told you I was going to bring you a surprise. Look."

TO and Gene stepped forward for their turn for hugs and love. It was a holy moment. For almost an hour, we felt the presence of the Spirit of God all over the room.

TO asked Billy if he could read a few verses from the Bible. Of course, Billy slowly said yes. TO opened his Bible to Revelation 21 (CSB) and read,

> Then I saw a new heaven and a new earth; for the first heaven and the first earth had passed away, and the sea was no more. I also saw the holy city, the new Jerusalem, coming down out of heaven from God, prepared like a bride adorned for her husband. Then I heard a loud voice from the throne: Look, God's dwelling is with humanity, and he will live with them. They will be his peoples, and God himself will be with them and will be their God. He will wipe away every tear from their eyes. Death will be no more; grief, crying, and pain will be no more, because the previous things have passed away. Then the one seated on the throne said, "Look, I am making everything new." He also said, "Write, because these words are faithful and true."

When TO finished reading, there was a moment of silence. Billy looked up at Gene and said, laboring with his words, "Gene, I will hug you now. God is going to make all things new." Gene walked over to Billy, and they embraced in an eternal, life-affirming hug filled with declarations of "I love you" that I'm confident echoed through the halls and the promises of heaven.

Before leaving, we assured Billy we'd come back the next day. We asked what he liked to eat. Billy wanted Mexican and a Coke. Bobby, Billy's brother, a taco addict who seriously needs a 12-step group, fully supported the idea. It was a plan.

Later that night, as we processed through our time with Billy, TO said, "The curtain was pulled back a little." That summed it up. I learned that day that looking into the eyes of unimaginable hardship is where I get one of the most transparent pictures of eternity. We were reminded of 2 Corinthians 4:16–18 (MSG):

> So we're not giving up. How could we! Even though on the outside it often looks like things are falling apart on us, on the inside, where God is making new life, not a day goes by without his unfolding grace. These hard times are small potatoes compared to the coming good times, the lavish celebration prepared for us. There's far more here than meets the eye. The things we see now are here today, gone tomorrow. But the things we can't see now will last forever.

The next morning, TO was concentrating on a sermon outline he would be preaching at his home church the following Sunday. I'm in awe of this man. The Lord has redeemed his past and made him a conduit for knowledge and wisdom. His understanding and thirst for a relationship with the Lord are incredible. He remembers everything he studies. It's incredibly annoying. Somehow, I didn't get that genetic marker. Every time I read a scripture, it's as if it's the first time I've read it. Weird. I want to be there when the Lord hands him the "crown of exultation." I can only imagine the believers who will be in heaven because TO spiritually invested in them.

Gene and I spent time reading and catching up on where we were in life. Gene, most times, refers to the Lord as Abba, one of the most significant names in how the Lord relates to people. It signifies a close, intimate relationship between a father and his child as well as the trust a child puts in his daddy.

That is how Gene relates to his life and present condition. His Parkinson's disease has left him using a walking cane most of the time and sometimes a chair to move about. His body moves with uncertainty. But the light in his eyes screams of eternity and the joy of seeing Daddy for the first time face-to-face.

These are good men. We are three amigos who couldn't possibly be more different, yet we are bonded together, a three-stranded cord that can't easily be broken.

That afternoon, we made it to a Mexican restaurant and bought ten tacos, cheese dip, and guacamole. For three hours, we visited with Billy and his superhero brother, Bobby.

Bobby would say he's only a regular brother, but he's anything but ordinary. He has sacrificed and been there every time Billy needed him. Bobby makes sure Billy knows he's loved.

As we sat at a picnic table, Billy continually touched us, held our hands, and affirmed his love for each of us. Later, we sat around Billy and watched as Bobby carefully, with sacrificial love and patience, trimmed Billy's goatee. Billy reached up to hold Bobby's arm and proudly look in his brother's eyes.

Then, noticing signs that Billy was tired, we helped him into his bed. TO knelt next to Billy's bed and asked him what his favorite psalm was. Without hesitating for a second, Billy said

Psalm 1, and TO read those precious promises amid an occasional "Amen" from Billy.

Billy was tired. We knew he needed rest. I didn't mention it to the other guys, but I believe we all recognized it was probably the last time we would see Billy on this side of the veil.

TO and Gene each took a turn bending down next to Billy's bed and hugging him. When it came my time, I knelt beside him and took that courageous man in my arms. It was a fierce, life-affirming hug. He wouldn't let go. He kissed me on my cheek and whispered, "I love you, Tim. I love you so much. I've always believed in you."

When I let him go, tears streamed down my cheeks. Billy took my face in both his hands, and his eyes pierced into mine. At that pivotal moment, as Billy used his thumbs to wipe tears from my cheeks, the veil was pulled back, and my spirit gazed directly into eternity. I didn't see a table of food or hear angels singing. I didn't see a throne or seraphim. Those are surprises and delights yet to be unwrapped.

I felt the love and presence of Jesus, almost excruciatingly impossible for this frail human vessel to contain. Crystal pure. A prism of joy, hope, wonder, and expectancy. I pulled in one last time and kissed Billy on his cheek. Our eyes met once more, and I said, "Billy, if you happen to get home before I do, would you be standing there waiting for me?"

His whisper was almost a shout. "Yes. Yes, I will. And when my kids get there, we will all be together. And I'll say, 'See that man over there? He's the reason we're all here.'"

I said, "Yep, Jesus will be right there with us."

Bobby walked us to our car and thanked us for coming. We hugged him goodbye and quietly made our way back to the hotel.

Gene lay on his bed, weeping. TO stood beside the bed, holding Gene's arm. Gene thanked Abba for that time, and he affirmed both TO and me as men and as ministers. Then he said something I will never forget. As Gene lay there on that bed, his exhausted body racked with tremors, with tears flowing freely and bravely down his face, he said, "Parkinson's has been one of the greatest blessings of my life. His plan has perfect purpose, and I am overflowing with love." I don't know that I've ever encountered such courage and determination. Through the storms he's been swept through, he's trusted the Lord wholly, determined.

Hardship is part of our path to eternity. Abba allows difficulty and loss in our lives so we'll continue to lean on him, depend on him, and stay surrendered to him. And oh, how much sweeter heaven looks through that lens.

Here's the passage of scripture, Psalm 1 (CSB), that TO read to Billy:

> How happy is the one who does not
> walk in the advice of the wicked
> or stand in the pathway with sinners
> or sit in the company of mockers!
> Instead, his delight is in the Lord's instruction,
> and he meditates on it day and night.
> He is like a tree planted beside flowing streams
> that bears its fruit in its season
> and whose leaf does not wither.
> Whatever he does prospers.
> The wicked are not like this;
> instead, they are like chaff that the wind blows away.
> Therefore the wicked will not stand up in the judgment,
> nor sinners in the assembly of the righteous.
> For the Lord watches over the way of the righteous,
> but the way of the wicked leads to ruin.

We believed we were going to Nashville to make sure Billy knew he had made a difference in our lives, had made an eternal difference, and was loved.

Abba's plans were far better.

CONVERSATION STARTERS FROM DAVID AND MICAH RICE

We all live out in Ferndale, a small community outside Little Rock. We all spend a lot of time together. It's sometimes a little slice of heaven. David and Micah make it a deliberate point that whatever the activity, there must be a way to give God glory, whether it's music, prayer, small groups, or a bonfire. They love Jesus. They love telling people all about him.

1. Bobby's devotion to his brother is amazing. Are you prepared to care for your family in their days of deterioration? This may be in regard to finances, time and space, and your current state of friendship with them. Do you think that they know that without a doubt, you will be there for them?

2. Since hardship truly is part of our path to eternity, do you view your current hardships as a detriment to your life or as an opportunity to rely wholly on Abba's overflowing love and perfect purpose?

3. The brotherhood seen here is inspiring and vital to life. Whom are you engaging with and being engaged by? Or are you not making time and effort to be part of intimate community?

They Called Him Little Man

OKAY, SO I think I'm over the embarrassment and mortification enough to talk about the following now.

Yesterday I traveled down Maumelle Boulevard in rush-hour traffic to pick up Chinese food for the workers at the fireworks stand and myself. I stopped at a red light, glanced to my right, and saw a shiny new apple-red convertible right out of Hollywood. Entirely out of place.

I thought about my pooch Falkor staying at Dr. Peck's vet clinic during the day so he didn't have to be kenneled so long at home, and I imagined how he'd look in the passenger seat while I was driving. (See "Find My iPad.")

I call him "little man." I'll say it like four times in a row really fast. "Little man, little man, little man, little maaaan!" He goes berserk, jumping up and down with his tongue hanging out and his floppy ears flying, turning in circles.

For some insane reason, I started saying it while driving down the boulevard, over and over. Trying to save gas, I had all the windows down. I then, again for some unexplainable reason, started singing it to the tune of "Camptown Races": "Little man, little man, little man, doo-dah, doo-dah!"

Every mile or so, I was stopped by a red traffic light.

Next came "Summertime": "Little maaaan, little ole little man." That didn't work as well as I'd hoped, so I returned to "Camptown Races."

In my stream-of-consciousness exercise, I remembered loving Woody Woodpecker when I was younger and decided to resurrect Woody's voice in Falkor's honor. "HuhuhuHUhu. HuhuHUhu. Huhuhuhuhu, little man."

I spent the next couple of minutes, or traffic lights, trying to perfect Woody while calling out to my precious pooch.

My voice was a little scratchy at that point, so I went from Woody to Elmer Fudd while the tune inexplicably changed from "Camptown Races" to the theme song from *Flipper*: "Wittle ole wittle man, wittle man, wittle man, faster than wightning." I was cracking myself up.

At that point, I was stopped once again at a light, actually laughing out loud at myself. It was maybe the fourth light since I'd started down the boulevard.

I felt compelled to perfect my cross between Woody Woodpecker and Elmer Fudd while singing "Wittle Man" to the tune of *Flipper*.

At this juncture, I truly believe it was, in fact, the Holy Spirit, who next instructed me to sing "Happy Birthday" to little man as performed by Katharine Hepburn impersonating Elmer Fudd. I can't even begin to type out how that sounded. But I was insanely proud of it.

I stopped for a moment to catch a breath and heard faraway laughter.

I looked to my right and recognized the same red convertible from the first light, also with its windows down. The first thing

I noticed was the woman in the passenger seat. She had her head leaning back against the headrest, laughing so hard she was slapping her raised knee. The dude driving was just staring at me. I have yet to accurately figure out his expression. Not disgust or even a lack of understanding. His mouth was agape, and his brow was furrowed. It almost seemed there was a semblance of awe.

I gripped the steering wheel and stared straight ahead. I concentrated on the red light with everything in my being, as though I'd just graduated from driving school yesterday. The exact same shade of red rose from the back of my neck and traveled upward over my head and down toward my eyes. Thank goodness the light changed. I was able to raise my hand and wave fondly. They heard me proclaim as I raced down the road, "Th-Th-Th-That's all, folks."

CONVERSATION STARTERS
FROM JERROD PIKER

Piker gets my humor. We laugh at stuff no one else would find funny. We can't sit next to each other in church. Everyone needs a friend like Jerrod, a friend with whom you can escape the bonds of adulthood and occasionally, only occasionally, be a kid. Yep, that's Jerrod. Love my friend. He keeps me young.

1. How much would you pay for a video of Tim reenacting this, his proudest moment?

2. The song was inspired by Tim's best little furry buddy, his little man. What's the funniest thing your pet has ever done? What's the funniest thing you've ever done to your pet?

3. If they ever made a Who's Who list of people with funny and embarrassing stories, I think Tim would make the cut. This one's a doozy. What is the most embarrassing thing that's ever happened to you?

The Mighty Chest

I GOT MAD. I got mad, and I vented to and at God. I was already on edge, and I guess I didn't even realize my meteorically hazardous condition until I detonated.

I rarely lose my cool. But the past few months had been hard. I worked hard to trust the Lord; stay surrendered; and stuff down frustration, fear, and, frankly, a huge lack of understanding of his plan.

Rationally, I knew his plan was perfect and knew he was working, as he promised, for my good. I was cleaning house and knocked over my iron, and the lid to the water reservoir broke off. *Great! Yet one more expense I can't even think about managing.*

A few minutes later, I bumped a desk and knocked off a glass figurine given to me as a gift. It shattered.

That was it. I screamed. I cried and even uttered a few not-so-well-chosen expletives. I pointed my finger and poked the air, angry with God for not meeting my needs. I was tired, worn out from trying to wear the right stoic face in front of a Father who knows my heart better than I know myself.

After approximately ten minutes of my Paleolithic meltdown, I felt regret and guilt and crumpled onto the couch. I was a tired, worn-out pile of poured-out flesh. I apologized over and over for my lack of faith and maybe a little fear, remembering that God hadn't had a problem offing a bunch of wandering, whining Israelites over an embarrassing manna and quail incident.

I wanted an answer right then. I wanted God to fix my problems right then. Tired of the struggle, I felt I had grown enough through that season of seemingly constant heartache and stress, and it was time to rest.

So fix it, God.

My good friend Gene told me about a time when one of his sons was younger, maybe seven or so. A long-planned trip was coming up for them, father and two sons, to a NASCAR event. It was all they talked about for weeks.

The day before they were to leave, the younger son came down with a horrific stomach virus, and they were forced to cancel the trip. When my friend walked into the bedroom to break the bad news to his sick son, he was a little shocked by the reaction. As ill as he was, the little boy begged his dad to change his mind. When told he was too sick to go, the boy jumped from under the covers, ran to the end of the bed, and began to scream and cry. He beat his fists against his dad's chest, yelling that the decision was unfair and that his dad was mean.

When the child's body grew weak from fever, he collapsed into his father's arms and wept.

My friend knew how hurt his baby boy was physically and emotionally. So he took the pounding. He told me later that he was willing to take the punches because his child chose to come to his dad instead of the Enemy. He chose to go to the one he knew he could trust. He chose the one who would truly and completely understand. He chose to pull in close instead of running, hiding, and isolating.

I realized my old self would have done all those weak, foolish things—running, hiding, and isolating. Although I was still sorry I'd reacted in anger and resentment, I was relieved I had instinctively taken my rage and pain to the One who gets me and knows my love for him is real and honest. And he loves honesty. I still know there is a plan, and I will continue to wait on him— with him.

The Sunday morning after my conniption fit, my pastor gave the call for the offering. He spoke about real trust and about the one place in scripture, Malachi 3:10, where the Lord tells us to test him—to try him. To see if he will open the storehouses of heaven if we tithe.

During those months, I wasn't able to tithe regularly. It drove me crazy. I honestly love the feeling of giving 10 percent of my income. But it made no earthly sense to tithe when I was already in the hole.

Yet the Holy Spirit tugged at my heart. Six dollars was in my pocket—all I had to buy gas and survive till Wednesday, when I got paid. When the bucket passed, I prayed. *Here I am, Lord. The widow with her two mites. I don't know if I'm offering this to further your kingdom, to prove to myself that you're true to your promise, or to show you that you can trust me with more.* Maybe the truth was a combination of a couple or all of those. *I don't need a jug of oil that doesn't run empty. But my gas tank could use some help.*

I reached into my wallet and grabbed the bills between my thumb and pointer finger. Before I had time to think it through, I suspended my hand over the bucket. I took a deep breath and released the money. I watched the bills fall as if in slow motion, almost as if I could still grab them before they disappeared into the murky abyss. I was afraid. But I was okay with that. I've learned that doing something courageous has little to do with fear. Fear is just an emotion. Courage is an action.

That afternoon, a man I'd never met or even heard of got hold of me and said he and his wife were coming back from Fort

Smith. He asked me to meet him at a gas station just off the 430. We shared friends in common, so I wasn't worried.

When I got there, he blessed me by making my mortgage payment. Then he took my car over to the pump—I didn't tell him I was low—and filled the tank. Finally, he said they'd stopped on their way in and bought a gift card so I would be able to get fuel when I needed it. He verbally blessed me again, and they were gone.

I sat in my car with my hands gripping and my head leaning against the steering wheel. I cried, feeling Abba's big, warm, safe arms wrapped around his ragamuffin son.

Matthew 18:2 (MSG) says,

> For an answer, Jesus called over a child, whom he stood in the middle of the room, and said, "I'm telling you, once and for all, that unless you return to square one and start over like children, you're not even going to get a look at the kingdom, let alone get in. Whoever becomes simple and elemental again, like this child, will rank high in God's kingdom. What's more, when you receive the childlike on my account, it's the same as receiving me."

I feel certain El Roi—the God who sees—takes into account how bratty his kids can be from time to time.

CONVERSATION STARTERS
FROM CLIFF PECK
(DOUBLETREEVETERINARYCLINIC.COM)

Cliff is one of my bosses. More than that, we've been friends for a couple of decades. One of the most caring animal doctors on the planet, Cliff shows compassion and professionalism to every client who comes through the doors. I learn something new from him every time I work with him. He's a good, caring, giving human. He loves his wife, Deane, and his kids and throws a mean crawfish boil.

1. How many times have you felt the call to give but thought, *I don't have the full ten percent right now. I'll wait till I have it?* Did Tim's decision to trust God no matter what encourage you to do as Malachi 3:10 says and test God by tithing to watch him open the floodgates of heaven?

2. Has the Spirit ever moved you to do something completely out of the ordinary to go the extra mile for a stranger? Give examples.

3. When have you taken the time to pray thanksgiving for a problem and an opportunity to trust him and seen absolute evidence of his working a miracle in your life?

That TIME I ALMOST GOT SUCKED DOWN A BLOWHOLE

SPOUTING HORN BEACH Park, near Poipu, Kauai, lives up to its name. The giant blowhole can, depending on the tide and surf conditions, shoot a ferocious spout of water as much as fifty feet into the air.

Visitors can view this impressive natural ocean attraction from the top of a hill. There are guardrails and warning signs offering protection to keep tourists from wandering too close to the perilous spouting water and the subsequent mighty surge of the dangerous maelstrom as it swirls back through the hole into the ocean below.

When I was there, however, the Enter at Your Own Risk signs were nothing more than a green light to me—a welcome mat, if you will. Honestly, I don't even know why they put up offers of advice like that when I'm in the neighborhood. It's like a dare. I don't walk around looking for an adventure like that, but if it's put right in front of me, what am I supposed to do?

At that particular time of day, the tide was low, and the ocean level was way below the lava shelf's rim. So down the hill my friend Tricia Walker and I trotted. I was sporting the cool

297

flip-flops I'd bought four hours earlier and an equally fashionable gardener's straw hat.

No waves were flowing over the top of the shelf to wash us down the blowhole, and I knew I could back up far enough from the geyser when it blew to miss the churning, foaming maelstrom of water as it receded down the hole.

Tricia and I stood between the blowhole and the ocean, exploring the sharp, serrated, ancient lava formations, when I glanced up and saw fellow tourists waving at us from atop the hill. I thought it a kind gesture from folks I didn't know. So I did a bodybuilder pose, suspecting they were taking pictures of us, when I noticed some of them stop waving and begin pointing behind us.

I turned just in time to see a massive wave, much taller than the lava shelf, bearing down a mere handful of seconds from us. It must have been a freak minitsunami from some earthquake off the coast of Tasmania.

I screamed for Tricia to hold on to something. I lay back on the lava floor, planted my feet as firmly as I could against a small incline in the shelf, slammed my eyes shut, took in a deep breath, and waited.

The wave hit full force. Water gushed up the blowhole no more than fifteen feet from me. I found myself being shoved forward by the torrent of salt water pummeling against my back. Quickly, it all subsided. At that instant, I heard something ominous: rushing, groaning sounds and a sudden, violent gurgling—the ocean coursing its way back down the blowhole. I found myself being pulled along with it. I felt my feet come off the ground, out of my flip-flops. I dug in as hard as I could.

I have a distinct memory of some bouncy, horrified shrieking going on. I have decided to remember it as concerned sightseers atop the hill.

When the water finally subsided enough for me to know I wasn't going down the blowhole with it, I realized I was less than a foot from the hole, pretty much straddling it, watching my brand-new gardener's hat whirlpool out of sight. Tricia must have noticed my immediate sense of loss, as she attempted to grab it. I yelled, "Leave it!"

I never knew what happened to my flip-flops, but I have my suspicions. All I know is that my feet were cut to shreds by the dried, razor-sharp lava, and for the rest of my stay on that beautiful island, those feet were severely sensitive.

I've been told the blowhole is actually a sort of safety valve, much like the old steam engines that open if the equipment gets too hot or pressurized. This safety valve keeps the equipment from exploding and damaging the machines or causing injury to nearby people.

If the blowhole were not there to release energy, the constant pounding of ocean water underneath the dried lava would slowly disintegrate the shelf, causing it to break apart and fall into the boiling ocean below. So the safety valve itself became the attraction.

I sometimes experience that same beautiful, familiar feeling. It has become almost a motor response when I experience something that draws me closer to what I honestly believe heaven will be.

When my body becomes responsive to an encounter with Jesus, that can be experienced only because I know his Holy Spirit resides in my heart.

The closest earthly comparison might be sitting in the front car of a roller coaster—my favorite position—as it reaches the pinnacle of its slow, rhythmic, *clickity-clacking* climb.

The car slowly crests the hill. My adrenaline begins to pulse the moment just before I hear the release of the brake, and the car starts its insane plunge back to earth. I look down at the curved track far below. I inhale again—and scream. The exhilaration and anticipation tighten in my chest and move up into my face.

I, through sheer determination, raise my hands off the safety bar into the air and take in the deepest breath I can manage, because I know there is not one single thing I can do to get out of whatever happens next. The only thing I can accept at that point is the thrill of the ride.

After 45.5 seconds of sheer terror, the car comes to a screeching, abrupt stop, and my eyes fill with tears as I beg my fellow travelers to get back in line for one more ride. Why do tears fall when I feel such euphoria and elation?

I call it "the catch"—that moment when my emotion is at its peak and can't rise any further. I get the same feeling when listening to praise music. I fill entirely up with the maximum amount of joy, anticipation, and expectation my body can withstand, until I can't hold any more. I begin to shed tears with the certainty of the hope I have in Jesus. Why do tears come when I'm experiencing the pure joy of being in the presence of Jesus?

Praising Jesus and worshipping him is the closest I believe I will come to experiencing heaven here in this earthly body. It makes me look forward to the time when I'll not be restrained; my worship and praise will rise forever; and the lump in my throat, the catch, will no longer be a hindrance. My joy will mix unendingly with every voice and heart at the throne of King Jesus.

Praise is perfect for here on earth, but I long for more. I've finally figured out that tears are our safety valve, the catch. I'm convinced the Lord gave us this earthly escape valve because our bodies can't contain the magnitude of eternity.

Paul pointed it out in 1 Corinthians 2:9 (MSG): "No one's ever seen or heard anything like this. Never so much as imagined anything quite like it—What God has arranged for those who love him. But you've seen and heard it because God by his Spirit has brought it all out into the open before you."

I believe God created us to long for heaven and the release of our limited capacity to physically praise him the way we wish to. There have been times when I've stood in my living room with my hands raised, screaming praise songs, when my heart was about to explode with sheer joy. I didn't want the thankfulness and love I felt for him at that moment to stop. The final expression of my worship was with tears. It was a small reflection of eternity.

The safety valve, the catch—we weren't made to experience here what we will encounter there; our bodies can't contain it, so he gave us tears.

A moving picture of this expression of the safety valve is in Luke 7:36–50 (MSG):

> One of the Pharisees asked him over for a meal. He went to the Pharisee's house and sat down at the dinner table. Just then a woman of the village, the town harlot, having learned that Jesus was a guest in the home of the Pharisee, came with a bottle of very expensive perfume and stood at his feet, weeping, raining tears on his feet. Letting down her hair, she dried his feet, kissed them, and anointed them with the perfume. When the Pharisee who invited him saw this, he said to himself, "If this man was the prophet I thought he was, he would have known what kind of woman this is who is falling all over him." Jesus said to him, "Simon, I have something to tell you." "Oh? Tell me." "Two men were in debt to a banker. One owed five hundred silver pieces, the other fifty. Neither of them could pay up, and so the banker canceled both debts. Which of the two

would be more grateful?" Simon answered, "I suppose the one who was forgiven the most." "That's right," said Jesus. Then turning to the woman, but speaking to Simon, he said, "Do you see this woman? I came to your home; you provided no water for my feet, but she rained tears on my feet and dried them with her hair. You gave me no greeting, but from the time I arrived, she hasn't quit kissing my feet. You provided nothing for freshening up, but she has soothed my feet with perfume. Impressive, isn't it? She was forgiven many, many sins, and so she is very, very grateful. If the forgiveness is minimal, the gratitude is minimal." Then he spoke to her: "I forgive your sins." That set the dinner guests talking behind his back: "Who does he think he is, forgiving sins!" He ignored them and said to the woman, "Your faith has saved you. Go in peace."

The picture of the so-called sinful woman even being in Simon's house is worth noting. She came ready, prepared to see Jesus. If supper was to be at 6:30, she was there at 6:15.

She brought the perfume with her. It was not a last-minute decision. She knew who Jesus was, so she must have previously heard him speak healing and love to the hurting and forgotten.

She probably followed him from a distance, fearing he would shun her, as everyone with any amount of dignity and integrity would have.

She was not stalking a stranger. She withstood the scornful "What are you doing here?" looks from the others at the table.

Because it was the tradition for the host of the party to have the guests' feet washed and dried, she didn't bring water or a towel.

Instead, she must have thought she would finish the welcome by anointing his feet with oil. How surprised she might have been when she saw his road-weary feet covered with dust from his travels.

But her heart was too full to allow that to stop her expression of thankfulness. She knelt in front of the One, the only one who didn't look down on her. In fact, Jesus was the only one who showed compassion. All she could do was respond with a full heart of gratefulness that her earthly body couldn't possibly contain. Thankfulness that she would never be able to fully express in the manner she wanted.

She never spoke a word. Her love poured out in the only way it could humanly respond: tears. Her safety valve became the attraction.

She wasn't weeping tears on Jesus's feet to make it clear how sinful she was or how wretched a person she knew herself to be. She was holding as much eternity as her earthly body could contain—maybe more than anyone else in that room, except for Jesus.

He knew. He saw. He understood. I believe the owner of the alabaster box's tears were from a heart filled with thankfulness, repentance, and newly realized acceptance. She could see a future filled with hope, maybe for the first time; forgiveness; and a sense of self.

No woman of her status would have dared to do what she did. Newly discovered self-worth flowed from a life filled with adventure in the kingdom of love.

I'm satisfied that on the day she met Jesus in heaven, he gave her two gifts of her tears. He opened a great ledger and pointed to a specific time in history when he recorded her tears on his behalf, when no one else chose to wash his feet. Second, he gave her a bottle, maybe made of alabaster, in which he'd saved every single one of her tears, her safety valve, shed for his glory. And she was able to express her pure, real heart with the realization that she was finally home.

With the fullness of all eternity in front of her, she would no longer need the safety valve of a Hawaiian blowhole. She would finally exclaim, like the bride in Song of Solomon, "My beloved is mine. And I am His."

That's far more thrilling than a roller coaster.

CONVERSATION STARTERS
FROM DEBBIE REES

Kentucky butter cake. That pretty much sums Debbie Jean up. I can't remember a time at her house when there wasn't a Kentucky butter cake on the counter. I've never left without a couple of pieces in my belly and a couple of pieces on a paper plate. Debbie wears Jesus like a scarf and graciously wraps him around the cold shoulders of anyone who needs a hug, an encouraging word, a sandwich, or a big slice of cake. She's so pretty.

1. In what ways do we tend to want the momentary thrill-of-the-ride experiences in life, thinking they will satisfy the deeper needs in our heart? Do you come away from these times feeling fulfilled? Or do you find those exhilarating moments are short-lived and leave you wanting or needing more? Give an example.

2. Name a time in your life when you, as Tim did, willfully walked through an enter-at-your-own-risk situation, ignoring the warning signs placed there for your protection and safety. What was the outcome of that experience? Did it go as you expected or desired? What did you learn from it?

3. Describe a time when you were so filled with love for Jesus while praising him, as was Tim, or felt an overpowering and deep gratitude for what he has done for you, as did the "sinful" woman, that the safety valve of tears opened up and rolled down your cheeks.

4. As the "sinful" woman came to the Pharisee's house prepared and ready to see Jesus, how are you preparing for the time when you will see him face-to-face?

Questions

THE FOLLOWING WAS written by a friend who currently resides in a correctional unit. He has been through eight Celebrate Recovery step-studies and cofacilitates these studies alongside me. In eight years, he has never missed a single class. Never. He just keeps growing and coming back for more. I love his raw honesty and seeking heart. Does he have all the answers? I doubt it. But neither do I. What human does? What he does have is a hunger for truth and a continually growing, maturing relationship with Jesus. Read on.

> The Bible tells us that we can't even begin to fathom the ways of God. I agree entirely, 100 percent. However, I believe that from time to time, he gives us little still-frame images that display shimmers of his glory. Heaven forbid he expose too much of himself to us. The finite cannot contain the infinite. That's general physics and somewhat common sense.
>
> What blows my mind is how humans are conditioned to seek answers to everything, not realizing (or just ignoring the fact) that some

questions have no answers. We never grow out of that childlike state where we always seem to ask, "Why, why, why?" If you're a parent, you know the stage I'm talking about.

As I said, I don't believe we ever grow out of that stage. We only progress in the type of questions we ask. We go from questions like "Why do I have to eat all my vegetables?" to "If God is a God of love, then why do such terrible things happen in a world he created?" Two questions, very valid ones, light-years apart.

Life is unfair. It is a very cliché but intrinsic truth. We were not born into a world where the playing field is equal, and fairness is a constitutional promise. We live in a world where one child is born with a silver spoon, trust-fund life, and another child is born in a welfare line with a block of government cheese (which is delicious and one of the few perks of poverty). I'll speak more on this in a moment, though.

First, a quick shakedown on me. I'm a thirty-one-year-old man who is five years into a thirty-year sentence for first-degree murder. I work as a substance abuse and behavioral modification counselor in the therapeutic community at the correctional unit. I wasn't always like this. Possibly, you will have an opportunity to learn more about me and my whole story someday; only time will tell. I'm an ex-junkie, failed father, husband, son, brother, grandson, and friend.

I failed. I am the dregs of society, and the great State of Arkansas has a place for those types of people. Do I deserve to be here? Absolutely. Even though the incident that brought me to prison was an accident, I deserve to be here a hundred times over.

Today I am in recovery for a multitude of sinful behaviors and character defects. But I also work with men who are in the same position in life. We were (some still are) on our way to rock bottom. Chances are, a vast majority of you have never been incarcerated. But you likely know one or two who have seen the inside of a cell.

I am here today as a story of redemption. God has a calling for each of us, a vocation in mind. Some miss it altogether. I was one who, if not for chance and circumstance, would have been another one of those statistics. Life truly is beautiful how it works. Life has its own code of correcting what is wrong. Prison has humbled me very much.

But here is where I define my earlier point. The questions and their answers I often find myself asking are why it cost so much for such a simple lesson. Why did someone have to lose their life so I would get mine on track?

These seem like questions that have no answer or have multiple-angled answers. But one simple answer will not suffice.

I think Romans 8:28 (NIV) fits: "And we know that in all things God works for the good of those who love him, who have been called according to his purpose." But it's also so much deeper than displaying glory, because God need not show off to anyone. Seriously, what does he have to prove?

My cost? My freedom, my daughter, the passing of my grandmother, and my father. All are devastating to me. But they became less of a loss and more like victims when I chose my path. Wait—it gets heavier.

The conscious weight of knowing I am responsible for another human life and an innumerable amount of broken hearts dog-piles my guilt and shame.

Before I get overwhelmed by looking back, let me explain how cool God has been to me. He gave his Son on a tree so my and your soul could be redeemed. But he has afforded me a rare shot to redeem myself on a temporal level. Right here, right now.

So many people get lost in the chaos of life and never get that second shot. Others only need one shot. I am one of the chosen elite. A living, breathing testimony to his glory and graciousness.

That doesn't mean I will get back every relationship I ever broke and destroyed. Probably would be a safe bet to say most people will never forgive me. I did an excellent job of making myself a pariah. Some days are harder than others. Some days I feel insatiable. I have so many questions myself and no answers in sight.

But then God sends these sweet little nuggets. If we got our wish to know the answer to every question, what's the point of living? Without the mystery, there is no reason to stay driven. I tend to lose interest in books and movies I already know the ending to. It's when I think I know what's going to happen and then get a surprise ending no one, including me, expected. That keeps me coming back for more.

All these idle questions and philosophies, like "What's the meaning of life?" C'mon, man. Seriously? It's to live! You, me, us—we only get one shot at it. So rather than getting sidetracked and defocused by open-ended, rhetorical questions or questions that have no answer at all, why not focus on loving the here and now? Why not try to answer a question like "What's God trying to tell me here?" For five long years, I have been burdened by the heavyweight question "Why did it have to cost so much for me to wake up?"

Then God's answer hit me like a freight train.

He loved me so much that not only did he give his only Son for my sins, but he allowed an innocent life to be sacrificed, along with an entire host of family and friends who loved her.

This person who lost her life has been redeemed in his presence. There is not a single doubt in my heart. And I believe her family will be rewarded for their faith.

And you know, maybe that's not a good answer. Matter o' fact, maybe it's a terrible answer, and it's my logic and a form of self-preservation I use to cope and maintain in the midst of my guilt. But I doubt it.

You ever receive a gift, and rather than just saying, "Thank you," the first thing out of your mouth is "How much did it cost?" The answer I usually got was "Don't worry about what it cost. That's not important."

That's how God works.

So until a day when we can better acquaint ourselves with each other, I'm going to leave you with this: questions are good, and seeking answers is part of the human condition, but don't ever get caught up in trying to find answers so much that you forget to live.

You know the definition of *satisfaction*? Satisfaction is the death of desire. So once all questions are satisfied, will there be a desire to live anymore? God allows me to know what I need to know when I need to know it.

Nothing more, nothing less.

Hope that makes sense.

So much love,
William

CONVERSATION STARTERS
FROM BYRON SCHEIDER

We've shared some great food together, Byron, Sue, and I. Some folks make it easy to be around them. Byron and Sue are great listeners and wonderful teachers. They lead their ministries well.

1. What *why* questions have you been struggling with in your life?

1. What do you say to yourself about your mistakes that you would like to change?

2. A definition for *forgiveness* is "to give forth." In order to do that, you have to let go of the thing you've been holding on to. Through Christ, God has given forth. He has let go of your errors of sin, past, present, and future. Here's my last question for you: In what ways do you stop yourself from accepting that God has let go of your sin and still holds on to you?

The Night of the Twenty-Eight Salads

ALBERT SCHWEITZER ONCE said, "The purpose of human life is to serve, and to show compassion and the will to help others." I believe he's right. In fact, if we are to follow the example of Jesus, serving was his edict from heaven. Matthew 20:28 (MSG) says, "That is what the Son of Man has done. He came to serve, not be served—and then to give away his life in exchange for the many who are held hostage."

I've found in my life, and in our culture, that it's much more challenging to ask for help than it is to give help. Most of us jump at the chance, if we are able, to lend helping hands to those in need. But we tend to wear a fake badge of toughness if we are the ones in need of help. A judgment error I, like many others, have made is not asking for help when it's desperately needed.

A few years back, my water heater went out. Several days of rain had flooded under my house and blown the water heater up. Don't even ask why the water heater is under the house. That's a different story for a different day.

Anyway, I prayed and asked the Lord to help me out. I told only a handful of people. A couple of them offered to help get a new one. But I resisted, knowing the Lord would take care of the problem. A full year went by. I took cold showers in the dead of winter, feeling every bit the role of a modern martyr "for the Lord." The good news is that I never left the house not feeling totally, excruciatingly awake.

Life carried on like that for a year. Seriously, a solid year of taking many cold showers, washing dishes and clothes in cold water, and waiting for the Lord to come through. I didn't accept the help offered, because I didn't want to inconvenience others, and I didn't want to appear needy. How stupid is that?

Finally, my brother-in-law, Jim, called and said, "Go buy a water heater. I'll give you my card number. Your sister can't stand that you've been taking cold showers for a year. That's ridiculous. This is your Christmas present from us. And have someone else put it in. Do not, under any circumstance, attempt to install it yourself."

I went to the local home-improvement store and bought a heater. However, I did not have them put it in. The heater cost only $300. Having them put it in would have added another $1,000. So I finally broke down and called my buddy Cliff Peck and asked him for suggestions on whom to call. He knows pretty much everyone with a specific skill in our little corner of the world. It was Christmas Eve. Within an hour, Cliff and his son Beaux were at my house, rolling out the old heater and putting in the new one.

But something happened with my electrical system after they left. All the power to my whole house got knocked out. I called Cliff back, and he gave me the number of an electrician friend of his. I called Larry Ward, admitting I needed help, and he said he would come out the day after Christmas.

So I was out of commission for a couple of days. Since my whole house is electric, I was out of water as well. But I knew help was on the way. Larry came out and worked all morning the day after Christmas to get my electricity going again. The whole time, I was nervous about the cost. When Larry was done, I grabbed my checkbook and asked him how much. He grabbed my hand and said, "Merry Christmas."

He jumped into his truck, and as he drove out of sight, all I could think was *And to all a good night.*

I wasn't sure which to do first: cry or go jump into the hot shower. So I combined the two. Best shower ever!

This year, the week before Christmas, the water heater again started acting up. The belt on my dryer broke, and on Christmas morning, I began making desserts for Christmas dinner and found the bottom element of my oven had burned out.

I called Larry and told him I needed help. He came to the house and crawled under. After removing the heater cover, Larry informed me that the bottom element in the water heater was burned out and told me exactly what I needed to repair it. Again, he wouldn't accept any payment.

I went under the house to repair the heater, and when I pulled out the old element, I could see a lot of something white. I realized that my well water must've dumped a massive amount of calcium into the heater, burning out the element. I phoned Larry back, and he gave me the number of a plumber. I called him and told him I needed help. He told me he would leave a piece of rubber pipe out by the gate of his business. I could tape the red rubber pipe to a dry vac and vacuum out the deposits. He didn't charge me for the tube.

It took me a couple of hours, but I was able to vacuum out most of the sediment and replace the element. I went to a parts store about twenty minutes away and told the guy I needed help, and I got a belt for the dryer. I replaced it, and it broke in the first cycle, possibly because I put it on backward. Maybe. I went and got another one and a couple of other parts. The guy said, "I want to help you. I'm only charging you wholesale for these." I replaced the belt and, at the same time, got a new element for the oven.

So all is well right now. I'm learning that asking for help isn't a weakness; it's wisdom. Seeking help is the best way I can take care of myself. And there are obvious consequences in not seeking help.

As I've said, back in the 1980s, I worked at a restaurant in Nashville called Dalt's. It was the place to be back in the day. Everyone hung out there—country stars and contemporary Christian artists. The restaurant is still there, and when I visit Nashville, I always stop by to see how it's changed. Great memories. I could fill a book with the stories of our escapades, and fortunately, thanks to social media, I stay in touch with many of the folks I worked with.

One of my favorite memories is tied to the idea that it's always a good idea to accept help when it's offered.

We usually started the night shift with a ten-person waitstaff. As the evening progressed past the supper rush, we would OTLE (option to leave early). The manager used this option to have servers leave, beginning with station ten and working down toward station one, who was always the shift leader. It was the shift leader's duty to make sure every person leaving did OTLE duties, which included stocking, cleaning, and getting everything ready for the next shift.

One particular night, we OTLEed down to two servers. I was in section three and had just finished my shift. It was about ten thirty at night. We closed at midnight. That left only two servers on the floor. That was fine because on a weeknight, having a rush was a rarity.

I, having just clocked out, sat down to order my late-night meal at our customary booth, table number ten. It was directly across the aisle from the expediter counter, where we usually made salads. Steve Ford and Cindy Johnson were the only two servers left on the floor; Steve was the shift leader. He knew everything was stocked and cleaned, so the last hour and a half would be smooth sailing.

It was one of Cindy's first nights back after being gone for a few months. Several weeks earlier, late one night, Cindy had been on her way home from work and been involved in a horrible car accident near the restaurant. She'd broken her jaw and two bones in her arm and crushed a kneecap. Now, weeks after the ordeal, she came to work basically pinned together and proceeded with great caution.

When my food arrived, I sat back to enjoy it. I noticed a party of seven come in. Steve greeted them, grabbed some menus, and seated them at booth fourteen. He decided to take the table. Usually, when people came in that late, they just wanted appetizers and drinks or maybe a burger and fries. But no, these people wanted full dinners, all of which included dinner salads.

Steve came to the front and turned in the order. He then pivoted around to the salad station and proceeded to make seven dinner salads. I can't remember what Cindy was doing at the time, but I told Steve I could help carry the salads to the table. Because we at Dalt's all took pride in how many plates we could carry and because Steve was tall, with long arms, he said he could handle it.

I watched him prepare seven bowls of salad, stack four of them all the way up his arm, even above his elbow; perch one on his other wrist; and balance the final two between his fingers. I was impressed.

Carrying them with great aplomb, Steve walked around the counter; passed me at booth ten; whisked between booths eleven and thirty; and, for some unexplainable reason, fell flat on his back. I was excruciatingly proud of myself for not guffawing.

Those were salads one through seven.

Steve picked himself up and walked back to the counter. His face was beet red, so I chose to remain silent for a second or two.

A busboy magically appeared, sweeping up the garden of salad between booths eleven and thirty.

Once again, Steve made seven salads, and once again, I asked if he wanted my help. It was now a point of pride for Steve, who said, "No! I've got it."

Steve gathered up what was left of his composure and the salads in the same arrangement as before. Cindy, sensing impending disaster, grabbed a couple of them from him, and they walked around the counter, passed me at booth ten, and attempted to whisk between booths eleven and thirty.

From my perch at booth ten, I saw the whole ugly thing unfold as if in slow motion. Maybe Steve thought if he bent his knees and went into a knee-dip position, he would be saved. He even planted one elbow over the booth thirty railing, but to no avail. Unfortunately, gravity eventually won out, and he sat squarely and, I'm sure, less gracefully than he imagined on his rear end. Cindy, continuing at a full gait, promptly sat right on top of him. She managed to stand up reasonably quickly, and Steve jumped up with salad hanging precariously from his apron pocket and stormed back to the counter.

Those were salads eight through fourteen.

Steve acquiesced to yell, "Help on a run!" which really didn't matter. Cindy was standing directly behind him. She stood sweetly by as Steve prepared yet another seven salads. Obviously, he was getting help this time, whether he wanted it or not.

As soon as the salads were made, Cindy grabbed three of them, Steve balanced the other four, and off they went.

They rounded the counter, with Steve in the lead and Cindy safely behind him. They passed me at booth ten and whisked around the corner between booths eleven and thirty.

There must have been residual salad dressing oil swimming on the floor. To me, Steve appeared to be trotting as if on a treadmill before he fell face-first. As he staggered, his leg hit Cindy, who fell directly on top of him. It was performance art, culminating in a dazzling firework explosion of salad greens, bright red tomatoes, crumbled bacon and egg, shredded cheddar, and croutons in every possible direction.

My first feeling was horror because of Cindy's injuries. I jumped up and helped her to her feet as Steve, who had somehow miraculously ended up on his back with arms and legs flailing, conjured a startlingly good impression of an upside-down turtle trying desperately to right itself.

Those were salads fifteen through twenty-one.

As soon as I knew Cindy wasn't hurt, I saw Steve once again at the counter. His face no longer wore a look of determination or even embarrassment; it was more resignation. Caught in a *Groundhog Day* time loop, he would spend all of eternity making the same seven salads.

After yet another trip to the salad station, he changed direction. He asked Cindy for help. Together they carried all seven salads through the bar and around the host stand to arrive at booth fourteen, safely delivering what, in Dalt's folklore, became known as the Night of the Twenty-Eight Salads.

When the bedeviled greenery, cheese, and croutons were set in front of the now starving patrons at booth fourteen, booth thirteen was set by the host with four new customers. Steve, being as gracious as possible under the circumstances, took their order. Unbelievably, they all wanted dinners with dinner salads.

Because someone asked, Steve reluctantly rattled off the dressings: "French, Italian, blue cheese, ranch, Caesar, Thousand Island, and vinegar and oil."

One of the patrons innocently asked, "How's the Italian?"

Without hesitation, Steve, with chin quivering, muttered, "Slippery."

CONVERSATION STARTERS
FROM DR. PATRICIA KNOTT

Pat is a wife and mom. She and her husband, John, are quintessential hosts. Pat is a caring and compassionate doctor, makes me laugh at a moment's notice, shares teaching responsibilities with me in Creative Living Connection class, and, best of all, is a collector of all things *Wizard of Oz* (she had me at all things *Oz*). Dr. Knott is really pretty.

1. Has there ever been a time when you needed help but, because of pride, didn't ask for it? What happened as a result of not asking for help?

2. Can you remember a time when you needed help and saw God work on your behalf? Did it make it easier to ask for help the next time? Did you form new or closer relationships?

3. Have you ever been the one someone turned to for help in a desperate situation? How did it minister to you when you helped?

Juju Mommadawg

THIS MORNING, I carried Juju Mommadawg to the car and loaded her in the passenger seat. I've done it a thousand times over the past fifteen years. Driving with her beside me to Doubletree Animal Clinic, I passed the bend in the road where Mommadawg and three of her siblings were dropped off and abandoned a decade and a half ago. I'm not sure what became of two of them. I hope someone rescued them and gave them good homes.

I passed the bridge where I stopped one clear autumn night when I heard Mommadawg and Willie running through the hills under a dazzling harvest moon with their bays echoing at who-knew-what. I remember that specific moment; I prayed the Lord would help us catch those two pooches. I thought, *Remember this moment. Take a heart picture.*

A few months later, I was able, with the help of a sedative-filled pill pocket, to chase her drunk brother Willie through Fern Cliff Presbyterian Camp and catch him. He became a lifelong companion to friends from church. He died four years ago from cancer. I was able to take Mommadawg to the Herndons' home. She and Willie spent a couple of hours loving on each other before Willie made his journey home.

I passed the same Presbyterian camp where, a few months later, I found Mommadawg's first litter of five-week-old puppies curled up together in the roots of a downed tree. Those ten pups stayed at the clinic until they were old enough to find forever homes. Except for the last one. I brought him home. His name is Chester.

I passed a few places while driving down Ferndale Cutoff where we tried unsuccessfully to catch Mommadawg during her first two years. She was a wily, slippery foe. The same sedative-filled pill pockets that worked so well on Willie never worked on her. She easily slipped through our hands and ran into the woods. Every time. We knew she was watching. We just never knew where from.

Finally, during her third pregnancy (our small community referred to her as the Ferndale floozy) someone called the clinic and said they had trapped her inside a fenced-in area where a huge propane gas tank lived next to a local convenience store. Dr. Peck and Jenny immediately jumped into Dr. P.'s truck, raced to the store with a retractable rabies pole, and gathered her up.

They called me. I raced to the clinic, where we spent hours bathing Juju and picking ticks and fleas off her. There wasn't a square inch of her little body that didn't have a tick or flea. Dr. Peck sedated her for the procedure because she wasn't used to being touched. No human had petted that precious girl for two and a half years. We spayed her and gave her every med she needed to become healthy. We treated her for heartworms, which took more than a year to eradicate.

We made a comfortable home for Mommadawg in one of the outside runs. We turned a spacious cleaned-out trash barrel onto its side and filled it with blankets to keep her warm.

She became my project. Every day, I would open the gate of her run, and she'd scurry out to potty in the fenced-in area behind the clinic. She'd race to the grass and do her business, keeping a sharp eye on me in case I tried to get too close to her.

Then the chase would begin. The little storage building in the center of the potty area became her barricade. No matter which side I tried to surprise her on, she would dart away and run to the other side. I could not catch her. I'd grab stuff and try to build a fence made of boxes and old lumber on one side, hopefully trapping her so I could grab her. It never worked. She broke through or jumped over every time. She'd eventually tire of the game, jog around the back side of the kennels, and spring into her run. After closing all gates, I, gasping for breath and furious, would drag myself into her run.

Once again, vainly attempting to avoid me, she would jump on top of her barrel. I'd grab her and sit in the run with her across my lap. At first, she tried to wriggle away. But I held tight. I held her, hugged her, whispered to her, petted her, and loved on her until she finally stopped resisting and relaxed, settling quietly in my lap.

We shimmied through that dance for about an hour every day for months. All the friends I worked with at the clinic kept saying, "You're gonna keep that dog." I adamantly told them I wasn't.

About three months later, when I got her home, a whole new set of challenges began.

Mommadawg was a flight risk. I had to take her out on her leash, or she'd run. Late at night, no matter the weather, if she slipped out on her own, I was forced to leave the sliding door open a crack and turn off all the lights. After she romped through the woods for a couple of hours, baying at the moon and waking all the neighbors, she'd sneak back into the house. Then she'd jump up onto the couch, thinking she'd really gotten away with something.

Early on, I learned she liked potato chips, so trying to persuade her, I routinely made a Hansel and Gretel trail from the sidewalk all the way up the deck, where I'd end the snacks just inside the house. Mommadawg would cautiously eat the chips, chewing suspiciously, trying to ascertain which bush I might be hiding behind, until she stepped inside the house. I, with more agility than I'd known I possessed, jumped out of a corner and slammed the sliding glass door behind her.

But one winter night, she chose not to play fair. She wouldn't follow the trail of chips.

It was about midnight. The temperature was about 40 degrees. I was about freezing.

I had my bag of chips in hand. Mommadawg was just out of reach. I could see the cast of her silhouette in the safety light outside. I stood in the frosty grass and called her name as sweetly as my chattering teeth allowed: "Momma! Mommadawg!" She just sat there.

I got up and tried to mosey toward her, and she ran to the edge of the woods. I put a few chips on the ground. She smugly scowled at them.

I thought maybe she felt threatened by my being taller than she was. Maybe if I got down level with her, I thought, she'd feel less intimidated and come over to get the tasty chips.

So I lay down in the damp grass, put some chips on the ground at arm's length, and, because it was cold, sort of curled up into a ball. I started calling for her. "Momma! Momma! Mommadawg!"

Somewhere in the middle of that lesson in futility, I thought, *If the neighbors are looking outside right now, they're watching me lie in my front yard on frost-covered grass in the fetal position at midnight, calling out pathetically for my mother, cradling a bag of potato chips.*

I gathered the one molecule of dignity left in me, stood up, and slinked back inside.

I left the sliding glass door open a bit, giving all the heat in the house permission to leave. I lay down on the couch. Eventually, I heard Mommadawg jump up and perch herself on the sofa and gawk at me. She was cocky, as if she'd proven some kind of alpha-dog point.

Believe it or not, there was a lesson to be learned there.

Mommadawg could run for a while. She could try to be on her own and self-sufficient. But in the final analysis, she knew where she was loved and safe, and that was where she returned. Every time. Eventually.

It's good to know where we are safe. It's good to sense whom we can be safe with. It's vital that we have a network of forever family we know are walking this journey with us, the ones who call us to honesty and give us the freedom to not be okay. It's crucial that we know who will wait for us through the cold night.

When I first brought her home, Mommadawg basically lived under the bed until I put food out for her. She would crawl out, eat, and crawl right back under, unless I grabbed her and sat on the couch, continuing the petting and hugging process, which she hated. At night, I'd pick her up and set her at the foot of my bed. She would immediately jump down and under the bed, where she stayed all night.

One night, though, after several months of moving from fear to obvious obstinacy, she stayed on the bed all night. It was a miracle. I was happy.

That was our routine for a few months.

Then, one night, I woke up, looked at the foot of the bed, and noticed Mommadawg concentrating intently on me. We lay there for a long while, just peering at each other. I eventually cautiously held my hands out toward her. She considered the gesture for a bit. Then she stood up and walked toward me. She lay down next to me and gently rolled over onto her back. I rubbed her belly. All her fear and loneliness were gone. She discovered that being by my side brought her peace and contentment. From that moment on, she knew she was safe. All I had to do was hold out my arms, and she'd throw her head back, and those floppy ears would come running.

I drove Mommadawg to the clinic this morning. Her congestive heart failure betrayed her hard-earned skills of survival. I held her close to my chest for most of the night. A few times, through labored breathing, she gazed at me with so much love and acceptance that my heart broke. She knew it was time. She knew she was ready.

I wasn't.

I texted Dr. Peck at two thirty in the morning and told him I thought Mommadawg was telling me she wanted to go home. I asked him to text me when he got to the clinic.

He texted me when he arrived at the office this morning.

I drove Mommadawg to the clinic. I passed a bunch of memories on the way, and for the first time ever, I thought of something essential. In all the years I've fed, loved, hugged, and cared for her, Mommadawg never once growled. Never. She only bayed when she was running through the woods. The only time I ever heard her bark was at five o'clock every morning, almost to the second, to go outside. I never once heard her growl, bark, or snarl or saw her bare her teeth at the other pooches or anyone. Never. She never complained or reacted. She only responded with love, intelligence, and, I'm positive, thankfulness.

Even this morning, as I held her close to my chest at the clinic, she looked up at me and, in her precious, understanding way, let me know I was even then taking care of her and keeping her safe.

I held her gaze and said, "Juju, I love you. I love you. You have been my treasure. You're about to go on your greatest, most joyful adventure. Don't be afraid. You're about to see beautiful things and colors and people and animals. They will take care of you till I get there. You're going to see Jesus before I do. Tell him I love him and can't wait till we're all together. Lick his face. Jump around, and be happy. You've loved me so well. You did your job."

Dr. Peck prayed.

And now I hold on to this solid truth, this strong hope:

> That's why I don't think there's any comparison between the present hard times and the coming good times. The created world itself can hardly wait for what's coming next. Everything in creation is being more or less held back. God reins it in until both creation and all the creatures are ready and can be released at the same moment into the glorious times ahead. Meanwhile, the joyful anticipation deepens. (Romans 8:18–21 MSG)

CONVERSATION STARTERS FROM RITA STONE

I can sit with Rita and a big cup of kombucha and talk for hours. If it's not food, it's how God loves us through the good times and the painful times of life. We freely and openly pray for each other. When the Bramble needs decorating, which is often since mostly guys work there, we call Rita. She whirls through, and the place looks like a picture out of a home-and-garden magazine. She's got the class. She's got the style. She's so pretty.

1. God gave man the responsibility of caring for the animals. At what point do we realize that they also care for us? How have your pets enhanced your life?

2. Juju hated the process of learning to trust. Has there been a time in your life when you learned it was okay to trust again? Did you rail against it? How did you overcome the fear?

3. Has there been a time in your life when you determined to stay the course with someone (e.g., a child, friend, spouse, or relative) in order to show that you would always be there for him or her? Did staying the course mean letting the person go? Did you have the courage to let the person go, praying he or she would eventually come home?

4. How many chips in your trail would it take for you to make it through the front door?

Dream Catcher

THIS IS MY nephew, Tad. When Tad was eight years old, we decided to work on a project together. We went out in search of a way to build a dream catcher and found a kit to put one together. Tad was fascinated by the Native American legend: if a dream catcher was placed in the window of your bedroom, bad dreams would be caught in the web before they drifted into your sleep.

To be honest, I have few memories of the event. I do remember the joy of hanging out with my buddy Tad and spending a few moments investing in our relationship. Those moments are never wasted.

Every moment is a matter of perspective. If I keep an eternal mindset, every experience becomes essential and impactful. We have no idea how the Lord will use even the most inconsequential words or actions to permeate and permanently change a person's life. Something said or done, even off the cuff, at a moment's notice, can alter a person's day.

We hear about emotional and verbal abuse all the time, aimed not just at children but at adults as well. How often do we forget that as believers in Jesus, every footstep we take is drawing us closer to our eternal home? How often do we recognize that every breath we breathe is laced with opportunity to show that reality to others?

Even when we don't mention the name of Jesus, we are still representing him. What if I'm the only chance a restaurant server will have to see Jesus today? Will I leave just a little bit more on the gratuity, or will I fret over whether I should tip on the tax or not? Will I intentionally look at the person and take a moment to know him or her?

I have a great friend who is a pastor in Las Vegas. When Jimmy, Marna, and family go to supper at a restaurant, they always pray over their meal. Jimmy makes it a point to tell their servers they are about to pray, and he asks if there is anything he can lift up for them as they pray. It's usually a shock to the servers. But there's almost always a need offered up.

One day I was getting gas for my car. As I walked to the window to hand my cash to the young lady I'd seen in that same window many times before, I was suddenly struck with the realization that I never saw her smile. She was mechanical—not rude or unkind, but she pushed the same gas buttons every day and slid the cash drawer back and forth the same way day in and day out. No smile. Monotony.

When she slid the drawer back and asked if I wanted the full ten-cent discount per gallon the same way she probably had said it thirty times that day, I paused. She looked up for my response. I said, "Please don't think I'm creepy, but the Lord has blessed you with the most beautiful eyes."

It was an eternal moment. The young lady's countenance completely changed. She beamed as she broke into a big, heartfelt smile and said, "Thank you."

She might never remember it again; I don't know. But in that moment, I felt the presence of the Lord.

Sometimes we have to be bolder. Sometimes those eternal moments present an opportunity to stand up for the bullied or disenfranchised. Though I wish I were better at handling those situations, I almost always lean toward the underdog. The problem lies in my knee-jerk tendency to demean the perpetrator. What I should do instead is verbally accost the bully with love.

I remember one example vividly. With an empty, gnawing stomach, I saw a sign at my favorite chicken place that said, "Nine pieces for $9.99." For me, those pieces of chicken would cover three or maybe three and a half meals. (When I was younger, that much poultry would have been one meal, tops.)

Let me say, before you read the rest of this tale, I did say, "Ma'am," at one point. That will be important later and maybe show I did try to retain a semblance of integrity. My feeble attempt at accosting with love.

The drive-through was insane, so I figured it would be much quicker to go inside. In theory, that would have been correct. When I got inside, there was only one customer in front of me, obviously waiting for her nine pieces of chicken.

I placed my order. The two girls bravely operating the cash registers, clearly exhausted, tried their best to be sweet and professional. The girl taking my order said it would be a few minutes. I told her it was no problem. I saw cooks and servers dashing around behind the counter. Yep, they were busy that day.

The lady in front of me, obviously feeling a little more entitled than she should have, yelled, "Could you please find out how long it will be for the rest of my order? It's just two pieces!"

One of the counter girls, exasperated and deflated, sluggishly apologized. "It'll be just a few more minutes. They're trying to cook more."

The lady heavy-sighed, crossed her arms, shook her head, and leaned against the counter.

I was, at that point, mildly amused, and to be honest, throughout the rest of our encounter, that amused interest never left me. The lady huffed, "Well, I guess I'll just have to come earlier next time if I'm going to have to wait!"

The poor employee shrugged and almost whispered, "It wouldn't matter. It's been like this all night." I almost laughed out loud.

The lady turned to me and, with the most exasperated voice she could muster, said, "Can you believe this?"

The girls behind the counter looked at me, weakly waiting for me to agree with her. I furrowed my brow, focused on her, and said, "Ma'am, followers of Christ are being beheaded by horrible pure evil. People are dying excruciatingly painful deaths all over the world by the thousands from a grisly virus that no one should have to experience, only because they don't have access to a vaccine that can save them. Women and children in Sudan are abused and are dying from thirst or starvation because they refuse to deny their belief in Jesus. Dogs and cats are living together. And you, on the other hand, are all up in your feelings journal over a chicken leg. Seriously? It's a chicken leg!"

For the next few seconds, I'm fairly sure I heard a nightingale sing in Berkeley Square.

I glanced over to see both the workers resembling baby sparrows with their mouths agape, apparently waiting for the momma bird to toss chicken nuggets into them.

Fortunately, the awkward silence was broken by one of the girls sliding a bag with two final pieces of chicken across the counter to the lady, who was still staring at me as if my head had spun around and I'd ralphed up green pea soup. She sheepishly picked up her bag and skulked away.

One of the girls, with mouth still ajar, slid my box to me. I shrugged and said, "Sorry. Someone had to do it." She raised her fist in solidarity so I could give her knucks.

In the car, I did a HEART check: Was I hungry? Exhausted? Angry? Resentful? Tense? Apparently, I was starving.

I hope the lady who needed to hear words that might have been tough will think long and hard before she faults and berates others for petty circumstances out of their control. And maybe I will think long and hard before opening my mouth, even if it is the perfect rebuff. Or maybe not.

When I spent those few hours with my nephew, Tad—who, by the way, has grown into one of the best men I know—it never crossed my mind that it would be any more than a good time. Tad owned every Lego known to mankind. He would disappear for hours. None of us would worry about him, because he was never a rebellious kid. He never used drugs or abused alcohol. He was a really good guy. We would find him hours later, sitting in his room, surrounded by Legos, building an airplane or the *Millennium Falcon* or creating a labyrinthine safe house, totally content.

During Tad's kindergarten year, my sister made the tough decision to hold him back in school. He didn't do well that year, and she decided he needed a do-over. Because of that impossible decision, Tad made one B his entire school career. All the rest were As. He went on to study at West Point and became a Black Hawk pilot.

When Jacqui sent the above picture of Tad holding that silly dream catcher, she told me it had hung in Tad's bedroom his entire life, even on the wall in his room at West Point. When Tad was in the army, it traveled with him to Afghanistan and every other post where he lived.

I never knew about it. That's the important thing here. We have no idea about the ripple-on-the-pond effect. We never know how many of those tiny waves continue expanding until they reach the shores of heaven.

I'm convinced we will spend eons upon eons of time in heaven, if we have done the simple work of investing in moments here on earth, hearing people say, "Hey, I became a follower of Christ. I'm here because you invested time in our mutual friend." Or "Do you remember the day you silently asked the Lord to bless that small child walking down the sidewalk? My life wasn't always easy, but you listened to the Holy Spirit that day, and the Lord blessed your prayer, and he blessed me. And I'm here now. Thank you."

Hebrews 10:24–25 (MSG) says, "Let's see how inventive we can be in encouraging love and helping out, not avoiding worshiping together as some do but spurring each other on, especially as we see the big Day approaching."

So what will be the opportunity look like for you today?

The answer is this: don't look. Don't wait for the Lord to say, "Here's your chance to make an eternal difference in this person's life." You see, every moment is an opportunity. Every encounter you leave behind will be a chance for someone to say, "Wow, whatever they have, I want it."

When Tad and his precious wife, Abby, were expecting their first child at any minute, Jacqui was there, waiting to do what she was made to do: be a grandmother. She sent me the following picture.

On the wall is a drawing of an elephant being held aloft by balloons with this precious little boy's name, Thomas Allen Lefler, and under the picture, hanging just above Thomas's bassinet is a twenty-five-year-old dream catcher filled with a lifetime of dreams.

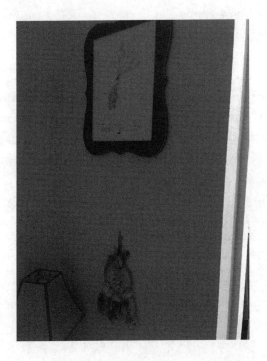

I pray Thomas's dreams will always be filled with visions of his eternal home in heaven and a Savior who knows him by name.

CONVERSATION STARTERS FROM ANTHONY AND LAURA HENNEN

Laura is an authentic encourager. I never talk to her without feeling important and validated. I never leave her without being sick from eating way too much cheese dip (and any other junk food we can think of). We laugh a lot. Next to asking Jesus to be his Lord and Savior, Laura is the best move Anthony ever made. I never hug her without her saying, "We love you." She means it. I love Laura. She's so pretty.

1. What would your response have been to Tim had you been the lady in the restaurant waiting for your chicken leg?

2. What opportunities do you face daily in which you can make a difference in someone's life with simple, kind gestures, even when you don't want to or feel like it?

3. How can you prepare yourself daily to be ready to encourage or inspire others you cross paths with during the course of your day?

CONVERSATION STARTERS FROM TIM e HOLDER

1. Yep, me. One more time. Truth be told, I couldn't, for the life of me, find who originally did questions for this story. But I finally did after I'd written some. I almost deleted mine, but I liked the way Anthony and Laura's questions

worked together with mine, so y'all get a twofer. Y'all are truly blessed!

2. Name a time when you acted on an unplanned chance to be kind or a time when you gave up something (e.g., time, finances) just to show someone attention. Did you find out later the difference it made in his or her life?

3. Does it matter if you never, on this side of the veil, know if it made a difference?

4. Have you ever been the benefactor of someone taking his or her time to make sure you know you have worth and are essential in this world? Have you taken the time to thank that person for his or her gift of love to you? Lately, have you thanked Jesus for willingly and freely taking the time to prove his love for you?

FaLKor the Adventure Dog

AS I'VE SAID, I live way out in the country on two and a half acres of woods with a winding creek and a small wood house I call home—*The Blair Witch Project*. It's a perfect setting for dogs, and normally, I take them outside and watch them run around and perform their regular constitutionals before coming inside.

Years ago, I decided to stand inside the door rather than venture out into the misty weather. One day my Jack Russell terrier, Gitli (Cherokee for "Dog"), a tornado of teeth and toenails, seemed to be taking a lot more time than usual to come back to the house. I went out looking for him.

I finally located him behind my house. He must have wandered there and encountered my neighbor's two dogs. Because I wasn't there to stop them, they brutally attacked and killed my precious pet. I've never gotten over that experience. Now I never, under any circumstances, let my pooches go out, rain, shine, sleet, snow, or ice, unless I'm there with them.

A while ago, I took two of my six out. My little blind one, the tiny rat terrier, Gawasi (Cherokee for "Grace"), was barking at me to pick her up, so I did. I carried her into the house.

Falkor wasn't out of my sight for more than one minute. He is what my veterinarian calls a Labasset: a Labrador head and a basset hound body. Completely black. Weirdest-looking dog ever!

I went outside to bring him back in, and he had apparently, and ill-advisedly, decided to go on an exploration adventure.

He never wanders far, never out of my line of vision. I calmly checked all the usual places he went, including the burn pile and the creek. I called and called. I walked around my next-door neighbor's house and to the street behind, where I'd found Gitli in a field years ago. I immediately began to tense up. I could feel anxiety and fear rising up my shoulders and into my throat. My mouth went dry, and my heart raced as the minutes turned into hours. I got in my car and drove around the neighborhood, looking for any sign of him. I stopped to ask neighbors if they had seen him: a black Labasset with a red collar.

Kids were playing in the front yard of the house where the dogs had killed Gitli. The owners of those dogs had moved out, and the youngsters were new to the neighborhood. I stopped my car, stuck my head out the window, and asked if they had seen a black dog with a red collar. They were sweet. They walked to my car and said no dog had come by with that description, but they would be on the lookout for him and bring him home if he came over.

I glanced up to see their father standing on the front porch. I yelled, "I promise I'm not a predator! I'm really looking for my dog. I live right behind you. I love Jesus, and I'm in the choir."

He smiled and gave me the thumbs-up sign. I thanked the kids for helping me search.

Then I hollered up at their father, "By the way, they probably still shouldn't walk up to the car of someone they don't know!"

He laughed and said, "You're absolutely right."

I drove on down the road a bit, turned around, and headed back. As I passed, I saw the father on his knees with his kids, obviously having a pertinent and timely discussion. They all smiled and waved.

I was beginning to panic. I walked through the woods all around my house, screaming Falkor's name, the whole time praying, *Please let him come home. Please let him be okay.*

My brain reeled with unsubstantiated, unhealthy thoughts. *What if those neighbors with the pit bull tied in front of their house down the way are actually dogfighters? What if they caught Falkor for bait?* Possible but totally irrational. I couldn't stop praying. The what-ifs were not impossible. Not probable but possible.

I came home, sat on the front porch, and drank Dr. Pepper and prayed. More than two hours passed. He never had been gone so long. My whole body trembled. I couldn't get past the awful thoughts and pictures in my head.

I finally realized the experience was entirely out of my control. I knew the only place I could go was to the Lord. And I didn't need to be alone with my fear and anxiety, so being the junkie that I am, I went to social media and posted Falkor's picture. I asked my friends to pray with me.

Immediately, posts began to pop up from my precious friends and family: "Praying for a safe return," "Praying," "What a horrible feeling. Praying," "Oh, Tim, I'm so heartbroken," and "Praying for Falkor's safe return and peace for you." They went on and on.

At that point, I realized my entire body had reacted to fear. I realized my brain, which is supposed to be used for problem-solving, was being bombarded by the what-ifs, which are never good in a situation like that.

I thought of 2 Corinthians 10:5 (ESV): "We destroy arguments and every lofty opinion raised against the knowledge of God, and take every thought captive to obey Christ."

I always believed that verse was just for evil thoughts concerning unforgiveness, lust, or any number of ungodly mental failures. It never occurred to me that it could refer to fear. Fear and anxiety are as faithless as any other feelings and are equally capable of pulling me out of obedience to Jesus.

I realized I had many faithful believers who loved me and were petitioning our Father and going to him on my behalf. They were all praying over something that would seem a trivial matter to most people. I felt my heart slow down, my chest untighten, my breathing go back to some semblance of normal, and the sweating stop. I closed my eyes. *Lord, I can't control this. I have to let it go. I just ask that you hear the prayers of your people.*

It seemed everything slowed down for a while. It wasn't that I was okay with my sweet little pooch being lost. I just knew the One who'd created Falkor was in control no matter what.

About four hours later, as I watched the sunset, I still needed God's presence. Every time I felt the fear begin to bubble up, I would pray, *Give me your peace.*

Then, about eight o'clock, up sauntered Falkor, soaked. Obviously, he had been swimming in the creek. He looked obnoxiously sheepish.

When he saw me sitting on the deck, he stopped short. He knew he was in trouble. I just let him stand there, dripping, staring at me, while I calmly went to social media on my phone and let everyone know he was home safe. Then I hugged him while people all over the world typed, "Yay," "Hallelujah," and "I'm so glad. Praise God!"

The next day, there were still consequences from my letting fear take the place of faith no matter the outcome. My body literally ached. I was sore all day long.

Once again, obedience to Christ is proven through my weakness.

My memory verse this week is Isaiah 41:10 (MSG): "You're my servant, serving on my side. I've picked you. I haven't dropped you. Don't panic. I'm with you. There's no need to fear for I'm your God. I'll give you strength. I'll help you. I'll hold you steady. I'll keep a firm grip on you."

A few weeks ago, between services at church, I listened to a message on my phone from the correctional unit where I do volunteer work. It was my weekend to be on call. An inmate's cousin had died at a correctional unit where she was incarcerated in Missouri, and I was to inform him of her death. It's never easy. But I've done so many of these interviews over the years that it's not as devastating as it once was. I have the conversation down, and I can pretty much do it by rote. I fight not to become so callous that it ever becomes just a nuisance or even an inconvenience.

My plan for the evening included teaching at the women's unit just down the road from the men's. That gave me a convenient opportunity to meet with the gentleman who'd lost his cousin. Although it was hard, he handled the news reasonably well. His cousin's death was not expected. I gave him a few minutes on the phone with his family to grieve together. Those few moments are genuinely touching.

Then, before the evening service, I settled down to put final touches on my notes for the service. I called a couple of inmates, my cofacilitators who lead Celebrate Recovery with me, down to the office so we could start planning our upcoming step-study. About the time we got into the planning, I got a call from the women's unit. One of the ladies there had lost a family member, and I needed to come talk to her before she could read the obituary in the newspaper the following day.

I sent the guys back to their barracks and sat back in the chair. My stomach churned. This one seemed impossible. Reporting the death of a cousin couldn't hold a candle to what I needed to tell Traci.

I drove the quarter mile to the women's unit, and as I walked through the chain-link gate, all I could do was pray. I told God this one was too hard. I didn't want to do this one. I wasn't angry; I just felt an overwhelming fear, leading to almost immediate weariness. I recognized the pattern.

I walked into the barracks area and told the officers the purpose of my visit. I usually take the inmates into the chaplain's office alone, break the news, give them a few minutes to process, let them call a loved one, pray with them, and send them back to their barracks. This was different.

I asked the officers if one or two of them could stand outside the door in case Traci became too inconsolable. The captain walked to the barracks door and called her name: "Mason, to the chaplain's office."

There are a few things I can count on when I have to deliver devastating news to inmates. First, if they're called to the chaplain's office, there's a 99 percent chance it's not going to be good news. I've done so many of these interviews that I know the thought process as they approach me. They are running through a litany of people in their lives, wondering who it could be. Who's been sick?

Who's oldest? Was there some kind of accident? An overdose? Murder?

As they approach, I see the excruciating anxiety and fear in their faces. They search my eyes for any sign or clue as to whom they are about to begin grieving.

I also know they are lining themselves up internally. No matter what the news, the inmates can't show their grief. They can't show weakness or fear of any kind. They can't allow anyone in to walk with them, for fear of owing.

My heart broke as Traci walked toward me. I introduced myself. "Hi, Traci. I'm Chaplain Tim. How are you today?"

Traci, already no bigger than my index finger, seemed to fall in on herself and became even smaller. She smiled weakly. "I'm okay. But I think I'm about to not be."

I closed the door behind us and motioned to an empty seat for her. I sat with the desk between us, which, at that moment, seemed to separate us by miles. "No, I'm afraid not. Traci, there's no way for me to make this easy for you. We got a call today. Your son, Benjamin, chose to end his life."

There is always a moment of silence. One thing I've learned in life is that silence is usually better than trying to fill a space with well-meaning but nonetheless empty platitudes that, more often than not, go unheard.

So we sat, with those few moments as distant and distinct as the space between us. Traci locked her eyes on mine, and I watched as tears pooled in her eyes. She finally whispered, "Thank you for telling me."

She started to get up, and I said, "No, sit here with me for a while."

I waited for the tears to momentarily subside. Then I asked Traci questions about her boy. All the good things she could remember. I asked about his favorite things in life. He'd loved the Razorbacks and pretty much anything with a motor. I choked back tears at several of her memories.

I prayed with her and told her how important it was going to be for her to find ways to lean into God for hope and strength. I prayed God would place angels in strategic places around her to whisper peace that only he could give her hurting heart. I prayed that as impossible as it seemed, she would find peace instead of fear.

The last thing I told her was that I would continue to pray for her. I would pray that she find a way to show the glory of her Father in the midst of this devastating situation. That she would press into him and give him the chance to be her safe place, the only One she could truly trust with this pain. Traci gave a half-hearted nod, unconvinced. It was, after all, prison. She wiped her face with her government-issued white sleeve and walked back to her barrack.

I watched as she made her way down the cinder-block hallway. I heard every step of grief echo through the building. I listened to the heaviness of her barrack door as it closed behind her. Her lowered shoulders, bearing more weight than one lonely woman should ever have to carry, spoke volumes. One more defeat in her life.

I looked toward the officer at her door as she watched Traci plod slowly to her rack. The officer turned toward me and said, "Traci went straight to her bed and started brushing her hair."

I went back to the office. "Lord, you've called me to this ministry. I do love it. But I don't ever want to do that again."

A couple of hours later, at the evening service, I stood at the door, welcoming all the ladies to the visitation center. Mentally, I was only halfway there, trying to realign my troubled heart for the teaching I was about to do.

As the welcome line progressed, I looked up to see a tiny lady walk in. Her eyes were red and wet with tears. My throat closed, and my eyes stung as I struggled with the words.

"Hi, Traci. I'm so glad you're here."

CONVERSATION STARTERS
FROM STEVE HOLDER

Steve is my older brother. Steve is a retired band director. In order to get to their schools, Steve and his wife, Julee (also a retired teacher), would travel down Pleasure Street and then pass through the town of Joy to arrive at their schools in Rosebud. If they went just a few miles farther, they'd stop in Romance. No wonder they've been married so long. Steve and Julee have three great kids and a couple of adorable grands. Julee is a gifted artist. She's really pretty. Steve walks five miles a day. I walk to the mailbox occasionally.

1. If you're old enough to remember, as children, we used to go find an adult if we were lost or hurt. We instruct our children to stay away from adults they don't know (stranger danger). What happened that makes today's world so different?

2. We live in a world beset by pandemics, economic stress, racial strife, and countless other forces that threaten our happiness. Prayer can be a tremendous road back to peace. Don't wait. Compose your own message to God. Put it in your spiritual backpack, and have it ready for when it's needed. Use it as often as required. Then add to it based on the current situation.

3. Scripture teaches us that just like Falkor or Traci, we're all going to get lost sometime. How far have you ever traveled away from your heart and God? And how did you journey back? Are your prepared for your next adventure?

Obvious Places

ONE OF THE lessons—maybe the most important discipline—I've learned from being part of Celebrate Recovery (CR) for more than twenty years is the discipline of listening. I think it's a habit of our culture to have a pithy phrase at the tip of our tongue for every situation and every problematic occasion. We do it for basically one reason: the comfort factor. We don't like to feel uncomfortable. In effect, we have learned not to listen.

I remember realizing for the first time that as soon as someone began talking to me, I started the process of formulating a response. Providing a response, any response, would make me feel better and more comfortable. I believed if I felt better, then the person in crisis would feel better.

James 1:19 (MSG) gives a perfect picture of the inverse of this deadly habit we, as a culture, have cultivated: "Post this at all the intersections, dear friends: Lead with your ears, follow up with your tongue, and let anger straggle along in the rear." James says it's so important we should post this life-giving advice at every intersection: Yield, Stop, Caution, Lane Ends Ahead, and Listen. He tells us to lead with our ears and then follow up with our words.

I learned through the guidelines of CR that I don't have to have a response. As a matter of fact, allowing other fallen humans the respect of hearing their pain, really listening, makes them feel valued and important. Some, for the first time in their lives, feel heard and not interrupted.

So I listen. And most times, I learn.

A residual blessing from this discipline of active listening—and I believe all blessings have residual blessings—is that I've learned to give this same respect to God. When he told us to lead with our ears, maybe he wasn't just talking about listening to each other. It's part of his "Be still and know that I am God" philosophy.

The madness of living life tends to drown out our ability to hear him. Along with trying to formulate a correct and life-altering response to a person's appeal to be heard, we think that catchphrases are a healing tonic. But now I believe God is seen, felt, and heard most clearly in the silence. After all, it wasn't in the hurricane winds, the massive earthquake, or the mighty fire that Elijah heard him. It was in his still, small voice. And that still, small voice moved Elijah to action.

I often pray the Lord will place me in strategic places on any particular day where his presence is undeniable and where I can make a difference. Not for me but for him—for his glory. I don't believe I hear them every time, but sometimes they are pronounced, and he always shows himself in unexpected, unusual, spontaneous, surprising, and sometimes challenging ways.

Heading to Fort Smith for a business meeting once, driving down a relatively deserted road, I happened to look to the shoulder and notice a large bird in a ditch, writhing, obviously in pain. I was running a little late, so I just hoped it would be okay.

About a tenth of a mile later, I realized I would be miserable if I didn't take care of it. So I turned around and went back. I saw the bird trying to walk. It must have been hit by a car and left to die.

Sidebar: I won't go into how furious this makes me. Just imagine torture and perhaps a small amount of permanent maiming.

I got out of my car and walked to the bird. Recognizing a young turkey, I reached for her, but she crawled away. Wearing slacks and a dress shirt, I chased behind her through briar patches into the woods.

After a bit of chasing, I caught up with her, picked her up, and carried her to the car. I drove her to Doubletree Veterinary Clinic, where I worked, and took her inside. The good Dr. Peck made a quick exam and shook his head sadly.

I said, "Look, I was in the right place at the right time. Now fix 'er!"

Jenny, the vet tech, said, "You mean like with dressing?"

I left the critter there and yelled back over my shoulder, "Fix 'er!" as I walked out. I thanked the Lord for letting me pass by that spot at just the right time. I went on to Fort Smith, did my business presentation, and headed back.

I was traveling down the interstate and got stuck in rush-hour traffic and a major amount of road work. I was tired, annoyed, and frustrated that it was taking forty-five minutes longer to get home than I wanted.

But as I got into town, I passed Walgreens, when I saw a couple of men in the grass, bending down and looking at a sweet little dog lying in the grass. I immediately knew the sweet pooch had been hit. I thought I might be able to take it to the clinic to have Dr. Peck look at it. But I pulled into the Walgreens parking lot and saw them covering the little pup up. The little animal was gone.

Just then, I saw a lady sitting behind them in the grass with her head in her hands, sobbing. Perhaps she'd hit the dog. I couldn't tell. But I did notice a couple of other women approach her and try to comfort her.

I walked to the men and asked what had happened. They said it was her dog, and it had jumped out the car window while she was parked. It had run into the street during rush-hour traffic.

I walked over to the grieving woman and sat in the grass near her. By then, a small crowd had gathered, including a child, all wanting to comfort her. I spoke first. "What's your name?"

"Suzie." She continued sobbing.

I let a couple of minutes pass. I felt the Lord prompting me to say or do something; I just wasn't sure what. So I waited. I listened.

The little girl looked up at me and said, "Her puppy is with Jesus."

I got all misty-eyed and said, "You are one hundred percent right. I have absolutely no doubt." Just then, I knew what the Lord was asking me to do. "Suzie, do you believe in God?"

She looked up at me with her eyes filled with tears and nodded.

I said, "Would it be okay if I prayed for you?"

She suddenly looked relieved. At the same time, everyone else said, "Yes!"

Suzie reached out and put her hand on mine. Everyone there threw his or her hand in, and I prayed. I prayed for Suzie's peace and that she would feel God's strong arms wrapped around her while she grieved. I prayed he would send his angels to protect her, and I said even though we didn't understand why these things happened, God was still on his throne and grieving right along with all of us there.

In that unlikely but holy place, five strangers held hands. We prayed while, fifteen feet away, rush-hour traffic flew past us on Highway 10. How many of those drivers wondered at all the people praying?

Suzie was still shaking and overwhelmed, having just lost her precious little friend.

Someone got a box from Walgreens, and I put the little one inside, wrapped in a plastic red-and-white-checkered tablecloth Walgreens donated. I put her in the back of my car and then drove Suzie home in her car.

There was another dog in the car, a big boxer. Suzie wasn't sure Roxie would be okay with someone else in the car. I told her I felt safe. I got in, and Roxie came right up to me and started licking my face. Suzie smiled through her grief and said, "Wow, she never does that."

I told her to just call me the dog whisperer. She laughed a little but cried most of the way home. I listened. She was upset that the woman who'd hit her little pup hadn't even stopped. Even though I again had fleeting thoughts of torture and a little maiming, I told her she mustn't dwell on that. Seven people had stopped, total strangers who cared. I reminded her that she'd loved her sweet little one better than anyone else could have. The pup had loved her unconditionally, and she had to remember all the happiness they had brought to each other.

One of the other ladies followed us to Suzie's apartment. When we got out of our cars, Suzie spoke through tears. "I'm overwhelmed by your goodness."

I told her, "Oh, Suzie, don't thank me. I'm not good. It's all about the Lord. He even made sure I was held up by road work so I'd pass you at just that time."

She asked, "You really think so?"

I smiled. "It worked, didn't it?"

She hugged us both. The other lady drove me back to my car. I drove to the clinic and left Suzie's precious little companion there.

I love days like that, even when they're hard.

Once again, God surprised me with his goodness. I know this to be true: I will never lead as well with my words as I do with my ears. I will never have the wisdom to give affirmation, hope, mercy, and grace if I speak before I hear.

And I mean really hear. Not just the parts for which I have a canned, ready response but everything.

Butterball the turkey (yes, that's what they named her at the clinic, which scares me just a little) went to a rehab clinic for wild birds. Dr. Beach gave her some meds for a few days and then set her at the edge of the woods. He watched as she took flight and soared over the trees and into the woods.

Hey, God!

CONVERSATION STARTERS
FROM NELDA ALEXANDER

Nelda, former state rep for Celebrate Recovery, is now the founder of Healing Her Wounded Heart (healingherwoundedheart.com). She's an addiction, life recovery, and mindset coach. We have traveled many miles together as Celebrate Recovery reps. But the greatest gift is our friendship, which has lasted a long, long time. She's so pretty.

1. Healing begins when we feel heard for the very first time. Really heard—with the heart. Have you been there? Do you remember what that felt like? Did that help you realize that God hears you?

2. Have you ever been in the exact place where God needed you to be, at the exact right moment, to share God's message and then listen with your heart as someone shared things he or she had never shared with anyone—ever—as God opened his or her heart? Pray for those moments, and then be still and listen.

3. How easy is it to feel out of control when everything around you feels chaotic? Have you been there? Focusing on him brings it all back into perspective. Have you learned to practice that habit? Intentionally be still, and know?

CONVERSATION STARTERS
FROM RON ALEXANDER

A fellow recoverer and one of the hardest-working men I know, Ron is the picture of a servant heart. Wherever he's needed, he's there. He always shows up and always has the best attitude. He refuses to give me his secret herb recipe for chicken rub. I've forgiven him. For the most part.

1. Are you one of those who often speaks when you should be listening?

2. In what situations have you seen an opportunity or felt the Lord's prompting to show his kindness but passed it by because you were too busy or didn't want to become involved?

3. Identify at least two steps you can take to improve your listening skills.

Waiting

FOR SEVERAL YEARS, I sold fireworks in a tent in West Little Rock. The days usually stretched to twenty-two hours, allowing me just enough time to run home, take a shower, let the dogs out, and feed them. I didn't have time to love on them, which made me feel like a terrible dad. It was hot. I was tired.

Every year, I entered that venture knowing full well the amount of work involved. I went in prepared to live on French onion dip, Ruffles, and Slim Jims from the dollar store.

By the time I helped load up the leftover fireworks on July 6 at ten o'clock at night, I'd be running on pure adrenaline. I didn't mind. I met amazing people and had engaging conversations with friends who'd stop by and sit in the extra white-with-green-stripes lawn chair. I sat under a three-poled tent with the flaps rolled up, thankful for a rare breeze to chill the sweat on my forehead. Tropical Skittles on the counter and an ice cooler filled with bottles of water—not bad at all. In fact, I looked forward to it every year.

One particular year was harder, though. In the midst of preparing to get the tent going, I heard of the passing of a dear friend from Nashville, Greg Murtha. Greg suffered for more than four years with colon cancer. He endured more than seventy rounds of chemo, two heart attacks, and other ailments. But Greg showed more exceptional courage, belief, faith, and absolute joy during his terminal sickness than any human I've ever known, including biblical characters. Greg never failed to vigorously look for places to show the heart of Jesus. He believed in celebrating and celebrating big.

Greg was right. When the prodigal son came home, he didn't get a pat on the shoulder and a "Welcome back" key ring. They threw a party. A lavish party. An impressive celebration. Greg believed, and so do I, that any celebration for any reason should be big. He said he'd been to too many memorial services that were morbid and solemn. Even forever family—faithful followers of Jesus—had to settle for Kool-Aid drinks and store-bought cookies at the reception.

But Greg's memorial service that August rang with pure joy and triumphant celebration. It was a party to end all parties. Greg made plans before he died. He hired his favorite band from Nashville and catered a massive blowout with lots of great food.

I will never say Greg was. Greg is. He waited and found purpose in his weakness. He wrote the book *Out of the Blue*, which contains one of my favorite quotes: "There is no better place to be than to truly, truly say YES to the prompting of the Holy Spirit, whatever He tells you to do. The answer is YES because we get to join Him on the adventure. It could not be better."

One day, when I finally feel the verdant grass of home, Greg will be standing right alongside Jesus and many others in my great cloud of witnesses welcoming me to my forever home.

Within a few days of learning about Greg traveling to heaven, I learned that a college friend had suffered a massive heart attack in Baton Rouge and died. Two days later, I was doing a live feed on social media, talking about the fireworks stand. An old friend of mine chimed in and asked about the stand. I told him to come visit. He said, "I'll see you soon."

I couldn't wait. I was excited to spend time with my friend, as we went to different churches and hadn't been around each other for several years. It would be good to catch up.

The next morning, I realized he never had come to the tent. I figured he was just busy. A few hours later, I got a message from his niece that he'd also suffered a massive heart attack at work, and the doctors had been unable to save him.

I was stunned. It was a moment when I just had to sit back and ask, "Why?" Greg, only fifty-one, left an amazing wife and son. Both of my other friends were living life while completely unaware that their time was limited.

Why? Why now? I wasn't questioning God's wisdom or his will. I know that somehow, somewhere, there is good for those who love him. I wasn't doubting that he had a plan and that it would unfold according to his timing. I guess I was wishing these things were more manageable, as a human being, to digest and understand.

I talked to my friend Debbie Ganus and said, "I'm beginning to get the feeling we aren't going to make it out of here alive."

She responded, "Me too. But sometimes I wish we got a countdown clock."

I said, "That would be nice. I'm just glad I can't really think of anything I would need to change."

The spiritual side of me totally gets it. The human side of me wants and needs answers. It would be great if all the pieces fell into place, even for a minute. I know how my story ends. In fact, I know that it never does. I know that living, for me, goes on forever. There is no termination.

I also know that no part of my journey will ever be isolated. I will never be alone. I guess the best we can hope for on this side of living is the waiting.

The more I thought about waiting, the more I looked at the myriad of verses that speak to that concept. Isaiah 30:18 (ESV) says, "Therefore the Lord waits to be gracious to you, and therefore he exalts himself to show mercy to you. For the Lord is a God of justice; blessed are those who wait for him."

Notice it does not say, "Blessed are those who wait for an answer." It doesn't say, "Blessed are those who wait for a blessing." It says, "Blessed are those who wait for him."

Lamentations 3:25 (MSG) says, "The Lord is good to those who wait for Him, the soul who seeks Him."

I spend too much time looking for reasons in life and too little time waiting for him. Too much time seeking the path for my life, when in reality, he is the path. Too much time wanting the pieces to all fall together without having to waste too much energy forcing the square peg into the round hole. Psalm 33:20–22 (ESV) says, "Our soul waits for the Lord: He is our help and our shield. For our heart is glad in Him, because we trust in His holy name. Let your steadfast love, O Lord, be upon us, even as we hope in You."

Probably few people can say their lives have turned out exactly the way they planned. Some may not have turned out as well. Some turned out far better. As important and necessary as planning can be, it doesn't come close to the peace, joy, and adventure of waiting on the Lord. I can only imagine the joy and laughter he must get out of the grand surprises he throws at us if we take the time to look. Sometimes they are so subtle we really have to scrutinize closely to see them. But sometimes they are so astonishing that all we can do is say, "Hey, God!"

Waiting is not passive. Waiting is hard work, especially when we realize that waiting might not be resolved in this part of our eternal lives. But we should wait expectantly and be prepared for the surprise of unexpected results. Wait in the Word. Be still. Be strong. Be willing to be courageous. Pray, and be thankful for the blessings you are going to receive. Isaiah 40:31 tells us that if we wait on the Lord, our strength will be renewed, and we will rise up with eagle-like wings. We will never grow tired in the running, and we won't grow weary in walking the path he has for us. Whether the waiting is long or short, we can be encouraged that the best is yet to come.

Susannah Spurgeon, wife of Charles Spurgeon, wrote,

> The Lord has strewn the pages of His Word with promises of blessedness to those who wait for Him. And remember, His slightest Word stands fast and sure, it can never fail you. So, my soul, see that you have a promise underneath thee, for then your waiting will be resting, and a firm foothold, for our hope will give you confidence in Him who has said, They shall not be ashamed that wait for me.

As I reeled from the deaths of three friends, I wasn't questioning God. I was looking in every crevice and corner for the good he has promised. I waited.

Psalm 33:4–7 (MSG) says, "God's Word is solid to the core; everything he makes is sound inside and out. He loves it when everything fits, when his world is in plumb-line true. Earth is drenched in God's affectionate satisfaction. The skies were made by God's command; he breathed the word and stars popped out."

Star Breather is intimately interested in every molecule of our journey and knows precisely where and how the good will all be bound together.

I got the following story from Joseph Watson, a friend who travels the world as a teacher for Youth with a Mission (YWAM). It brought me to tears.

Whoa! Check this out! Whenever I teach for a whole week, my rule for myself is to never start teaching till I've memorized everyone's name.

To help me learn their names, I've written over a thousand icebreaker questions.

Almost every week, someone in the school will pick number twenty-three. And whenever that happens, I know it was God who had them choose that number. Never more so than this week.

Question twenty-three reads, "Who would you most like to get saved?" Whenever that question is chosen, I know that God wants the whole class to take a moment, and all of us together pray out loud for the person the student says.

Sheila, nineteen, one of the students, picked this question and answered, "My sisters." And so we prayed.

When we finished praying, I told her in front of the class, "Look how many prayers just went up for your sisters! God heard every one, and his promise is that his arm is not too short to save, nor are his ears deaf to our cries. Expect to see God move on their behalf, and you let us know what happens."

Well, God started moving immediately. One of her sisters we'd prayed for is a prostitute in Brasilia. Only hours after we'd prayed, a man paid the going rate to take Sheila's sister to a restaurant for dinner. But rather than him being another john, he talked gently to her about Jesus and how much God loved her. He wanted nothing more from her.

After dinner, she went back to her apartment, where she lives with her two little sons. In the middle of the night, her two-year-old awoke from a dream, crying out, "Jesus! Jesus!" Prior to this, she'd never even allowed the name of Jesus to be uttered in her home. But hearing her little boy right after the surprising dinner caused her to pray. She said, "God, I don't know if I believe in you or not. But if you are real, then cause Sheila to mend her relationship with our birth father."

The backstory is that Sheila had never before met her biological father. She had spurned all of his efforts to reach out to her, angry at his having abandoned them so long ago. But yesterday Sheila felt from the Lord to reach out to her birth father for the first time. Over the phone, they asked forgiveness of each other. Sheila knew her birth father was suffering from a terminal illness. But unbeknownst to her during the conversation, he was gravely ill. In fact, a few hours after they spoke, her dad died—but not before letting Sheila's sister know about his reconciliation with Sheila.

Now the two sisters have plans to talk about all these things after their dad's funeral tomorrow. Only an all-loving Father God could weave these pieces of broken hearts together. Have I mentioned lately that I love my job?

The postscript to this story is that Sheila's sister is now a former prostitute, working a better job, and pursuing the Lord. Wait for the Lord. His plan for you is perfect.

I wait for the Lord, my soul waits, and in
His word I hope; my soul waits for the Lord
more than watchmen for the morning,
more than watchmen for the morning.

—Psalm 130:5–6 ESV

CONVERSATION STARTERS FROM NELDA ALEXANDER

I rarely ever talk to Nelda when she's not up to something new and exciting, whether it's counseling someone who feels damaged or broken or chalk-painting an old, worn-out, discarded piece of furniture. Actually, that's kind of her thing. That's her gift.

1. Have you prayed about a specific person or situation and felt God wasn't listening or didn't really care because he didn't give you an immediate answer? Are you looking for that answer outside yourself? Have you thought maybe the answer has more to do with you—what he wants to change in you—than with the other person or situation?

2. Do you have a prodigal loved one you need to be preparing a celebration for?

CONVERSATION STARTERS FROM RON ALEXANDER

Ron is the laid-back friend. Everyone needs at least one Ron in his or her life. He is full of good advice. He rarely gives it without being asked. He's thoughtful and respectful of everyone he knows. I always know I can trust him. I feel certain he's left the recipe for his chicken rub to me in his will.

1. Has the Lord revealed to you his purpose for your life? If so, write it down here. If the answer is no, ask the Lord to reveal this to you.

2. When you have an important issue to address in your life, do you wait on the Lord to reveal his plan, or do you move ahead under your own understanding? Share a specific example.

3. What can you do while waiting on the Lord for answers?

What Good Looks Like

ONE OF THE colossal mysteries of life is the ease with which most humans find fault with themselves. I include myself in that number. It's even easier for people to point out the frailties of others, maybe because it makes them feel better about themselves and their own weaknesses. In the economy of the world, we've lost track of what it means to outdo one another in showing honor.

I have been the recipient, on several occasions, of someone saying, "Oh, I was just kidding," after delivering a hurtful, damaging statement, as if kidding heals the cut. Just for the record, so you'll know, your children will know, and your children's children to the fourth generation will know, "I'm just kidding" is always a lie. What if we deliberately chose to live by Romans 12:8 (ESV): "Be devoted to one another in love. Honor one another above yourselves"? Those words are simple yet profound. How often do we purposely take the time to tell others that we recognize a specific strength or gift that sets them apart from the rest of the world?

I've done this a few times lately, and I get fascinating responses: either they shut me down because they fear being vulnerable to encouragement or are surprised anyone would notice something good about them, or they are confounded and embarrassed because it's much easier to believe the bad. After all, the bad far outweighs the good. I sometimes get the feeling they think I have some sort of untrustworthy agenda for encouraging them.

Over the years, I have taken an insightful personality inventory called Servants by Design. I say "over the years" deliberately. I've taken the inventory several times and even tried to occasionally cheat. I come up with the same results every time. According to the assessment, there are six distinct floors to our house. The original floors were Achiever, Persister, Catalyzer, Dreamer, Harmonizer, and Energizer. The names have been changed in recent years, and now they are Thinker, Persister, Promoter, Imaginer, Harmonizer, and Rebel. Everyone has all six of these personality types, but there is one dominant trait that is your default. It will always be your ground-floor level. You can move up into other floors, but you can only stay there for a while before you return to your foundation to recharge. Guess which trait is my dominant? Rebel! Someone wondered if that label made rebels sound like mischievous rascals. I said, "Not if you're a rebel." Then again, maybe it does. I'm good with that.

We all have specific strengths. If we are aware of them, they can help us experience the unique way we were created and how our strengths influence one another. These strengths are based on positive human functioning rather than behaviors that need repair.

Ironically, any of the six traits I could use for making money, such as Achiever, Persister, and Promoter, are top floors of my personality house—like way up there in the attic. On the unwise occasion I try to settle in one of those areas, I quickly scamper down to my foundation of Rebel and marinate there for a while.

My prayer is that understanding the areas of my giftedness that bring me life will help me enhance the lives of those I come in contact with and those who travel this journey of life alongside me.

Even though I want to use my gifts for good, I find the foundational problem of being good persists.

A few years ago, I worked under a supervisor at a church who gave evaluations regularly. There were several categories to discuss, with ratings from 1 to 10. When I went in for my first evaluation, he started the conversation by saying, "Just so you know, I will never give you a ten in any category, because if I do, you will never have room to grow."

My immediate thought was *Then why would I try?*

If we want to see people and see ourselves thrive and grow, we accentuate the positive. I have facilitated many Celebrate Recovery step-studies over the past twenty years. I'm telling you this not so you'll see me as some sacrificial, ace superhero twelve-stepper. The fact is, in actuality, the more step-studies I do, the more I find places in my heart and mind where I need to grow.

A couple of items in one of the step-study participant guides get responses that never surprise me but intrigue me. One says, "Name the negative things you've done in your life." In every study, the guys can write pages about the atrocities they have committed and the accompanying shame, guilt, fear, and consequences that come with those experiences.

It's the next item, specifically designed to balance a participant's inventory, that is interesting: "Name the good things you've done in your life." Their responses are significantly shorter, and many times, the space provided is left entirely blank.

What do we consider good? Doing good, in many people's lives, seems to mean significant, life-changing, world-shattering events. Believe it or not, God created this amazing, magnificent world full of good things that are not humongous.

I decided to come up with my own list of good things I've done. I read them to the guys before we read aloud our answers to those questions, so they may realize that good things in their lives can be moments of joy or beauty, a smile, or a remembered moment of peace.

Here's my incomplete list of good things:

I have been to the South Island of New Zealand four times, where I sang backing vocals for the number-one-rated television show. I also sheared a sheep there. Not on the show. At my dear friends Jeff and Margie Rea's farm. I won dance contests with gorgeous Maree Humphries. I have sung backup at the Grand Ole Opry. I have facilitated CR step-studies at churches and prisons, and in fact, I just finished my thirty-first step-study at a correctional unit. I have cooked lasagna and white chocolate bread pudding for inmates who are step-study graduates. I have baptized men whom society would deem unworthy. I have watched the lightbulb turn on as they work the program and realize that they are, in fact, worthy.

I pick up pennies. I have walked in the sand by ocean waves and watched a mile-wide moon rise from the horizon. I have rescued more abandoned dogs than I can count from living in the woods. I have held the hands of pet owners and cried with them as their precious pets have been put to sleep.

I have seen the dirt-floored cinder-block homes of families in Brazil. I've seen the dirt-floored hovel where my father was born in Texas. I've held my father's hand and told him I loved him, and most importantly, I meant it, even though his expression told me he couldn't remember me.

I've planted trees. I've hugged my friends and family. I've cooked great meals for them. I've hugged my dogs. I had two speaking lines in an Academy Award–winning film. I've learned the beauty of listening well. I have consciously chosen integrity over gossip. I've forgiven and been forgiven.

I've sought God and listened for his voice. And I've oftentimes heard him. I've kept quiet when I could have given a great answer. I have learned not to give advice unless explicitly asked. I've learned and am learning the eternal value of speaking words of life, not words of death. I have learned there is no in-between.

I've paid bills on time. I've read great books and watched great movies. I've played Boo Radley twice in *To Kill a Mockingbird*. I played the role of C. S. Lewis in *Shadowlands*. I portrayed Polycarp, one of the first Christian martyrs, in a Good Friday production.

I've spent quality time with Jesus. I've learned that he is profoundly crazy about me. I've moved toward community instead of isolation. I have deliberately chosen kindness over revenge. I have learned and am learning to accept compliments. I've made tithing a habit and watched the Lord perform miracle after miracle through that discipline.

I've learned to accept others as much as they are able to give and not put expectations on them to respond to me as I think they should. I've learned to respond and not react. I've learned and am learning to use my gifts exactly how the Lord created me and stop wishing I was in possession of someone else's.

I have grudgingly and finally come to grips with the fact that I will never be a half-pipe gold medal snowboarder or an Olympic figure skater. I've learned that God made the earth not for me to enjoy but for his glory. And he lets me enjoy it for his glory.

I've learned to receive well and to give in private.

I've learned that Jesus loves me. This I know. Yes, the Bible tells me so. But so does Jesus. I have learned that Jesus is everything. I've learned that if I look closely, I can see him in everything.

Jesus provided the most potent character theme in history. It was not weakness that held Jesus to the cross; it was his strength. His unparalleled, matchless power.

I say Romans 12:10 (NIV) often to remind myself of the following: "Be devoted to one another in love. Honor one another above yourselves."

The next two verses may encompass one of the most compelling commands in the Bible: "Love from the center of who you are; don't fake it. Run for dear life from evil; hold on for dear life to good. Be good friends who love deeply; practice playing second fiddle" (Romans 12:11–12 NIV).

Good manifests itself differently from person to person in any given experience. Love from the center of who you are. As impossible as it sometimes appears, find the good. Do good.

Jesus is the center. You can rest there.

CONVERSATION STARTERS
FROM TERRY BAKER

Terry is a state rep for Celebrate Recovery. She is incredibly vigilant, working her own recovery program, and she lives her faith freely in front of anyone she comes in contact with. Her words are seasoned, wise, and full of the Holy Spirit. When I have a question about handling a recovery issue, Terry is one of the first people I call for counsel. She knows her stuff. More importantly, she lives it. She is acutely aware of where her hope lives. She is one of the best examples I know of how God redeems the past and uses it for his glory. Such a pretty lady.

1. Have you ever been the recipient of a statement or observation about you that was less than flattering, with the tacked-on statement "Just kidding"? If so, what do you think the speaker's motive was?

2. What is your response when receiving a seemingly sincere compliment? If you struggle to receive it graciously, what is in your belief system that causes you to discount the good being said about you?

3. Did any of Tim's Servants by Design strengths resonate with you? If so, why?

4. Make a list of your good things, with a minimum of five things. If you can't find five, ask friends and family.

5. What keeps us from wanting to play "second fiddle?

6. The morning after I sent my questions for this essay to Tim, I found myself soul-searching as to which is my default drive. I came to the conclusion that some days,

I naturally look for the good in people and voice it to them, but other days, not so much. One could surmise that looking for the good in others and voicing it to them is an admirable trait. Is that your personal default mode? If you answered no to that question, what is your theory on why? Additionally, what are some ways you could acquire a more positive and kind default mode?

ThE ROCK GOd BUILdS

GINGER ROGERS DEMARIS has been my sister's best friend since they were in the second grade. For as long as I can remember, she has been part of our family. There has never been an event, joy, or grief in which G has not played an integral part. I proudly introduce her as my sister because she is, in every respect, one of us.

G makes cakes and beautifully unique centerpieces for anyone in our family getting married. She makes some of the best cookies I've ever eaten.

One thing that sets G apart from many of our friends and family is that she possesses minimal filter. She is loud and has never shied away from voicing her opinion.

I know if I'm ever in need, she'll be there as quickly and surely as my other siblings. She loves Jesus. He has become fundamental to her in the past few years. I love it when she calls me with a question about the Bible. Because we were raised in the same church, she questions many things we grew up believing.

So she calls and asks—and I'd better have a sound biblical response. Breaking away from some aspects of what we've believed all our lives is hard. It's scary. Ofttimes, when we're talking, I'll offer a response that categorically differs from our first beliefs.

If G feels she's standing at the edge of a cliff, staring down into blackness, hearing the Lord yell, "Jump! I'll catch you!" she still asks, "Are you sure?"

I love saying, "Yes, I'm sure."

Trust me, G's questions always compel me to be sure. Many times, I have to say, "Let me get back to you on that one." Then I study before telling her what I believe scripture teaches. It's a good balance. It's that iron-sharpens-iron thing.

One of G's sons is working through his belief in God's presence, not just in his life but also in the world. He questions whether God cares enough about us to intervene in our lives or even if God has the power to help us at all.

G called me one day with the age-old question that all students of philosophy ask when they want to stymie their opponent. She hit me with a question from her son: "If God is all-powerful, if he is omnipotent, could he make a rock he couldn't lift?"

Surprised, since I hadn't heard that question in eons, I figured it was like an internet hoax that keeps resurfacing and just won't die. I said, "Yes, he can. And drugged travelers wake up to find themselves in motel bathtubs filled with ice and a kidney missing."

I told G that he's asking the wrong questions, and I have two responses.

First, everything God does has a purpose. Everything has a plan and serves a God-given reason down to the smallest, most seemingly insignificant speck in the universe.

Proverbs 16:4 (MSG) says, "God made everything with a place and purpose," and Ecclesiastes 3 tells us emphatically that there is a time for everything, and God is in control of it all. We can choose joy and peace in the midst of life's adventure. God gives the faith we need to make it through.

The bottom line here is that G's boy is asking the wrong question. The question is not "*Could* God create a stone he couldn't lift?" The question is "*Would* God create a stone he couldn't lift?"

Why would he? What would be the purpose? It would be counter to his very nature. And if nothing else, God will always be true to his nature. Being inconsistent in his nature is probably the one thing he can't do. Malachi 3:6 (NIV) says, "For I the Lord do not change." Numbers 23:19 (ESV) says, "God is not man, that He should lie, or a son of man, that He should change His mind. Has He said, and will not do it? Or has He spoken, and will He not fulfill it?"

The good news is that God can create a stone as big as he likes. And the even better news? God can lift any stone he chooses to pick up.

Here's the second part of my response: it seems to me that we mortals are the only ones who create stones we can't pick up. We build skyscrapers, sculpt statues, and erect monuments, great architectural masterpieces we will never be able to lift with our own hands by our own strength.

And it is we mortals who have built stones the Lord can't lift.

We have, all humans, picked up stones that seem small and easy to lift, believing we can move them anytime we choose, only to find them far too heavy to free ourselves from. Over time, without our even being fully conscious of it, we can no longer lift them. Resentment, bitterness, anger, drugs or alcohol, fear, shame, pride and self-righteousness, doubt, stress and anxiety, depression, codependency, buried wounds from childhood, hate, envy, dependence on religiosity and haughty principles—the list goes on.

These are just a few of the stones the Lord can't lift—not until we ask him to. Until we realize the futility of our attempts at moving them. Until we find ourselves buried underneath them, unable to breathe.

I believe that more often than not, people find life more manageable if they can blame-place God for all their problems.

They can attempt to minimize his power by asking him to perform a miracle diametrically opposed to his nature, when in fact, this gracious Father is waiting just around the curve of the mountain to move it out of their lives.

That place where we find ourselves is what we recoverers call "rock bottom": the moment we realize we are buried, crushed beneath the rubble of our sin, and are helpless to move or get out from under it. It's the moment we realize our lives are out of control, and we have no option but to put pride aside and surrender to the only One who is able to lift the rock and move us into security. It's a scary, humbling place to be. But the freedom, peace, hope, and expectancy we gain make it eternally easier to keep those pesky little rocks from returning.

It's about having faith. The Lord even promises to provide us with the confidence we need to believe, even with legitimate questions to God, such as "Did you call it sand because it's between the sea and the land?" or "How long did it take Jesus to be potty-trained?" or "What exactly were you thinking when you made the avocado pit so big?"

Personally, I almost think that last one is a valid question. I know God has a good reason for everything, but that colossal avocado pit is a waste of functional avocado space, in my opinion. Think how much more avocado there would be if the pit were the size of a mustard seed. Most people have never seen a mustard seed, so this lesson would be much easier if the scripture said, "If you just have faith the size of an avocado seed, you can say to that mountain, 'Get on outa here,' and it will be done." Everyone would say, "Oh yeah. I get it."

Or, in the context of our story, "How long must I wait for this rock to be lifted?" It's all about asking the right question. We will, all of us, have rocks that need to be lifted at some point in our lives. Where will you find the strength to be rid of yours?

Will you continue asking questions that need no answer? Or will you surrender your pride and will to the One who is waiting to move the mountains for you?

> Is this not the fast that I have chosen: To
> loose the bonds of wickedness, to undo
> the heavy burdens, to let the oppressed go
> free, and that you break every yoke?
>> —Isaiah 58:8 KJV

> Cast your burden on the Lord, and
> He shall sustain you; He shall never
> permit the righteous to be moved.
>> —Psalm 55:22 NKJV

> For I, the Lord your God, will hold your right
> hand, saying to you, "Fear not, I will help you."
>> —Isaiah 41:13 NIV

CONVERSATION STARTERS FROM RANDY GRANDERSON

One of the reasons our Sunday Connection class is so great is because we have incredibly gifted teachers. It's one thing to have life experience we can relate to, but leaning heavily on the Word of God as the catalyst for every teaching keeps us all grounded and reaching for more of Jesus. Randy is one of those teachers.

1. If God can do anything, can he make a person accept him who has no desire to do so? Is this a rock God cannot move?

2. What role does faith play in your everyday life? Do you see a correlation between faith or a lack of faith and acceptance of God? Explain.

3. Are there stones in your life too heavy for God to lift? Give examples (e.g., rejection of God, lack of faith, a belief system you adhere to, an addictive behavior, a mental health issue, family dysfunction). Do you blame or trust God in regard to these? Discuss.

The Trombone Player Wore a Bouffant

SOMETIME IN THE summer of 1972—I'm reasonably sure it was mid-August—I remember it being blistering hot. Sweltering, eggs-frying-on-a-sidewalk hot. I was leaving junior high and heading to sophomore status at Searcy High School, a period of life when everything was changing: school, body, and definitely attitude. Everything in life was abhorrent, hilarious, loathsome, fun, and rebellious. Friends were the ultimate expression of loyalty and cutthroat exploits. Friends were the center of the known universe. Parents knew nothing and could do nothing right. I didn't honestly think they were ignorant; they just thought they knew everything (anything).

One particular Saturday, I was just finishing summer band rehearsal at the practice field, which was just behind Ahlf Junior High. Mom informed me as I threw my trombone into the back and jumped into the front seat beside her that it was way past time for a haircut. No big deal. She would drive me to Hickmon's Barber Shop on Race Street, a little ramshackle wooden shop, as I recall it, with maybe only two chairs. I can't remember anyone ever working there besides Mr. Hickmon. One seat sat empty every time I was there.

At any rate, we were not going anywhere near Race Street. In fact, we barely went the length of a football field before turning into a house adjacent to the stadium. I immediately recognized the sign out front: Merlene's Beauty Shop.

Merlene Barker was Mom's dear friend from church and the manufacturer of most every woman in town's coif. For some reason, she apparently never had recovered from the death of John F. Kennedy, because most every woman coming out of her salon was channeling the exact same flip Jackie had a full decade before. Except for my mother, who insisted that much like the basic black dress, the beehive would never go out of style. She usually said that at bedtime while wrapping her head in toilet paper.

For some undefinable reason, as with a rabbit when it senses danger—a coyote or woolly mammoth—every ligament and tendon in my body tightened into defensive mode. "What are we doing at Merlene's?" Somehow, I knew we weren't there to pick up one of Merlene's amazing casseroles, the culinary marvels she was famous for making when there was sickness or a death in the family. "Why aren't we going to Hickmon's? And where's Andy?" My little brother was almost always in the mix when it was haircut time.

"Hickmon's is closed today for some reason."

I can't remember if Mr. Hickmon was sick that day or out hunting with his boys, but I've never entirely gotten over the resentment of what transpired over the next hour.

Mom tried to sound excited. "Andy was finished, so I dropped him off at J. R.'s while I ran some errands." J. R. Betts was another friend of the family. She'd dropped my little brother off at J. R.'s gas station while she came to get me. "Merlene wasn't busy today, and she said she would be happy to do your hair."

Do my hair? My breath caught in my chest as I remembered the time Merlene had given my little sister a perm and burned her hair off at the crown. To this day, Jacqui still calls her "Mom's old-lady hairdresser."

"Mom, I can wait till next weekend. It won't get that much longer."

"I've already paid her, so get in there."

Many people, when they are in an unnatural, albeit nonfatal, accident, will experience flashbacks. They recall small bits and pieces, pictures of the event, and not the entirety of the cataclysmic, life-shifting episode. As I walked into the room, my first thought was to wonder why my mother didn't whisper, "Dead man walking," as I shuffled to the chair in the middle of the room.

Merlene was thrilled to see me and exclaimed how excited she was since she rarely ever got to work on boys.

I couldn't compartmentalize any of the smells in the place: a mixture of bleaches, dyes, and—what? Burned hair? Merlene began her ritualistic persecution by strangling me with a pink-and-blue-striped plastic apron thing. Before I could instinctively rip it off, the chair was jerked back into waterboard position. I have to admit, the hair washing wasn't half bad. I think I fell asleep, until the chair was unceremoniously thrust back into an upright position, and Merlene began circling me with a pair of scissors and a comb.

No clippers?

Merlene absentmindedly conversed with Mom while she snipped at my head. They talked about church and what someone had worn to someone's funeral. They laughed and giggled, which was annoying to me—stupid stuff.

Then Merlene began performing some kind of sardonic treatment to my head, as though she were raking it with a fork, as if she were combing it backward or something. I asked, "Are you teasing my hair?"

She joked, obviously for the hundred thousandth time, "Oh no, honey. If I were teasing your hair, I would be doing this." She pointed her fingers at my head and said, "Nyea, nyea, nyea, nyea, nyea nyea."

I assumed at least one person over the past several decades had found that hilarious. I, however, did not.

I rolled my eyes as she continued to tease my hair. The entire time she was teasing, she was spraying me with some kind of lethal toxin. My eyes were burning with the fires of a thousand volcanoes, and I was unable to take in air, gagging as I gasped for what I felt sure were my final two or three tattered breaths.

Just before I went unconscious, I had two thoughts almost simultaneously. The first was *This is what females go through weekly, and they rarely come out of it genetically altered, as if they grew up next to a nuclear power plant China syndrome meltdown disaster.* The second thought, as I glared at my mother, who was mysteriously absorbed in a *Southern Living* magazine, was *For the love of all that is holy, I am your son. Why aren't you doing something to save me?*

Finally, it was over. Merlene stood back, crossed her fleshy arms, cocked her head to the side, and exclaimed, "Oh!"

Mom lowered her magazine, looked up for the first time, and furtively murmured, "Oh."

Then, almost as if deliberately adding intentional punishment, Merlene held up the mirror, and I morosely said, "Oh." I thought, *Please. No. Let me wake up or die. Please.* It was like vainly attempting to look away from a train wreck. Only I was on the train.

Growing up, I possessed a weird tic. I would laugh at the most inappropriate times. If someone told me his or her mother had died, I would stifle an insane urge to guffaw. There was no way to politely say I would rather have had my eyelids stapled to a railroad track than look in that mirror. So I froze. The next thing I knew, I was laughing.

I looked as if Patsy Cline and Lady Bird Johnson had given birth to a poodle, only my bouffant was way more poofed up and solid. It was hard, remarkably stiff. If I had been Samson, the entire trajectory of history would have been altered; Delilah would never have been capable of shearing that monolithic concrete from my head. If I raised my eyebrows, my whole scalp migrated backward. I was a guy—in junior high school!

Somehow, in my near hysteria, I mumbled, "Thank you," which came out sounding vaguely like a question. I slinked out the door, almost crawling, praying that no friend—actually, no other human—would see me before I got to the car. When Mom got in, I dove into the floorboard and began trying to flatten my hair down with my hands and spit. But it was like scraping a concrete yard gnome. I think my fingertips bled.

Mom yelled at me to leave it alone. "You need to keep it just like that till tomorrow, so Merlene can see it at church."

There was about as much chance of that happening as hell getting a Baskin-Robbins. I figured I could leave it alone until the second we got home, and then I could drown myself in the shower with a jackhammer.

Again, however, the car wasn't going toward home. We were heading down Race Street. It wasn't until we pulled into J. R.'s service station on the town square that I remembered my little brother. Mom, frustrated at me for futilely attempting to get the mutant off my head, said, "Go in, and get Andy."

I hope you're getting the emotional picture here. I was fifteen years old and about to enter high school in a town of about ten thousand people, where everyone knew everyone, and I looked as if Merlene had dipped my head in Aqua Net and dragged me through a donkey barn. And up until this experience I thought zits were the most evil scourge of the Devil. I said, "I am not walking into that gas station. It's not happening. You can pull out a couple of hairs from my head right now and stab me in the heart with them if you want. I'm not going in there."

"Timothy Eldridge, get out of this car this minute, and go get your brother."

She'd used my first and middle names, so I knew the battle was over. I prayed that a freak tsunami would splash through Arkansas, washing away the entire town, including my hair.

I walked toward the firing squad, which was actually a glass door. I pushed it open to see three gas station attendants wiping tears from their eyes, looking toward the opposite corner of the room. I glanced over and saw Andy in the farthest chair, curled up in a ball, with exactly the same bouffant as mine. Every greasy gas station attendant in the lobby turned and saw me. One of the good ole boys snorted and said, "How can I help you, Miss Sinatra?" The hilarity started all over again.

Andy and I tried to beat each other to the car. I jumped in first and stammered, "Okay, let me get this straight. You actually allowed this hairdo thing to happen twice?"

"Oh, well, now, it doesn't look that bad. It's just ..." She trailed off with a heavy sigh.

The remainder of the ride home, Andy and I avoided eye contact. It would only have ruined the false hope that we didn't have the same alien on our head. Andy would have burst into tears, and I would have burst into uncontrollable laughter.

Mom barely had the car parked before Andy and I raced into the house and stood in our respective showers for about forty-five minutes. Although I'm sure Mom only took us to Merlene's little shop of horrors, torture, and humiliation out of convenience, no boy from our family ever stepped foot in that place again.

The only consolation I felt from the experience was at church the following morning, when I marched in and watched Merlene's look of shock. There might have been a snarl on her face, as if I'd deliberately defaced a masterpiece. I might as well have drawn nose hairs on the *Mona Lisa* with a Marks-A-Lot or taken a chisel to the statue of *David*. At any rate, fortunately, right about then, the old tic set in again, and I burst into peals of hysterical laughter.

We all have specific moments in our lives that define us. If you ever wondered why it doesn't faze me for a single second that my forehead recedes to the back of my neck, now you know.

CONVERSATION STARTERS
FROM PAM SMITH

Pam and I grew up together but didn't know it—same town, same school, same church, and same university. We became good buddies many years later, when we were on staff at the church we attended. Pam kept the worship department hopping and running. She did her best to keep me out of trouble. That took up much of her time in any given week. Pam and I are founding members of the much-coveted lunch posse. Pam is one of the friends who never stopped encouraging me to do this project. I love Pam. Pam loves marathons. She's so pretty.

1. Have you ever tried to fry eggs on a sidewalk? Have you ever tried to test out any other sayings from your youth? Did they work? For instance, I put salt on a slug and immediately regretted it, so I poured the whole box onto him to try to make it go faster. Ugh!

2. What was your favorite grade in school? Why? What was your least favorite? Why? Are the memories that cause you to classify them as most or least favorite related to the people around you or the schoolwork in front of you?

3. What is your favorite church-lady potluck casserole dish? Why do they call them potlucks? When is the last time you went to one? Where have all the church lady cooks gone? Do you have a church cookbook with all the potluck recipes in it? Was the food that good, or did the fellowship make the food better?

4. Summers in Arkansas are hot and humid. Do you think that taking Tim for a haircut in a small in-home beauty shop after his band practice on the field was the act of a true friend of Merlene? What fifteen-year-old boy would dare go anywhere after a few hours of blowing his horn on a football field in hundred-degree heat without a shower and a few drops of Brut cologne?

5. How do you respond to embarrassing trauma? Laugh? Cry? Scream? Curl up in the fetal position and never show your face again? What is one embarrassing moment from your junior high years? Everyone has a story to tell.

6. As a child of the South, Tim was taught at an early age to always say, "Please," "Thank you," "No, sir," and "Yes, sir." It's an automatic reflex of good parenting. Tim responded to his horrific experience with "Thank you." Was that just good manners? Did Tim really care what Merlene thought, or was he flat-out lying to keep his mom happy? Is that a lie?

7. Did your mother use your full name to signal that you were in trouble? How does that make you feel about your full name now? Do you like your middle name? If she didn't call you by your full name, what signal did she use to let you know you were toast?

8. Do you think the toxic chemicals in the hair spray had anything to do with Tim's disappearing hair, or was that a direct result of the genetic trait that is supposed to come from one's mother? Does that mean Tim's mom is at fault for his shiny head regardless?

CONVERSATION STARTER
FROM TIM e HOLDER

1. Did you blame subsequent decades of intensive therapy and heartrending counseling on this experience? (Asking for a friend.)

Trust and Obey

BOB PERKINS AND I have been friends for more than forty years. We were in college theater productions and were Chi Sigma Alpha brothers. I was his pledge master. He swallowed a lot of raw eggs—rough night. I love Bob. I love his heart.

Sweet Tim,

How's my own favorite angel?

So not to lay too much need on you. But I've been thinking about folks who believe that God is in control. Then I ask them to help me understand what that means for them. Definitely not asking folks to defend or justify that belief. Just asking different people what that means for them. I'm someone who would love certainty but doesn't really expect it. And who, on my best days, is content with and intrigued by mystery.

So even if "God is in control" is really more of a prayer than a certainty for someone, that's worth knowing to me. But if it means something more definite, perhaps if it's based on some experience or even revelation, that would be worth knowing too.

This is a super long way of asking: When you have time, would you mind telling me what it means to you to say God's in control? I don't know that I can say that. Surprise. Why else would I be asking?

I guess I can try my best to align my faith with Dr. King's and Gandhi's assertion that the long arc bends toward justice. And I'm pretty sure I believe that "in the end, there is love." Though I wonder if I could hang on to that if it was really tested for me.

I don't like what feels to me like my weak faith; possibly as much because I struggle with wanting stronger faith but not really being disciplined enough to do the things that I expect would help strengthen it: much more prayer, meditation, letting go of things that make me feel unworthy or unholy, etc., etc.

I'm scared enough by the state of the world that I have turned into a not very good sleeper anyway; it's very common for me to wake up at 4:00 a.m. and not be able to get back to sleep. Which would be okay if I didn't have to work regular hours and be available to my family.

Do people of deep faith and attachment to God, like, oh, say, you, usually sleep well? Maybe strong people feel more or less like I do and just move ahead anyway.

Anyway, I'm starting to ramble. I just wanted to ask you that question. No need for a quick reply if you want to take time to think about it. Man, oh man, do I love knowing you.

I wrote back,

Earlier this week, I read your post about your dad leaving this life, and when you said other people have a clearer idea about what's next than you, I shed more than a few tears. Mostly because I can't bear the idea that someone I dearly love wouldn't know, dream, and have visions of what our future home will be. I know I prayed at that moment that you would have that absolute faith that would help you sleep better.

And by the way, no, having faith doesn't always assure one of eight straight hours of peaceful slumber. I wish I could hug you right now. But know this. I prayed last week that you would have a clearer understanding of faith. Today you asked. It's interesting, and not coincidence, I'm positive, that you would ask that question now.

November of 2006, the week before Thanksgiving, my body went crazy and began to shut down. I felt like I was getting the flu and went to bed, feeling very sluggish and feverish. For the next twenty-four hours, I ran to the bathroom every hour or so with severe diarrhea. TMI, I know. But hang with me. Then my bowels completely stopped. Within hours, my bladder completely stopped functioning. Then fatigue set in to the point I couldn't function at all.

I was scared.

I was sent to a cornucopia of doctors over several months for MRIs, CT scans, spinal taps, and x-rays. I visited urologists, internal medicine doctors, a gastroenterologist, and, finally, a neurologist. Five months of uncertainty and fear. My neurologist finally diagnosed a disorder called transverse myelitis (TM). It's a first cousin to multiple sclerosis (MS). The recipient of this disorder experiences the same symptoms as MS. As a general rule, though, those symptoms don't progress like MS. And depending on where the virus strikes across the spinal column is how severe the symptoms are. Everything below the strike zone is affected.

Very few professionals really know about TM, because only one in eight cases out of a million is diagnosed with it. During the five months of not knowing what was wrong, I leaned heavily on my extensive experience with paranoia. Every exotic disease known to mankind would soon result in my inevitable demise.

During that confusing, challenging period, I never questioned, "Why?" I never got mad at God. I never doubted his love, sovereignty, or grace. I didn't ask, "Why me?" I know that earlier in my life, I may have wondered. But during this time, I said out loud, "Okay, Lord, how do I use this to show your glory?"

I finally gave myself permission to grieve. One afternoon, I sat on my deck and cried. And when I say cried, I mean ugly sobbed. Snotty-nosed, pillow-over-the-face, wet-T-shirt-contest (and not in a good way), gut-wrenching, powerhouse, blubbering-mess sobbing.

Then I stood up, took a step, and moved forward. I had to figure out what a new normal was going to look like for me.

It's not now, nor will it ever be, easy. It's called an invisible disability for a reason. I don't talk about it often. Most people are unaware that I deal with it. Chronic fatigue is the worst symptom. I will always be tired, and I never know when a severe case will hit. Some days I can barely get out of bed. I will never do many things that used to bring me joy.

I don't have much of a bucket list anymore. But then again, I don't really need one. The joys of heaven will make any wish here seem less than a shadow. I don't think the Lord will use me to part a sea and save a rogue nation from approaching enemies. I won't run a marathon, although I'm considering a half marathon someday—maybe. I doubt I'll teach in a packed stadium where thousands will give their lives to the Lord. To many in the world, I suppose my life might even look like a failure. Because they don't know.

I don't necessarily see myself as a man of great faith. I'm not even sure what that means. I do have faith. I do my best to be faithful. And I recognize that even the faith I do have comes from God. I regularly ask for more.

Over the past years, I have learned a few lessons. But those lessons, as is often the case with most people, have been gleaned through fire. Allowing myself to be refined by it. Depending on an ever-deepening relationship with Jesus to keep my spirits, occasionally sinking in a sea of despair, buoyed in his ocean of mercy and grace.

I know that I trust him. I know for certain that he is working all things for my good. But believing that truth doesn't necessarily mean the experience is pleasant.

Look at Abraham.

Abraham, seventy-five years old at the time, whose name in Hebrew means "Father of many nations," heard clearly God's promise that he and his sixty-five-year-old wife, Sarah, would have a child. Twenty-five years later, Isaac was born. Promise fulfilled finally.

But then God threw a wrench into the plan and told Abraham to offer Isaac as a sacrifice. I have read this story a hundred times and heard it from the pulpit as many. I always thought Abraham, this great man of faith, merely took Isaac, who carried the wood for his own execution, up a hill behind their house, and, once there, with knife-wielding hand hovering over Isaac's prostrate body, felt the hand of an angel grab his arm and save the day.

That's not what happened at all. Well, not emotionally anyway.

Abraham knew God's voice. He'd heard it many times before. So he knew the command was from a friend, not an enemy. He had to obey. God told Abraham to take his "only son" (the promised one) from their home in Beer-Sheba to Mt. Moriah and there kill him and burn him as a sacrifice to God. Far from a quick two-hour jaunt up a hill behind their home, Mt. Moriah loomed in the distance, three days away.

Three days.

Walking beside his son for at least seventy-two hours, Abraham found himself on a journey he couldn't possibly understand. He had plenty of time to process. God had promised he would have a son.

Abraham had waited a quarter of a century for that promise to come true. And now, many years later, he was asked to not only see his dream of becoming the father of a great nation die, but a knife in his own hand would be the thrust that ended it.

Abraham sat in confusion beside a campfire for two nights, watching the deep, steady breathing of his sleeping heir. According to God's commitment to Abraham, Isaac's legacy would include being the first star of billions. And Isaac slept in perfect confidence, knowing his father kept watch over him and would protect him from harm. How Abraham must have grieved. Silent tears for what was to come.

Anger. He'd waited decades for Isaac. And he'd already lost one son.

Confusion. What was God doing? Where was the plan?

Bitterness and resentment. God shouldn't have led him on without revealing the outcome.

He was old. Would he live to see God's promise fulfilled another way?

How could God cut Isaac's life short when there'd been so much hope?

Would God miraculously raise Isaac from the dead?

This seemed an exceedingly unfair, harsh, grim way for Abraham to prove devotion.

Even if God had a different plan, Isaac was Abraham's beloved son. How could Abraham survive the loss, the absence of this gift he'd prayed for, waited a hundred years for, raised, invested in, and unconditionally loved from birth? How could he reconcile the faithfulness he'd experienced from God with his anger and resentment focused toward this same God, who now commanded him to kill his child? The God he'd raised Isaac to obey, worship, love, and trust.

Abraham's heart battled for equilibrium between the assurance of God's faithfulness to his promise and the desolate, bleak inevitability that lay a few miles ahead. Afraid to sleep, through tear-glazed eyes, he scrutinized embers as they swirled and floated upward and away from a dying fire. Maybe he prayed God would speak to him from the flames, as he had spoken to Moses from a burning bush. As the cold black of a starless night enveloped him, he felt the creeping chill of loneliness surround him. Abraham's prayer went unanswered.

Somehow, we've missed—or forgotten—the concept that biblical characters were just as human as the rest of us. We want to believe we understand the complete trust that those faithful figures exhibited. The confidence in God we long to emulate. We read stories in the Bible of

God's people doing outrageous things for him. Something that often, he specifically commanded them to do. Yet sometimes we believe we've failed spiritually if we experience adverse or weak emotions in the midst of the fire.

You see, I spent way too much time in my life trying to be happy and comfortable. And the reality is that I was never made to be 100 percent comfortable here, only reasonably happy. I don't really belong here. I believe the Lord has left a space in my heart, a longing—a hankering—for something I'll never find here on earth. It will be realized only when I see him face-to-face. Then, and only then, will I be totally fulfilled. The Lord never called me to seek total happiness in this life. He *has* called me to be obedient. And like you, I think I have in the past fought valiantly to stay in control. Do it all my way.

But I have learned that surrender to Jesus is my safe place.

My health will never again be in my control. It never really was. Jesus is the one place I can go for assurance that I'm loved despite my weaknesses, disappointments, failures, and anger. And there alone is where I ultimately find absolute peace. There will always be issues I have to give up to him.

But the point is that these things always turn my gaze back to him. It rereminds me to remain, as much as humanly possible, in a state of brokenness and surrender if I really desire to be healed and whole. I've learned that suffering isn't ennobling; a relationship with Jesus is.

So now it is almost out of a sense of adventure that I embrace those moments when the Lord reveals previously uncharted areas of my heart where I need to give him jurisdiction. I have learned that every moment of every day, I'm creating my own history. And the choices I make today will be a great predictor of my future. If I can, in the moment, remember that, it will make a vast difference in how I respond to any given situation.

I can choose to respond with a Christ-regenerated character, or I can revert to old knee-jerk defensive posturing that got me to the position I was in many years ago: a lonely, desperately precarious, and discouraging season, pleading with doctors and God for a diagnosis, filled with uncertainty, hurt, resentment, confusion, and fear.

I don't know about tomorrow. But today I choose dependence. Whatever happens, I choose to allow it to turn my eyes toward Jesus. And I courageously make the choice to continue my adventure with him. Ten years from today, I want to look back at this historic moment and know that I chose the security of wiser actions, love instead of judgment, and acceptance instead of condemnation of others or myself.

I choose dependence. I accept relationship instead of feeble, worn-out patterns that led to frustration and powerlessness at best.

So that's about it for now. I don't know if this will help you, my good, well-loved friend. I think I just needed to process for a bit, and you were there at the perfect moment. You need to know that it wasn't a mistake. Thank you for being there for me.

Bob, I pray and will continue to pray you find what I've found: an unfathomable and mysterious grace that willingly sustains us forever through love and acceptance.

I hope you'll experience, as I have, how God is in the resurrection business, even for dreams that have died. The infinite possibilities available with Jesus. I pray you'll find the humor and wisdom that a life lived in real community with him and others can offer. I pray you learn the savage beauty of forgiving and being forgiven, especially by yourself. That you will courageously risk sifting through every heartache and victory, as sloppy, broken, and precious as the process can be.

To finally find the way to show God's glory.

I pray you will be delivered from chains of the fear of letting go and allowing God to be in control. It's safe there. I pray you would be freed from the prison of isolation and the dark, dreary dread of an uncertain future into the arms of a ridiculously wild, fiercely passionate, and outrageously unrestrained love affair with Jesus Christ.

I pray you will find what I have discovered: hope!

At what point can we identify the faith character of Abraham during the turmoil? In one sentence.

As they climbed Mt. Moriah toward the site where Isaac was to be sacrificed, Isaac reminded his father that they had flint and wood. And then he innocently asked Abraham where the sheep was for the burnt offering.

With one of the most heartbreaking responses in all of scripture, and filled with the horror of this truth, Abraham told Isaac, "God himself will provide the lamb for the burnt offering, my son." The declaration was valid enough. But I believe the entirety of Abraham's wounded heart was wrapped up in those final two words: *my son*. The hope. The promise. My child.

Abraham trusted God. The only altar on which Abraham could pour out his anguish was his belief that God was true to his nature. God had always been faithful. And it would be impossible for him to be anything other than constant and consistent.

The truth of God's nature was more reliable than Abraham's situation. Knowing and believing that essential fact legitimized Abraham's final act of faith.

Climbing Mt. Moriah, which in Hebrew means "Seen by Yahweh," Abraham chose obedience above emotion. He chose obedience over what he could see. He chose obedience instead of disbelief. In the face of the impossible, Abraham chose to believe. And he chose to obey.

It's all about being obedient. There have been scant few times in my life when I've had a clear picture of what was around the next bend. The next curve. The anfractuous nature of life always seems to catch me by surprise. I never know what God is doing. What he is up to. There's no security there. I've found the only protection in this life is resting in who he is. And I rest knowing he is for me.

I believe in his promises. I know he's done what he promised. He's my God. And he provided the Lamb. So I choose obedience.

My prayer for you, my good brother, is that God will give you enough peace to accept his promises, his perfect plan for you. Mostly, I pray the great Star Breather will lead you to an ever-growing understanding of his peace and security. Your only responsibility? Trust and obey.

When God gave Abraham the promise of Isaac many years earlier, Abraham believed. He was obedient.

And the Lord counted it to Abraham as righteousness.

CONSERVATION STARTERS
FROM MICHAEL NOLAN

If they ever do a movie about my life, I want Mike to write the screenplay.

1. What part of Abraham's story resonates with you? What part do you find most disturbing?

2. You've probably never faced a situation like Abraham, but when have you felt that circumstances required more faith than you felt you had? How did that play out? If it's unresolved, describe where you are right now spiritually and emotionally.

3. When faced with significant challenges, what's a familiar but unhelpful strategy you've tried? What results from that path? How do you rebound from that course toward something more effective?

4. Contrary to some traditions, you can be angry toward God without reprisal. (Even heroes of the Bible have survived such.) How do you, through words or actions, express your anger toward God?

5. It seems to be human nature to ask, "God, why did this happen?" Rarely does God offer an answer that suits our rational minds. It's been suggested that a more appropriate question is "To what end?" It's a question that embraces hope and the future. Think back to a time when your "Why?" questions were not answered; did anything noteworthy come to pass in the aftermath?

power

AS I'VE SAID, before the beginning of January, I always choose my word for the year. This year, I chose *power.* I never get a clear idea of how impactful and far-reaching the word I choose will prove to be. I'm always surprised how the Lord broadens my vision of him, the world around me, and even my own personal study of his Word.

This year, I wrote down on note cards Bible verses specifically using the word *power.* On the headboard of my bed, I have Colossians 1:11 (RSV): "May you be strengthened with all power, according to his glorious might, for all endurance and patience with joy." I've found this verse particularly significant while enduring many of the events happening in the world right now, including having to endure masks; watching the dark abyss called politics; and having to say, "See ya later," to my precious pup Chester. I feel as if 2021 is saying to 2020, "Hold my beer."

The wardrobe in my bedroom has 2 Peter 1:3 (RSV) taped to it: "His divine power has granted to us all things that pertain to life and godliness through the knowledge of him who called us to his own glory and excellence." Knowing this helps me remember that he has the power to help me navigate these perilous times and find peace in the midst of the turmoil. I have verses taped to the microwave, the bathroom mirror, and the front door of my house. I even have one on the top left corner of my television screen: 1 Corinthians 4:20 (RSV), which says, "For the kingdom of God does not consist in talk but in power." The verse on my bathroom door reads, "Therefore I tell you, whatever you ask in prayer, believe that you have received it, and it will be yours" (Mark 11:24 NIV). That verse doesn't specifically use the word *power*, but I wrote these verses the day the Powerball was close to a billion dollars, and frankly, after hearing the announcement of a winner, I had a hard time feeling the accuracy of that particular verse.

One of my favorites hangs on my bedroom door: Revelation 5:13 (NIV), which says, "Then I heard every creature in heaven and on earth and under the earth and on the sea, and all that is in them, saying, 'To him who sits on the throne and to the Lamb, be praise and honor and glory and power forever and ever!'" This verse became a safe harbor during January.

Mom left for heaven on Wednesday, January 13, 2021. The previous Saturday, she enthusiastically fussed at her TV, completely wrapped up in a Razorbacks game with my brother-in-law, Jim. On Sunday, she was not feeling well, so her caregivers decided to move her into a hospice environment and attempt to regulate her meds. On Monday, Ginger called, telling me I needed to get there as soon as possible. I packed up right then and headed to Fayetteville.

We all knew Mom had been living on borrowed time for a few years. We knew congestive heart failure continued to sap her energy and ravage her body more and more. But she always rallied when surrounded by her kids and grandkids.

I'd spent a few days with her just a couple of weeks earlier, during the Christmas holiday. She was alert and thrilled every day I walked through the little apartment my sister, Jacqui, and bonus sister, Ginger, painstakingly decorated for her.

Relaxing in her recliner, which most times doubled as a throne, Queen Eunice watched the Game Show Network or browsed through the *Arkansas Democrat-Gazette* on her iPad. Word puzzles and fill-in-the-blank Bible studies littered a little table comfortably within arm's reach beside her.

She would light up in a radiant burst of life when any of her kids or grandkids walked through the door. Leaning forward and taking our face in her hands, Mom assured us of how much we were loved. Her pride in her family never went unvoiced. We never left her side without knowing how important and valuable we are.

To the right of her recliner, on a little side stand, sat a digital picture frame, a Christmas gift from my brother a few years earlier. She motioned us down onto the love seat next to her, and together we watched picture after picture scroll through the frame. All her kids knew the email address for the frame. We imagined her unbridled excitement when she discovered the treasure of a new picture or two added to her priceless collection.

On the small kitchen table behind her sat a large red bowl filled with candy. It was mandatory, almost a religious rite, that we leave her cozy abode with a handful of bite-sized goodness. Even the day she left her apartment for the last time, the guys wheeling her out on a stretcher were required to stop and fill their pockets.

Only two people were allowed in the hospice room at a time. Jim whispered his love to Mom, switched places with me, and went to his car to wait. Jacqui and I sat on either side of Mom's bed, each of us holding one of her hands in ours. We stroked her face and arms as she slept and labored to breathe. We quietly declared our love for her and promised we would all look after one another. We prayed and asked Jesus to welcome her home. We encouraged her, reminding her of all the precious friends and family she would be hugging soon and the applause, whoops, and shouts of excitement and welcome she would hear as her own personal angel carried her to the shores of heaven.

Jesus, standing there to meet her, grabbing her up in his arms, with a twinkle in his sparkling eyes, would say, "I've been waiting for you. I'm so happy to see you. You did such a good job. Welcome home."

Mom took her last breath.

We sat silently for a few seconds as we sensed the electric power of the Holy Spirit envelop the small room. Jacqui and I reached across Mom and grabbed each other's hand. Tears flowed freely as Jacqui calmly pressed the call button. We waited for the nurse to come in, place her stethoscope against Mom's chest, and listen for a pulse. I watched quietly and was finally able to say, "Is it over?" The nurse nodded and told us she was sorry for our loss.

Jacqui and I stood at the end of the bed, holding each other tightly, waiting for the nurses to come prepare Mom to be moved to the funeral home in Searcy. I looked at Jacqui and said, "I don't know how people who don't have the hope we have survive this."

At Mom's visitation, friends we'd known all our lives, school buddies, Mom's coworkers, college teachers and classmates, and even several of my precious friends from church and Creative Living Connections class came to support me and my family. If you ever have wondered if taking a few minutes to be with someone makes a difference, trust me, it does. John and Pat Knott showed up. I determined before I arrived at the funeral home that I had cried enough and wouldn't need to during the visitation, until I looked up and saw them walking down the aisle. Then Randy and Janet Granderson and David and Cheryl Richards came in. I started up again.

My most vivid memory of the day is talking to David. He said, "If you want to see what your mom's legacy looks like, look around." I did. The room was not a room of sadness, mourning, or grief. People were hugging, laughing, telling stories about Mom, and catching up with each other. Each person there, each relationship, connected through the love and care Mom's unique personality had exuded. The atmosphere emanated exactly the warmth and joy Mom always had hoped everyone around her would feel during her journey on earth. It was comfortable. It was healthy. The friends and family gathered that day experienced a bit of the lightheartedness, comfort, and frivolity of heaven. Thankfully, my childhood buddy Sherry Barnett Hunter stood right beside me for more than an hour, reminding me of the names of people I couldn't remember or flat-out didn't recognize.

As I looked around, I was reminded of a quote from C. S. Lewis's final book in the Chronicles of Narnia, *The Last Battle*:

> The things that began to happen after that were so great and beautiful that I cannot write them. And for us this is the end of all the stories, and we can most truly say that they all lived happily ever after. But for them it was only the beginning of the real story. All their life in this world and all their adventures in Narnia had only been the cover and the title page: now at least they were beginning Chapter One of the Great Story which no one on earth has read: which goes on for ever: in which every chapter is better than the one before.

We followed Mom's body to a tiny cemetery in Romance, Arkansas, where she would be buried close to Ginger's mom and dad on one side and a tiny country Church of Christ on the other, which I'm sure gave her great satisfaction.

Another great friend of more than forty years, Doug Langston, brilliantly officiated the service. It was perfect. He is close to each of us siblings and offered tender insight on how Mom had influenced us and the world around us. His precious wife, Paula, was with him. Paula is another childhood friend. I attended church with her when we lived in Shreveport during our junior high years, before she and Doug met. I love how the Lord brings relationships full circle.

I would also like to add that as a gift to Doug, the family bought a gift card to one of Doug's favorite hangouts in Searcy: Wild Sweet Williams Bakery. Seriously, they have some of the best pastries on the planet. I bought the card for him. It was for $102.37. I thanked him in the card by saying, "I bought the gift card for you. Then I decided I really needed a cinnamon babka."

A couple of weeks ago, we kids were trying to decide what we thought Mom would want etched on her tombstone. One of my suggestions would have been "Dear Jesus, do not let her make meat loaf." Mom was a great old-school southern cook, except when it came to meat loaf. It was wretched. I decided it wasn't worth mentioning. Jim said he found out we could do a video hologram about basketball with a laser beam switch for $20,000.

After further discussion, we knew she would love a verse from the Bible, so we threw out a few ideas: "I have fought the good fight, I have finished the race, I have kept the faith" (2 Timothy 4:7 NIV), "In your presence there is fullness of joy; at your right hand are pleasures forever more," (Psalm 16:11 ESV), and "No eye has seen, nor ear heard, nor the heart of man imagined, what God has prepared for those who love Him" (1 Corinthians 2:9 ESV). I recommended the end verses of Psalm 23 (ESV): "Surely goodness and mercy shall follow me all the days of my life, and I shall dwell in the house of the Lord forever." I offered that if it was too long a passage, even the last part, "I will dwell in the house of the Lord forever," might be appropriate.

After finding out that we could get whatever we wanted etched, we decided those verses would be the best. We knew Mom would love it.

Jacqui kept Mom's Bible. Those sweet, ancient pages, worn with years of reading, studying, and memorizing, had cherished verses circled. A couple of days ago, Jacqui was browsing through and sent me a picture from Mom's Bible:

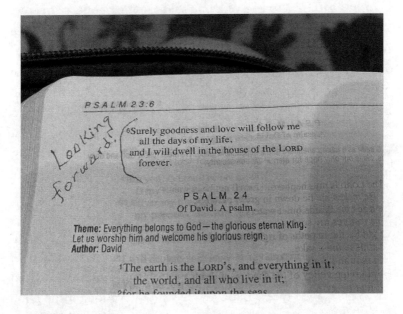

My last power verse is the following: "May the God of hope fill you with all joy and peace as you trust in him, so that you may overflow with hope by the power of the Holy Spirit" (Romans 15:13 NIV).

CONVERSATION STARTERS
FROM JANE HURLEY

Jane's life is so much fun to watch. She's always ready for the next adventure. She adds energy and purpose to every experience, and she loves including others. Her smile is radiantly infectious and full of Jesus. Jane is always there when a friend is in need. I'm thankful for her friendship. And she's so pretty.

1. Think for a moment about the time when you will transition into heaven. What do you look forward to most? Someone you'll see? A question you'll ask (e.g., "Why did you make ticks?")? Something you'll see, hear, or experience?

2. Which of Tim's power verses most resonates with you? Why?

3. Tim's mom circled the verse that became the epitaph on her tombstone, the scripture that encapsulated her life. Find a verse in the Bible you'd like to have etched on yours. Circle it.

You Can't Spell Funeral Without Fun

NOWADAYS, WHEN SOMEONE passes away, we gather together and have what we sometimes call a memorial service or going-home celebration. It's a bittersweet time to remember a life well lived in the service of Jesus. I've noticed in the last few years that the gatherings take the tone of the people who are no longer here. If they were Christians, their legacy continues in friends and family, and part of them lives on. It's a time of heart-swelling pride in knowing their lives are not over and never will be.

That stands in stark juxtaposition to the funerals of my childhood. I grew up in a small church and a Christian college town in a family of singers, and we were asked many times to sing at weddings and funerals, mostly funerals. Because Dad was a preacher for an even smaller country church, we sang for many country funerals.

When most of the kids from college were not in town during summer break, my family spent probably one day a week singing. Funerals back then were not hallowed festivals of rapturous remembrance and tribute. They were dismal, agonizingly morose requiems of lamentation and sobbing. Especially in the country, where nothing significant ever really happens, funerals were the grandest and most pretentious form of entertainment. Funerals were distressing and bleak. It was as though the deceased didn't just die; they ceased to exist, perhaps because the mourners never had heard what heaven is really like. Paul clearly says in 2 Corinthians 12 that a guy he knew was caught up to the third heaven but was not allowed to say what he saw there, so obviously, some thought, we shouldn't be dreaming about what heaven is like.

For most people, it seemed heaven was a place we looked forward to only because it meant we were not in hell. I couldn't imagine heaven being much more thrilling or energizing than endlessly jumping in a bouncy house or eating really good food whenever I wanted it, with the occasional drop-by visit of Jesus when he was making his rounds.

I think that's the reason funerals in those days were so devastating and even scary. Burials were only mentioned by our parents after they were sure we were intimately acquainted with the idea of death. This practice was clearly designed to be used as a punishment for bad behavior.

When my family sang at weddings, Mom would lean over, poke me, and whisper, "You're next." She thought it was cute and funny, until I started doing the same thing to her when we sang at funerals.

I'll never forget one summer after finishing my freshman year of college. All my college friends from the music department were away from campus for the summer. Some acquaintances in Floyd, Arkansas, asked Dad to preach for a funeral.

Dad asked if I could gather some local choir friends together to sing hymns. Without thinking, I said, "Sure." I began asking around and discovered the only people available were some friends still in high school. I enlisted them, even though almost every one of the eight was entirely unaccustomed to funerals.

I wasn't too nervous. After all, we'd all sung out of the same blue songbook our whole lives. I knew they would know the hymns. However, I'd lost my tuning fork a while back, so I borrowed one from my high school choir director. It might be relevant to note I grew up in a church that didn't use instrumental music for any church function. It was strictly forbidden.

I talked to Dad the day before the funeral and told him who was coming to sing. I strongly informed Dad that these kids were novices at singing at funerals. I wouldn't put them in a position of being uneasy. I told him he was to tell whoever was in charge that we would sit in the back of the church, far away from the casket. I also informed him we would leave before the final viewing. He said he would make sure the director knew my rules.

On the day of the funeral, I drove around to gather up all eight kids in the family Datsun station wagon.

Our big orange Datsun station wagon had been a gift to my sister, Jacqui, on her sixteenth birthday. Our dad had paid $170 to have it painted orange—really orange. We swore the vo-tech beauty was actually the front half and back half of two different cars soldered together and then spray-painted orange. It was a standard shift station wagon, and the back end had a decal that said, "Fully automatic." It looked like a dog loping with its hind legs slightly angled to one side as it ran toward you.

Dad gave me directions to the little country church, and we were off. As we turned down the well-traveled road to the church thirty minutes later, I thought it could not have been more picturesque. The small clapboard church with a white steeple rising just above the nearby trees seemed the most serene place I could think of for a funeral service.

Rain, pouring in torrents nonstop for three days before the funeral, had rendered the ground completely soaked. I drove down what used to be a dirt road, which was now slippery from the constant rain. The tiny church sat to my right. Directly across the street, to the left of me, was the cemetery, peaceful, quiet, and pastoral. It seemed a serene and undisturbed location for repose. I parked on the road directly between the church and the cemetery.

Dad was there ahead of us. As I walked to him, the other kids followed behind me, vainly attempting to avoid mud pits. Another gentleman ran out and took my hand. He was the funeral director and would show us where to sit. I glanced over toward Dad but saw him deeply engrossed in conversation with a mourner. As I passed through the front door, I noticed all the flower arrangements lining the back wall of the church instead of surrounding the coffin at the front of the small auditorium. *Odd*, I thought.

I heard the middle-aged man say to Dad as quietly as possible, "We had to physically pull her out of the coffin at visitation last night." Dad just grunted and avoided eye contact with me. The gentleman's comment left me a bit confused but nonetheless intrigued.

I kept walking as the funeral director ushered us down front and into a small, beautifully polished mahogany choir loft directly behind and above the podium, which sat straight behind and above the coffin. Before I could protest, the director scuttled off. I glanced back to see eight impressionable young kids looking down on the closed casket with eyes as big around as their open mouths. I whispered, "Y'all, trust me on this. In three years, you will have sung at so many of these, this will be nothing. I promise." Not one of them moved or blinked. I'm not sure they breathed. I knew we were in trouble. We sat quietly as guests trickled in.

Finally, it was time to start. The family came in as a unit. The men were staunchly holding up the female family members, exactly as they'd been taught from an early age, and the women all held kerchiefs to their noses, just as it should have been.

Then I heard her—before she ever got inside the small auditorium. From my vantage point, I looked down the center aisle to the back of the church. Into the building she came, held up valiantly by two men: the brother I'd heard talking to Dad earlier and another close in age, obviously siblings. As the brothers all but carried her down the center aisle, I sat almost in awe at the visage before me.

I couldn't decide if I was more disturbed by the mourning and wailing, which apparently emanated from Dante's third level of Gehenna, or her funeral attire. She carried the body of Aunt Bea and the voice of Almira Gulch. She wore a pencil-style black vintage dress, which I was sure she'd bought somewhere around forty pounds ago. Appropriate for a funeral, it did cover her shoulders—barely. She wore shiny, pointy-toed black patent-leather shoes, but it was her hat that was spellbinding. It was a pillbox hat with a short veil, but stuck inside the velvet band around the entire circumference were some kind of bird feathers that were not easily identifiable. They were varying colors and lengths, anywhere from a couple of inches to a foot high, not species-specific. I got the feeling she probably renewed the plumage for each occasion. *Poor birds!* Everyone else seemed determined to ignore the nest perched atop her head. I purposely turned away to keep from staring.

The brothers struggled as best as they could, one on each arm, stumbling as they maneuvered her to the front pew. The entire time, she wailed, "Oh, Daddy! Oh, Daddy!"

The brothers' futile attempt to console her included words of comfort. "Now, now, Auntie Christa. It'll be okay. Sit down, and hush now, Auntie Christa." At some point, I noticed the spiritual implications of her name.

Unfortunately, at that moment, one of the high school kids behind me discovered for the first time what it feels like to experience the embarrassment, guilt, and shame of uncontrollable and inappropriate giggling. At first, I thought she was just coughing. Then I realized she was trying to cover her wheezing snickers.

Fortunately, I saw the funeral dude signaling me to start. I grabbed the borrowed tuning fork out of my coat pocket, struck it against my index finger, listened to the hum of the fork, and gave the kids the pitch for middle C. I began directing the first hymn: "Oh, Lord, my God. When I, in awesome wonder, consider all the worlds thy hands have made."

Wait. It sounded at least a fourth of an octave lower than it was supposed to be.

"I see the stars. I hear the rolling thunder."

Even worse, all song directors know the fatal truth that no matter how fast you start a hymn, if you start it too low, it's going to slow down. After feeling as if I were hiking through molasses, I finally made it to the end of the song.

I was furious and wanted to take it out on someone, so I glared toward the back, where Dad was standing. He averted my scowl and quickly glanced out the open entrance door as if trying to read a tombstone in the cemetery across the street. I looked back at the kids, and they were all looking at me with confusion and maybe condemnation on their faces. One of them actually mouthed, "What are you doing?" And there was still the chuckling girl. Her shoulders were shaking, and she held a tightly clenched fist against her mouth.

Someone mouthed, "Pitch it higher."

I mouthed back, "I'm using the tuning fork." *It's right!*

Through all this, Auntie Christa was caterwauling, "Why? Why?"

I thought it best to go ahead with the next hymn. I pitched it in the correct key with the tuning fork and began. Somehow, it became an awkward duet with Auntie Christa. She would not be outdone.

"Low in the grave, he lay, Jesus, our Savior. Waiting the coming day, Jesus our Lord—"

"Oh, Daddy!"

"Up from the grave—"

"If I could hear him preach just one more sermon!"

"He arose!"

The song of celebration, still pitched embarrassingly low, became a funeral dirge, somehow oddly appropriate but not what I originally had envisioned. When it was over, I refused to even look back at the kids. I knew what they were thinking. It wasn't until I returned the offensive fork to my choir director later that I noticed I had been given a G tuning fork instead of a C fork. I was, in fact, starting every song a half octave too low.

After we finished singing, Dad took his turn. He walked to the front, deliberately averting my deeply furrowed brow, and stood at the pulpit, between us and the coffin. He gave a heartfelt message about death, which he was forced to scream, trying to be heard over the rivaling howling from Auntie Christa. The family no longer attempted to quiet her. A few kids close by her bent over, gathering up occasional tufts of bird fuzz that flew off her head.

Finally, it was done. I felt sure the funeral dude would escort us out before the final family viewing, but he did not. I sat in horror as he and his minion helper marched—and I do mean marched—to the front and opened the coffin.

There we were, looking straight down into the embalmed face of a ninety-something-year-old Baptist preacher, who, I'm sure, to the kids, looked astonishingly like the Crypt Keeper.

There was an audible gasp in unison. I turned around and witnessed eight sixteen-year-old kids metamorphose from well-adjusted high schoolers into clinical case studies.

A couple of them averted their gaze downward to the floor, but the others looked as though they were half expecting and hoping that Daddy would jump up and say, "Just kidding." Meanwhile, Auntie Christa was proclaiming to the entire congregation that she no longer wanted to live. At that moment, I was close to making her wish a reality.

I looked back and said, "Let's go," leading the procession of eager followers down the front aisle before the guests and family could parade past the open coffin. I felt compelled to get them out of there as fast as possible before they were forever mentally scarred. I would deal with Dad later. We passed him. I purposely avoided eye contact with him. He tugged my coat sleeve and whispered, "Um, the funeral director was wondering if the kids could carry the flowers to the grave site across the street before the family walks over."

I whispered back, "Dad, I believe you have successfully turned eight bright, well-adjusted high school students into Children of the Corn. We're going to do this one last thing, and then we're out of here."

At my direction, each kid grabbed a container of flowers, and we headed across the soggy, muddy street into the cemetery. The chuckling girl commented on the lovely white stones lining the walkway. I informed her that they were actually grave markers, and I walked ahead. Suddenly, I heard someone whisper, "Excuse me. I'm so sorry. Excuse me." I watched as chuckling girl passed me, apologized to each grave, and then long-jumped across them, precariously balancing her vase of flowers in her arms.

Something inside me snapped. I set my flowers down and laughed. In fact, I laughed so hard I leaned across a tall tombstone and continued with my own inappropriate guffawing.

Then I heard an excruciatingly loud whisper, "Tim. Tim!" I glanced up, wiping tears from my eyes, and observed Dad leading the procession of mourners across the street from the church toward us. All of them were looking at me with utmost disdain.

Suddenly, a haloed dome of feathers poked out from somewhere in the middle of the group, apparently to see what the holdup was. Auntie Christa, chagrined that someone else might be stealing her attention, abruptly howled and flailed her arms. She ran toward the open grave and deliberately fell just short of it, hitting the dry plastic grass in a dramatic dead faint.

Her road-weary brothers, obviously exhausted from the emotional and physical toll, just stood there. Everyone stared at her. When it was apparent no one was going to rescue her, Auntie Christa slowly raised her bird head and looked around. Broken and bent pinions and the few plumes left on her head wafted in the breeze. She looked less like a phoenix rising from the ashes and more like a deranged, run-over peacock. As her brothers wearily began the four-hundred-mile journey to pick her up, I looked at the huddled kids and jerked my head toward the car.

This time, as I passed Dad, we both avoided eye contact. I all but ran to the car, jumped in, and started the engine as the kids piled in. I threw the car in reverse and heard the dreaded spinning of wheels against mud. There was a definite groan from all the passengers in the car as I tried several times to put the car in drive, reverse, drive, and reverse. Nothing. So three of my guys jumped out and bounced the orange station wagon.

Someone yelled, "Gun it!" so I did. The car was removed from the deadly clutches of the offending mud, and everyone let out a tired cheer. I looked in the rearview mirror and saw my three guys covered from head to toe in slimy red Arkansas mud. One wiped it out of his ears, one wiped it out of his eyes, and the other just stood there. I was sad he didn't finish the tableau.

I glanced over and watched in fascination as the entire funeral company giggled along with all of us in the car, except, of course, Auntie Christa, who leaned morosely against her brother.

We drove off into the cloudy day.

In the years following, Dad and I never discussed the Floyd, Arkansas, funeral experience. Not ever.

CONVERSATION STARTERS
FROM CLIFF PECK

I've worked for Dr. Peck for the better part of twenty years. People drive many miles to his clinic, knowing there are other veterinarians much closer to their homes. Why? Because Cliff treats his clients and their precious pets exactly the way he treats his team: like family.

1. Have you ever found humor at an otherwise somber event? Explain.

2. How is it apparent in your life that God has a sense of humor?

3. Have you ever seen someone who reminds you of a comical movie character, right down to the animations? (Author's note: Dr. Peck was thinking of Eulalie Mackecknie Shinn. In *The Music Man*, Eulalie is the mayor's boisterous, attention-grabbing, snobbish wife, who isn't able to keep her opinions to herself. Reminiscent of Auntie Christa maybe?)

Y'all Come Go with Us

I'M A CHILD of the 1960s—not old enough to be a hippie but a young child of the '60s. For that reason, I remember how great the toys were back then. Imagination was a huge predictor of how long those toys would last.

I loved Slinky—not the cheap plastic ones they make now but the heavy ones made out of metal, which made that impressive, well, slinky noise when I held one end in each hand and passed it back and forth for about ten minutes. Then I'd force my little brother to hold one end while I backed up with the other to see how far we could stretch it, eventually pulling it completely out of its intended coil, rendering it useless.

I remember Mr. Machine Robot, a windup mechanical man that, when wound up, marched across the floor, showing all his inner workings through his plastic casing. You could take him apart bolt by cog by nut by wheel and then theoretically put him back together again. Theoretically.

Mr. Machine Robot lived in a bag in the back of my closet for five years because all the king's horses and all the king's men— well, you can guess the rest.

Then there was the miracle of Chatty Cathy, my sister's prized Christmas gift, the wonder doll that spoke three or four classic lines when you pulled the ring attached to the back of her neck. I also remember the big ole can of whoopin' I got for, with precision, surgically dismembering Miss CC to accurately identify where her voice came from.

Besides those glorious toys, I loved southern words and phrases from the '60s that have gone out of style or should've never been in fashion. Many of them I still use today when an opportunity arises. For instance, the following:

- Southerners don't say, "You guys." We say, "Y'all," or, for five or more people, "All y'all."
- We don't say *catty-corner*. We say *cattywampus*.
- We don't say, "Oh wow." We say, "Good gravy."
- We don't *have* a hissy-fit; we *pitch* one.
- Southerners won't tell you, "You're wasting your time." We'll tell you, "You're barking up the wrong tree."
- We don't hand you a Coca-Cola when you ask for a Coke. We ask, "What kind?"
- We're never "about to" do something. We're "fixin' to." Or we say, "Go fix your plate."
- We don't use the *toilet*. We use the *commode*.
- We never *suppose*. We *reckon*.
- Southerners don't call people *unintelligent*. We say they're "dumber 'n a sack o' rocks."
- Southerners don't check for food in the *fridge*. We look in the *icebox*.
- Southerners don't eat *dinner*. We eat *supper*. There's no such word as *dinner*. It's not biblical. We don't observe the Lord's Dinner.
- Southerners aren't "caught off guard." We're "caught with our pants down."
- Southerners don't *pout*. We get our "panties in a wad."

Julia Sugarbaker, on the 1980s sitcom *Designing Women*, proudly proclaimed, "This is the South. And we're proud of our crazy people. We don't hide them up in the attic. We bring them right down in the living room and show them off. No one in the South ever asks if you have crazy people in your family. They just ask what side they're on."

A few years back, my brothers and sister and I went to Texas to visit Dad. He was residing in a home for folks living with Alzheimer's. While there, we drove around Hurst, just around the corner from Fort Worth, and visited some of the old schools, churches, and houses we'd lived in when we were growing up.

On that trip, I thought about all the old southern words and phrases that add such richness to the language I grew up with. We drove by one house, and even the old white screen door looked like the same one from my childhood.

Everything looked familiar, except for one thing. I said, "I don't remember that big old tree being over on the side of the house like that."

My older brother, Steve, said, "Tim, we lived here fifty years ago."

"I know, but it's so big. I don't remember it at all."

"Tim, that was fifty years ago. A half century."

Even now, that doesn't compute with me. I guess part of the mystery is that I can still see myself looking out the front window of the kitchen while washing supper dishes. I could barely wait to finish. Only then did I have permission to go around the corner and find all my neighborhood friends to play hide-and-seek. We ran the neighborhood until Mom called us home, which was way after dark and fairly close to bedtime.

Sitting in front of the house that day, I remembered my favorite southern phrase. My dad was a preacher, and usually, on Wednesday nights, after prayer meetin', we'd go to different congregation members' homes for fellowship. We kids would have a dessert and drink cherry Kool-Aid while the adults drank hot, thick, aromatic coffee.

The only time I ever got to taste coffee when I was little was on the rare occasion Mom let me climb into her lap at someone else's kitchen table. She consented to allow me the dunk of my doughnut into her coffee. As a matter of fact, one morning, I woke up while visiting my mother many years later, in my early twenties, and she asked me if I wanted a cup of coffee—a passage-to-manhood moment for me. I took a heart picture that day.

Back in the '60s, as we prepared to leave the homes of our friends after goodbyes were said, I distinctly remember standing in the dark, just outside the glow of the porch light, and instinctively slamming my mouth shut for fear of kamikaze june bugs. After the small chatter while walking to the car, Dad turned around and said to the hosts, "Y'all come go with us."

That simple phrase, in my ten-year-old mind, was the perfect tagline to an ideal evening. It said, "We loved being with you, and we wish it didn't have to end."

The recipient of this declaration of friendship would reply with something like, "Well, I wish we could. The kids have school tomorrow. We better stay here and get 'em ready for bed."

As a kid, I thought it was the best idea ever. The reality never dawned on me the horror that would befall my mother if someone actually said, "Well, all righty then. Honey, go get the kids."

Even at an early age, I was thankful the Lord allowed me to take what I now call heart pictures: moments framed in my mind and soul, benchmarks of remarkable relationships, and perhaps even profound truth that wouldn't be realized for decades.

It's much more acceptable in today's climate and Christian culture to realize, possibly due to our not understanding when we were younger, that we must rigorously, deliberately seek out and nurture community. The truth is, we were never meant to walk this journey alone.

I don't think it was an easy task back then. The best my parents could muster to make someone feel important, needed, and valued was a simple declaration of unity, an acknowledgment of friendship that guaranteed "You're not alone," without actually having to be vulnerable enough to say it.

"We're in this together."

"Y'all come go with us."

Jesus says in John 15:12–13 (NIV), "My command is this. Love each other as I have loved you. Greater love has no one than this: to lay down one's life for one's friends."

James 5:16–18 (MSG) puts it in a more nuts-and-bolts configuration: "Make this your common practice." He doesn't say, "When you have committed a major public sin and need to repent by going forward." He tells us to make this a common practice: "Confess your sins to each other and pray for each other so that you can live together whole and healed. The prayer of a person living right with God is something powerful to be reckoned with."

Something powerful.

I sometimes wonder what draws nonbelievers to us or what should bring them to us. In a world that has become freakishly isolated, compartmentalized, and cubicle-like, it's imperative that they see us love one another and know one another.

Jesus said they would recognize him because of our love for each other, and he said that just after he washed the feet of his disciples.

Just before James's encouragement to confess sin, he says in chapter 5:7–8, "Friends, wait patiently for the Master's arrival. You see farmers do this all the time. Waiting for their valuable crops to mature, patiently letting the rain do its slow but sure work. Be patient like that. Stay steady and strong."

One of my favorite topics of conversation with friends—in fact, my very favorite—is how much I look forward to Jesus's arrival and what that moment will usher in for those of us who are his. What if we lived out the truth that our redemption is sure and solid? What if we encouraged one another with the accuracy and dependability of that truth, fervently excited?

When I talk about heaven and all the fun we're going to have and make plans to meet people for supper on a specific day a hundred years from now, trust me, that's not idle talk. I have a hope that it is real and that God is faithful to live up to his promise.

As time ticks by and I realize this motor of mine will one day stop ticking, the anticipation deepens. I think about all the people who will welcome me when I get there, especially Jesus. I think about my friend Greg Murtha, whom I've written about in this book. He's in heaven now after fighting a courageous battle with cancer.

Thousands of friends and family all over the world covered him in prayer and sacrificed countless acts of service to comfort his family. In one of his last posts on social media, instead of lamenting his circumstance, Greg wrote,

> Today will you take your neighbor a muffin or a potted plant? Will you buy that homeless guy a coffee? Will you linger a little longer over breakfast with your family, tell these people you appreciate them or, if you're bold, that you love them? Make today different while you're able.

I've written about a guy I'm in contact with who's in prison. He is one of society's outcasts who need and secretly long for freedom from the bondage of self-loathing, guilt, and shame and who refuse Jesus, not necessarily because they are callous to him but because they think he could never forgive them, much less love them. We all probably know these people imprisoned behind walls of inadequacy, self-condemnation, and selfishness.

I've told y'all stories about people I've met: a little girl racked with guilt over picking up trinkets in a store without paying for them; inmates, including a redeemed murderer and a grieving mom who lost her boy to suicide; the beautiful radio personality I loved to torment and make laugh on air; dear friends, including one fighting a battle with diabetes and dementia; the faith chaser; the tire changer; and the theatrical mourner. I don't know where some of these folks are now, but I hope our journey together isn't over. I pray I'll meet them again one day. I hope the winding, twisting, bending, anfractuous curves of our lives will crisscross once again. Even if we never physically see each other again on this side of the veil, when we're all finally home, I imagine standing at the throne, shouting my love to Jesus, and then glancing at someone next to me and exclaiming, "Hey, I know you! I remember you."

When I hang out with my peeps, it's a comfortable, mostly unspoken addendum to our journey together that this doesn't end here. We will enjoy this company, joy, and laughter and look after one another forever.

My prayer is that those living in silent desperation will recognize those eternal moments in our eyes. I pray they will give us the chance to share with them where the surety of our future comes from and how dearly treasured and loved they are.

Jesus is the great adventure.

I pray we will be able to boldly, with certainty, turn to them as we're leaving and say, "Y'all, come go with us."

CONVERSATION STARTERS
FROM NANCY J. KLINE

When we get home, Nancy will receive a million birthday cakes, with a candle in each one. Those cakes will be given to her by people who were, directly or indirectly, forever changed by the influence she graciously poured into their hearts. I will be right there waiting my turn, eager and impatient to present her with a cake.

1. What childhood memories were stirred as Tim described his glorious toys and southern phrases?

2. What has drawn you to someone who seemed to walk through life with joy and peace in all circumstances?

3. Greg challenged the living to "make today different while you're able." Can a muffin really be used to draw someone from behind his or her walls of inadequacy, self-condemnation, and selfishness?

Nancy wrote the following addendum to her conversation starters:

> Tim, this spoke to me, as I was taken to the memory of a heart picture when the mother of one of my Sunday school students met me for coffee on my birthday and produced a huge homemade muffin with a candle in it. This was probably thirty-plus years ago. I remember feeling so accepted in that moment. The shame of living as an abused woman lifted, and I was an

innocent child being nurtured by my friend who cared about my birthday.

My mother died when I was three years and ten months old, leaving me an orphan soon adopted by my aunt and uncle. When I was forty-seven, I received a letter that had lain in a family member's drawer for all those years. My aunt had written a description of a scene shortly after my mother's death and a couple weeks before my fourth birthday. She quoted me as saying with my head down, "I guess I'll never have another birthday cake now that Mama is gone." But then, lifting my head, looking around at my aunts and grandmother, and brightening, I said, "But you're my mama, and you're my mama, and ..."

Happy October birthday, my friend. You are going to continue blessing and leading many of us closer to the Lord as we celebrate suppers together.

Nancy

Combines and Concubines (Bonus Story)

IT'S IMPORTANT HOW we define a word and how we use it. Looking at a word or phrase the way we've always looked at it isn't necessarily the same way the Lord wants us to look at it. We need to be absolutely sure our words are used correctly.

Several years ago, my sister took all of us who worked for her travel agency to Little Rock for supper. I was in the front passenger seat while she drove. Three ladies sat in the back.

Conversation part 2 follows.

Don't look for conversation part 1. There isn't one. Two reasons: (1) part 1 was not as important as part 2, and (2) I have no memory of part 1.

So picking up in the middle of the conversation, the girl in the middle of the backseat said, "Oh, that's awful. Yeah, I knew this guy once who was riding his motorcycle through a cornfield, and he ran into a concubine, and it poked his eye out."

Crickets.

I said, "You mean *combine*, right? He ran into a combine?"

She replied emphatically, "No! He ran into a concubine, and it poked his eye out!"

I said, "Well, um, in the Bible, a concubine was a kind of second wife. She wasn't actually a wife, though. Didn't have the status of a wife. She was more like a servant usually, who was around if the man of the house wanted extramarital dalliances. King Solomon had, like, hundreds of them."

Crickets.

She asked, "So what's a combine?"

Children, take heed. Consider this critical warning carefully: stay away from concubines; they'll poke your eye out.

CONVERSATION STARTERS FROM GREG AND JULIE HILLEGAS

Greg and Julie are fun, Jesus-loving people. When you're around them, you feel special. Not only do they deliberately work to make you feel important, but they actually want you to know you're important. They are genuine and filled with wisdom and kindness. Everyone on the planet could learn from them what marriage, communication, and friendships—all relationships—can look like. And Julie is so pretty.

1. When have you mixed up words or their meanings? Give examples out loud.

2. Share an embarrassing moment using an autocorrect text.

3. Is there a word or phrase in the Bible you've always questioned and would like a clearer understanding of?